THE CHARISMATIC GYMNASIUM

THE CHARISMATIC
GYMNASIUM

BREATH, MEDIA,

AND RELIGIOUS REVIVALISM

IN CONTEMPORARY BRAZIL

Maria José de Abreu

DUKE UNIVERSITY PRESS *Durham and London* 2021

© 2021 Duke University Press
All rights reserved
Printed in the United States of America
on acid-free paper ∞
Designed by Amy Ruth Buchanan
Typeset in Minion Pro by Copperline Book Services

Library of Congress Cataloging-in-Publication Data
Names: Abreu, Maria José de, [date] author.
Title: The charismatic gymnasium : breath, media,
and religious revivalism in contemporary Brazil /
Maria José de Abreu.
Description: Durham : Duke University Press, 2021. |
Includes bibliographical references and index.
Identifiers: LCCN 2020020640 (print)
LCCN 2020020641 (ebook)
ISBN 9781478009719 (hardcover)
ISBN 9781478011347 (paperback)
ISBN 9781478010296 (ebook)
Subjects: LCSH: Anthropology of religion—Brazil. |
Leadership—Religious aspects—Catholic Church. | Religion
and politics—Brazil. | Christianity—Brazil.
Classification: LCC GN470.A274 2020 (print) |
LCC GN470 (ebook) | DDC 306.60981—dc23
LC record available at https://lccn.loc.gov/2020020640
LC ebook record available at https://lccn.loc.gov/2020020641

Cover art: Photographs by the author.

For Lina, of course.

CONTENTS

....

PREFACE: BREATHE IN. BREATHE OUT.

....

Like millions of others, I am under lockdown in response to the spread of the coronavirus. From my apartment in New York City I look down a deserted Broadway. The avenue is one straight line for ambulances speeding by, but there is little more. Yet the edges of this central artery within Manhattan look slightly out of focus, a trembling of contours I associate with the heat of fever. It is as though global warming's continued muffled cry has eventually downloaded into humans in the form of a virus affecting our breathing and our average temperature. If something will become apparent in the years to come, it is that air is not just an empty dimension within which humans exist but the substance through which existence itself is possible.

In such times it is not lost on me that the organizing concept of this book is *pneuma*, the Greek term for air, breath, or spirit. Written under the signature of gratitude to my 86-year-old mother, she will just miss its release. As I write these lines she is in hospital infected with COVID-19. COVID exposed a tumor. A doctor informs me over the phone that the situation is irreversible. For all the powers of digital media to offset our physical confinement, I am told that no communication technologies are available in her ward, the same one where she worked for nearly forty years. I wake up to the fact that she never owned a mobile phone, and I ask an old friend from my hometown to bring one to her. This technological interface seems to be the only way to share airspace with my mother, as though the digital has become the great air reservoir of the world. Despite agreeing to bring the device to her bed, the hospital staff tell me that she is disoriented and isn't making any sense. "And who isn't disoriented?" I ask in frustration. But I realize there is no point in arguing. I am smashed by the complexity of it all, my daughterly love finding solace only in the memory of a woman who loved silence and lived it soundly, especially in the later years of her life.

Breathe in. Breathe out. A fine balance keeps us alive. And yet for most of our lives we are hardly aware of its mechanism. Air partakes in eliding the conditions of the very reality it enables. Yet the air we breathe today is becoming closer to our thinking, no longer the mere (read: vital) background substance through which thoughts are possible but instead the very element that aligns our lungs to our brains. One good example of this is how performative paradoxes dominate our thinking, as though one side of a pressure seeks to draw balance from a pressure on the other. I sustain my condemnation of corporate capitalism through books I buy online from Amazon. I teach my students not to doubt the benefits of methodological doubting. I tell my son to think with his own head. Because of the virus, I'm in confinement in the name of a common good that exposes my economic privilege. Conscious of it or not, we have grown sick of hearing about performative paradoxes. And yet our sickness itself is symptomatic of the fact that, ubiquitous and insistent, the performative paradox has gradually lodged itself in our chests. It hosts itself in the structure of our breathing. For what is breathing—the alternation between opposites—if not a performative paradox, civil war in our lungs.

The rule in religion, politics, media, or the market is no longer simply to discipline or regulate the rhythms that animate public institutions and populations but to infuse them with what William Butler Yeats once called the "antithetical multiform influx," that is, an undecidable veering that draws us to its middle. The image is that of the swing of a pendulum whose oscillation from tick to tock does not tell time, less so where things are going, but constitutes itself as time by means of the very motion.

Bearing this in mind will help make sense of contemporary authoritarian populism in Brazil and other parts of the world. When Jair Bolsonaro and Donald Trump talk about the threat of coronavirus, their words are not pronouncements that take place in the present tense. Insomuch as the present is disjointed, the virus is always already both a dire danger and an overblown nuisance. To say that Bolsonaro and Trump are deniers of the virus is to fail to see how entangled their denial is in the already tomorrow when they will be saying the extreme opposite. To accuse these rulers of being paragons of contradiction is to miss the point entirely. That would be to impart them with grounds they actively disavow. A contradiction would assume a subject without caesura, a form of singularity that aspires to be self-identical. But sovereigns like Trump and Bolsonaro are deeply fractured; indeed they wield their sovereignty by upholding the rift like a war trench from which to launch their semiotic terrorism, even to the point of auto-annihilation.

In an odd twist of brutalist aesthetics, the cracks in the system are exposed, and not in purview of transparency but so as to allow for the total and organic identification between a subject and his praxis. As long as we fail to see the strategic coupling of opposites at the heart of contemporary governance, we won't be able to grasp how the Right operates its extremism. The epistemic leap I see necessarily involves something like a reconceiving of the political through the problem of substance. In this sense, the operations of breathing that COVID-19 is making apparent, like some powerful reagent, may also lend themselves to better grasping how power works today.

—New York City, April 17, 2020

ACKNOWLEDGMENTS

....

This book began in conversation with a crew of faculty members and colleagues at the Amsterdam School of Social Science Research. Thanks to Birgit Meyer for inviting me to be part of the international research group she ran on religion and media in that institution, in whose dynamic and intellectual bosom many of the ideas in this book were found. Thanks to Peter van der Veer for his advocacy on my behalf. I am grateful to Johannes Fabian for his teaching and for his trust in my project when doubt threatened to engulf it. And to Ana Lindo for graciously introducing me to the city of São Paulo. Special thanks to Irfan Ahmed, Marieke Bloomenberg, Alexander Edmonds, Ajay Gandhi, Anouk de Koning, Suzanne Kuik, Rachel Spronk, Shifra Kisch, Olga Sezneva, Olga Soudi, Malini Sur, Marleen van Ruijven, and Marta Zogbi for friendship and comradeship.

I want to thank those who, at one point or another, read and talked with me about my writing, transforming it for the better: Ananda Abeysekara, Alena Alexandrova, Courtney Bender, Thomas Carlson, Elizabeth Castelli, Thomas Csordas, Marleen de Witte, Iracema Dulley, Claudio Lomnitz, Eduardo Dullo, Abou Farman, Francio Guadeloupe, Lotte Hoek, Stephen Hughes, Mette Løvschal, Eileen Moyer, Valentina Napolitano, Bruno Reinhardt, Emilio Spadola, Patricia Spyer, Martijn Oosterbaan, Mattijs van der Port, Michael Taussig, Otávio Velho, and Samuel Weber. Special thanks to Rafael Sánchez for his intellect, Peter Geschiere for collegial sustenance, Rosalind Morris for brilliance, Brian Larkin for inspiration, and Jeremy Stolow for stalwart encouragement. Carlo Caduff and Angie Heo have been a source of friendship, spirited engagement with ideas, and support all the way. I have often asked myself whether I would be where I am now had they not been on my horizon. I am thankful everlastingly to Charles Hirschkind for being a seriously critical interlocutor and generous reader for many years. Rosa Norton has been a diligent proofreader and concept polisher too. One last read of parts of the manuscript by Emily Ng sharpened the idea of the project. Thanks to Gisela Fosado and Alejandra Mejía at Duke University Press for trust and direction, and to my project editor Lisl Hampton for patiently and valiantly traversing the gaps between the worlds of the book, the readership, and my nonnative English. This work has been possible thanks to funding support from Fundação Para a Ciência e a Tecnologia, the Amsterdam Institute for Social Science Research, and the Forum for Transregional Studies of the Wissenschaftskolleg of Berlin.

In New York, Daniella Gandolfo and Jason Pine are two angels whose guidance I hold tight. To my friends Cristina Barros, Orquidea Calisto, Paula Caspão, Paulo Domingos, Paulo Ferreira, Sandra Guarda, Patricia Guarda, Anabela Ribeiro, Luis Ribeiro, Pedro Santos, and Eric Woodley, I am grateful for years of sustaining care and affection. To Sota and Marie-Ritchie the pleasure of long walks under the Dutch sky, and for the laughter. In Michael Vatcher I found love and an entry into the vibrant worlds of jazz music. To Louis, my darling son, I am grateful for years of tremendous joy (he really is so funny) and for being one with my foolish heart. I dedicate this book to my mother in whose brave life I see the predicament of many women.

This journey wound into the Department of Anthropology at Columbia University, which I joined in 2017. I am grateful for the formidable crew of thinkers, colleagues, and friends there. I have long believed—as I could only do—that the best arrivals are those that bring one to a place of realization about how much more is out there to learn from. This never-finished endeavor is perhaps the gift the immortals speak of.

INTRODUCTION

....

We are showing people that this here, oh, oh [*he pummels the image*], look here, oh, oh, this here [*he kicks the image, holding it by the head*] does not function, this here is no saint. . . . Do you think God could be compared to such an ugly, horrible doll?
—PASTOR SÉRGIO VON HELDER

It was with these words and gestures that Pastor Sérgio Von Helder, on the October 12 religious holiday dedicated to the Virgin Mary, sparked a controversy that would become known in Brazil as the Guerra Santa. On that day in 1995, while millions of pilgrims were heading to the Basilica of the National Shrine of Our Lady of Aparecida, dedicated to the patron saint of Brazil, the evangelical minister brought a 42-inch replica of the saint to the studios of RecordTV (owned by the Protestant Universal Church of the Kingdom of God), with the aim of ridiculing it on live national television. Starting with verbal insults, the pastor moved on to physical aggression: holding the image by the neck, he administered, rhythmically, eight blows and twelve kicks. *Thwack, thwack, thwack . . . kick, kick, kick, kick . . .* Other local TV networks quickly appropriated the video of the attack on the statue and looped it endlessly on prime-time news, provoking outrage and protest throughout Brazil.

Time and again the media reproduced the scene of the kick. Widespread accounts and recollections of "the kicking of the saint" (*o chute na santa*), as the televised episode became known, claimed that the statue suffered a shattering blow. But even though he indeed struck the icon several times with the side of his shoe, Pastor Von Helder never came close to smashing it to pieces. And yet that is not how most people remember it. It is as though the very reproducibility of such a moment had the power of affecting its perception. As the weeks went by, the magnitude of the injury became ever more dramatic among various publics. I heard accounts ranging from the claim that the statue was merely broken to its head having been cut off (reminiscent of how three fishermen first found a statue of Our Lady in a river in 1717).[1] Defending his actions, Von Helder asked people to examine the footage again to verify that he did not shatter the icon, as everyone was claiming. But the more he proclaimed his innocence, the more the scene was replayed. At stake was what the operation of mediation itself can do to images, the media's power to transfigure the realities it depicts. In the end, the image could not hold up against the hammering force of serial repetition produced by its relentless rebroadcast. The more often the scene of the attack was broadcast, the more the statue disintegrated, the deeper the cut into the flesh of the nation, of Our Lady of Aparecida.

〰〰〰〰〰〰〰〰〰〰〰〰〰〰〰〰〰〰

This book sets out to show how the cut wrought by Guerra Santa opened up a space for the rise and expansion of a form of Catholic revivalism in contemporary Brazil. Best known as the Catholic Charismatic Renewal, this movement rose to popularity in the mid-1990s, a period of great structural change dominated by conflicting visions and tendencies in religion, politics, and aesthetics. Combining theological concepts with mass media and with bodily exercises, Catholic Charismatics would enforce a particular logic of value that prizes the ability to articulate and extend things in view of a certain suppleness of form. Much like the gymnast works on stretching her limbs to the utmost limit so as to expose the network of the joints and articulations of the body, Charismatics set to work on the elasticity that will bring the church back in form. This orientation toward elasticity is the central idea behind what I call the *Charismatic gymnasium*.

Applying the uses of the Greek gymnasium to Christianity, I explore the dawn of a new regime of devotional practices designed to build spiritually fit Catholic devotees in contemporary urban São Paulo (see Forbes 1945; Dutch 2005). I document the central role of *pneuma*, the Greek term for "breath," "air," or "spirit," in a vast respiratory religious program—popularly branded as "the aerobics of Jesus"—in reforming Brazil's Catholicism in doctrine as well as in conduct. Gathering in stadiums, big tents, sports venues, or old hangars, Charismatics transform spaces into gymnasiums for devotion. Their programs consist of well-orchestrated juxtapositions of choreographed bodily gestures and exercises, with mass media technologies, popular culture repertoires, and elements from Greek Orthodox theological doctrine. Their religious practices hinge on a productive semantic slippage between "going to the gym" in the sense of "building mass" and doing gymnastics as in developing elasticity, coordination, and proprioceptive awareness. This practical elasticity that underpins Charismatic theology and practice functions as the adequate foundation of a particular power structure. The implicit aim of this structure is to produce religiously fluent bodies congruent with the rise of neoliberalism in Brazil.

Von Helder's assault on the nation's patron saint and most revered Catholic icon offers an opening into the worlds this book explores. Through the power of shock, he initiated the rise of a dramaturgical epoch within Brazilian society, politics, and culture, one that is still unfolding today. This dramaturgy is characterized by a disavowal of the powers of representation, favoring instead the regimes of operation—the technical apparatuses—involved in the reproduction and circulation of things. Thanks to the repetitive viewing of the scenes of Von Helder kicking the statue, what was held to belong to the order of the visual became in fact musical, suffused with rhythm: the rhythm of mass mechanical reproducibility. What the eye, time and again jolted by the staccato repetition of the same scene, did to perception, so Walter Benjamin (1968) wrote, technologies of image reproducibility in the modern world do to the integrity of images. Reproducibility—the *ability* to reproduce—alters the limits of time and space. It erases the uniqueness and distance that was thought by the spirit of an epoch to preserve the sacrality of things.[2]

In being subjected to such rhythms, the statue of Our Lady subjects the circumscriptive borders of its being in a time and in a place to a new power configuration. What before was held as rigid and three-dimensional becomes reimagined as a two-dimensional medial space. More than a representation of the sacred, what becomes available in this two-dimensional sphere is the manual of operations—the "how" of the image—through which "imaging" itself is possible. Thanks to the power of shock, the rigidity of the statue can now accommodate a new graceful malleability, and it is this malleability that Catholic Charismatics will channel into institutional form.

In the context of this book, the shock of mechanical reproducibility opens up the aperture—the cut—through which the Charismatic gymnasium appears. It is as though in the perceptive disintegration of the statue of Our Lady Catholic Charismatics were able to reconnect, as though through a breach, with an older doctrine of doings—an orthopraxis—and therein pave the way for a project of renewal. This project of renewal links pneumatic theology to technological processes and then these to breathing exercises as the essential components of the Charismatic gymnasium. What is crucial to keep in mind, as you go throughout the chapters, is how a focus on operations opens onto a theological doctrine of the gymnasium among Charismatics in contemporary Brazil. In that effort, the main protagonists of this book are the operations that integrate the Charismatic gymnasium: reproduction, citation, recursion, interruption, overlapping, retarding, folding, bending backward and forward, the alternation between falling and restoring, among others.

Based on a theology of practical belief, more than argumentative reasoning, Charismatics' doctrine of the gymnasium hinges the breathing body to an entire network of relations, the prime aim of which is to expose—and thereby thematize—the "spirit" of renewal under which it functions. In the spaces of latency thus exposed, flesh and artifice, life and the machinic, not only cannot be differentiated but are seen as mutually constitutive of the operative logics of incarnation. A recursive imbrication exists between mystical *wound* and technological *cut*, between theology and technology, such that to talk about one is necessarily to talk about the other. Ramifying at the level of the doctrinal and the sociopolitical alike, these theo-technological operations are at the core of this investigation.

In times of contradiction and disputation such as those that led to Guerra Santa in 1995, Catholic Charismatics were faced with the challenge of deciding between extreme poles. On the one side, there was the Catholic Church losing its long-held hegemony over other credos—above all, over Pentecostal denominations. On the other, there was a clear sense that a paradigm change was underway within Brazil and the world writ large. Without saying that the pastor of the Universal was right in his attack on the rigidity of the statue, it was becoming clear for a certain strand of Catholic conservativism that the institutional body had to be renewed, trained in flexibility.

Neither liberation theology nor its practical mission in the form of grassroots ecclesiastic communities (seen by some as too worldly, by others as too caught up in stoic moralism) seemed to find the necessary vigor to hamper the rapid advance and penetration of evangelicalism and televangelism into key areas of the social, political, and economic spheres in Brazil. In turn, the aesthetics of scandal, often associated with a mediatic fascination with corruption stories, seemed to be the very force facilitating the penetration of televangelism into Brazil. In an ironic twist from the aims of modernism, radically reformative conservativism came forward in the public scene by way of an avant-garde engagement with interruption and shock.

But the more shocking the interventions, the more stunned and melancholic the local institution of the Catholic Church seemed to appear through its talking heads. A tension was arising between those two sides, and this opposition was, in a strong sense, what the attack on the statue on live TV and its subsequent renditions performed through a series of retaliations and nationwide public debates. The time was ripe for a new dynamism, and this dynamism was the terrain on which the Charismatic gymnasium would unfold with a determining influence.

Walter Benjamin ([1963] 1998a), who insisted on the necessity of anachronism for an accurate understanding of history, offers powerful clues in *The Origin of German Tragic Drama* to how a counter-reforming baroque sensibility rose up to a formal stiffness in the seventeenth century. As Benjamin notes the modern baroque sensibility first erupted in places like Germany and Spain out of the need to undo "a massive ornamental layer of truly baroque stucco" (1998a: 78–79). Prone to oscillation and political indecisiveness, the baroque craved more fluid mechanisms, supple logics apt to accommodate, even if grotesquely, all sorts of opposites and adapt, even if poorly, to all sorts of contingencies. The baroque virtuosity consisted in propelling the swaying motion, thanks to which "heroes are always able to turn around the order of fate . . . [and] like a ball in their hands, contemplate it now from one side, now from the other" (Benjamin 1998a: 84). Such a layer of stucco, Benjamin writes, "conceals the keystone" to "constellations" that "only the closest investigation can locate" (78–79).

But whereas Benjamin associated such "constellations" with the progressive energetics of the "dialectical image," I see the engine for a new power arrangement that more closely resembles a form of paradigmatic totalitarianism. As I argue this power arrangement expresses a notorious ability to deploy the extreme. What is key about this deployment of the extreme is how it is transformed in the process. Such transformation consists in a striking ability to consider extremes only to deprive these of a particular place or position. Abstract as this idea may sound, this is the key to the door of the Charismatic gymnasium and, as far as I am able to tell, the very essence of the political theater in which Bolsonarismo unfolds.

Underpinning the complexity of the Charismatic movement in Brazil is a command to hold tension through opposites. Such an orientation, however, is the applied formula of an older strand within Orthodox Catholicism called the *complexio oppositorum*: the principle by which thesis and antithesis endure their antagonism without mediation into a higher third. In *Roman Catholicism and Political Form* ([1923] 1996), Carl Schmitt described how the complexio allows Catholicism to embrace antonyms—the natural and the mechanical, the spiritual and the institutional, self-effacement and conspicuous propaganda, humility and arrogance, poverty and entrepreneurship, authoritarianism and capitalism. This capacity to draw vitality from the simultaneity of opposites explains, according to Schmitt, an "elasticity that is really astounding" (4). What is distinctive about the complexio is the methodological opportunism with which it draws on the extreme.

Significantly, if it takes things to an extreme, it is only so as to test the elasticity of its structure in becoming closer to what seems to oppose it. The more extreme it goes, the more able it is to assert the center (epitomized in the figure of Rome) from which it simultaneously wants to distance or decenter itself. Through such a mechanism the church revitalizes its institutional status—its muscle power—via what seems most radically opposed to it. Accordingly, tension and conflict are not to be seen as deriving from the meeting of opposites. Rather it is the pragmatic application of a particular kind of power that draws on tension as such. Hence, pneuma—and its respiratory logics—is reincorporated into the heart of the institutionalized body it simultaneously criticizes and distances itself from.

Given the Brazilian Charismatic Renewal's conspicuous investment in mass media, how can one reconcile that orthodox principle, the elasticity of opposites, with a model of communication? Charismatic Catholicism draws on the institution it simultaneously opposes as a way to resignify the communicative model through which to think the concepts of tension and opposition. This happens through an enabling abstraction that consists in displacing the powers of the argumentative—as classic liberal theories of communication have it—into the physiological mechanisms of the breathing body. As is the task of this book to show, Charismatics are interested in the "how" of communication, the pneumatic operations that enable communication as such.

What is so profoundly significant about this move is that it allows Charismatics to step outside the modern frame of dimensionality that undergirds protocols of argumentative reasoning into the mechanisms of fluidity and substance. Accordingly, pneuma does not warrant signification in referential terms. But neither are such mechanisms about a turn to ontology or materiality in a radical alterity to transcendence (see Reinhardt 2016).

At stake, rather, is a theology of mechanisms—a theo-technocracy—that must never succumb to either one of those sides but use every opportunity to activate and expose (indeed, pneumatize) the fluidity of the "how" itself. In Charismatic practice, in sum, communicative "tension" enters the circuitry of the breathing body so as to be rendered in gymnasium-like idioms such as tensile, stretchable, malleable, workable. In being reduced to its abstract elemental operations, this religious movement can move in all sorts of directions and accommodate many repertoires at once and without the slightest sense of contradiction.

I cannot emphasize enough the key importance of the complexio in Charismatic theology, practice, and rhetoric. Distilled into a theology of the gymnasium, the old complexio is responsible for the miracle of elasticity that undergirds much of Charismatics' contemporary media and religious programs. Charismatics' option for the elastic enables a deliberate instability. It promotes a pauperism of structures that precisely strengthens a neoliberal ethos. The complexio sustains a vigorous impoverishment of ways and things, a pliable modality detectable in myriad manifestations: the flooding of aphorisms in Charismatic daily talk, of trite and crude analogies, tropes, contorted semantics, stretches in logic, obsessive repetitions, grotesque puns and spoonerisms, infatuations with archaic media equipment (often mirrored in the povera of Saint Francis/Saint Clare of Assisi as a figural operation), a fondness for brutalist aesthetics and for precarious structures. For Charismatics, the function of such stylized impoverishment is twofold: it *both* draws on a Christian tradition of self-effacing asceticism (*ascesis*, training) *and* approximates the latter to the powers of potentiality intrinsic to Brazil's socioeconomic and political era. Impoverishment, thus conceived, is not a status or an identity one can own or locate. It is power's own flexible expression: impoverishment not as socioeconomic condition but as the condition of the socioeconomic.

Catholic Charismatics would come up with their own counter-reforming solution, one that would not embrace the shock of iconoclasm but, more ingeniously, *make shock internal to a pragmatic theology of compromise*. To the demands of having to decide whether to be more Catholic or more Pentecostal, more "option for the poor" (as proclaimed by liberation theology) or evangelical vitalism, more institution or more spirit, more stucco or more electronic media, Catholic Charismatics set out to produce a synthesis that sees undecidability not as an obstacle but as an energetic expression of the system itself. This synthesis that offers a throne to the powers of the undecidable draws on an old key strain in Orthodox Eastern Christianity, notably, the Byzantine. It's an extraordinary leaping operation. Yet such operations bolster the elasticity that Charismatics never stop emphasizing in their day-to-day versatile religious practices.

Arising out of a synthetic diplomacy within Christianity (specifically between Western Catholicism and televangelist Pentecostalism), the Byzantine provided Charismatics with a theology of compromise, or better, the compromise of noncompromise. The powers of the gymnasium lie in this outstanding encircling of incompatibilities, its attempt to articulate two traditions within Christianity. What pneuma awakens in the body through aerobic prayer, the Byzantine—itself born of tension between iconoclasts and iconophiles—legitimates. It is what mystics like Saint John of the Cross, also called gymnasiarchs, formulated as a test of the pliability of the soul (Largier 2007; Faubion 2013).

Far from pacified or repressed, therefore, unalloyed oppositions are emphasized as part of a discipline of revival. Rather than opting for a decision in either/or terms, Catholic Charismatics embrace an inclusive both/and. But then again, the both/and structure is not propositional. Rather, it informs the tenor of a bodily discipline that draws on the basic operations of pneumatic breathing. Practically, it would not make sense to speak of *either* inhaling *or* exhaling but rather of the *movement* that in actually alternating between one and the other pole potentiates the *coming to pass* of breath. What takes place then is the *holding-together* of a tension between opposites that must itself play out in Charismatic practice. This is how Catholic Charismatics in Brazil are able to wield the most abstract-concrete (both/and) unit of life, such as the event of breathing, to an all-encompassing and universalistic Catholic Spirit. In its semantic slippage among spirit, breath, and air, pneuma is the fundamental criterion for the practicing gymnasium.

The staging of operations involved in Charismatic revivalist reform runs across this book. With pneuma as its central protagonist, the book closely describes how media montages, speech, gestures, spaces, and objects are construed to render explicit the principles—the logical dispositive—that cause them to be. Throughout these pages I show how those elements are made to be in constant communication with their cause, so that each scenic manifestation becomes a witnessing of the underlying operations—the infrastructural underpinnings—of what Charismatics associate with spirit (pneuma). The progression of scenes in each chapter is designed to expose the persistence of this pattern in Charismatic religious media practice. It shows the continuity of action that characterizes the Charismatic gymnasium: the power of re-iteration by which the thing described enforces the very logic that propels it.

Such a procedure inevitably affects the style of analysis and narrative. My focus on the episteme of operations draws its motivation from the very phenomena under study, from having the object influencing its methodology. There is peril in this performative move in that the analysis risks participating in the (self-referential) logic it tries to elucidate. At the same time, theories of performativity have precisely shown us the limits of the Western episteme in shaping the canon of critique. Relying on a transcendental outside, the liberal critical subject has a hard time bending to the self-enunciating nature of the performative, that is, in its ability to excite into being the very reality it names. Such limitation, however, also opens an alternative path to critique, one in which we critically test the distinction between the analyst and the object of study itself as an intrinsic requirement to the task of examination. As Johannes Fabian (1983, 1991) reasons, the intrinsic value of anthropological theory lies in its ability to speak the language of the very traditions it seeks to criticize, for it is precisely in that echo from within that transformation may ensue.

What I take to be particularly instructive about Catholic Charismatic revivalism lies less in its particular sociological components than in the epistemic mode through which it operates. My goal is not to historicize or sociologize the events on the ground, which other studies on Catholic Charismatics in Brazil have done proficiently, but rather to submit these to a conceptual treatment that will help us come to grips with the principles of composition they adopt in their practices. If this idea sounds abstract, it is because abstraction is the operation in question. And I hope to be able to show how the powers of abstraction conjure tremendous political force in today's theological and political configurations of the social, not just in Brazil but elsewhere in the world.

Such a focus requires addressing the problem of what is meant by abstraction in the particular case of Charismatic Catholicism and what frames such a notion more broadly in the history of Western thought. If abstraction in the latter is often confined to the realm of ideas, far removed from the bodily, the mechanical, and the physiological, Charismatics instead proceed to effect abstraction as intrinsic to basic operations of the breathing body. The prime operational model of this abstraction, which they extract from the biblical Book of Acts, is "the act(s) of breathing": the oscillating and paradoxical movements of expansion and contraction. As I show at different points, the centrality of pneuma in Charismatic thought and practice is associated with a loss of eschatological dimension—the loss of a sense of ending—in favor of the promotion of an ongoing middle: a highly dynamic middle (*meio*, as homologous and homophonous to *medium* and *midst*), where elements move a lot without going anywhere in particular. This loss of eschatology, tied to a Westernized narrative-teleological conception of history, results in a transformation not only of what we mean by abstraction but also of the theatrical elements and the structure of the dramatic form to which it is attached.[3]

For example, Charismatics are fond of analogical thinking. They often bend the past and the present, bringing them face-to-face as mirror images. Yet they do so not out of a penchant for structuralist thinking, the kind that holds that the secular is a modern version of the theological or likens special effects to secularized miracles, only to reintegrate them in a linear conception of time. That is not the kind of abstraction in question. Rather, Charismatics are interested in how the structure of analogy can be effectively embodied as an exercising of the members—both in the sense of laypeople/membership and in the sense of limbs. Thus when Charismatics say, as they do in chapter 1, "Let us launch the nets," they are not simply making an analogy between the fishing nets of the apostles according to the Book of Acts and the nets of media technology today. They literally work it out on the level of a bodily act, turning analogy and other rhetorical devices into an aerobic exercise of sorts.

Such stylistic devices are important in Charismatic power rhetoric insofar as they enter the flesh of the participant. Importantly, entering the flesh does not mean it becomes a yielding to presence but instead it becomes a rhythmic partaking. What distinguishes "partaking" from "presence" is the "leave-take" quality of the former. In repeating certain phrases (as when they verbalize "Let us launch the nets" ten times according to the structure of the Byzantine rosary) in prayer and sermons Charismatics explore language's capacity to act and give form: to build up. However, building up does not mean becoming more present to oneself. Rather, it means to be better at exposing the undecidable structure of "leave-take" in incarnational partaking. As we learn from performative theory, "citational practice" produces a double effect: it both joins and displaces. *It joins in displacing.* It both adds to what was before and transforms it into something else.[4] Ideally, for Charismatics, formal aspects of language and referential meaning enter a relation of recursivity between constative and performative in that the act of reciting itself is seen as the act of weaving the net—a net*work*—it is proposing to launch. In sum, the aim of practice is to transfigure the subject who *actually* acts and yet in acting also ensures a certain virtuality for transformation. Analogies and other duplicitous forms such as resonances, mirrorings, and equivalences are not to be understood through a frame of identification between entities. These are the effect of a synthesis in the acting body itself.

This is also why the notion of mediation that informs the vast majority of theories on religion and media cannot do justice to the aspect of "incarnated operations" that concern Catholic Charismatics in Brazil. Terms like *mediation* and *immediacy* are often treated as collaboratively involved in bringing the sacred into presence across religions (Meyer 2011, 2012; Witte 2011, 2018). Yet such collaboration among mediation, immediacy, and presence confounds the desire to efface mediation with that to bypass it altogether (Morris 2017). The effacement of mediation places immediacy as the trading technique, the trick, that mediation itself allows. But an assumption of the primacy of mediation excludes the fact that there are forms of immediacy that are irreducible to mediation, even when it involves technology.

Such becomes apparent in how Charismatics draw on media technologies not to mediate the sacred but to expose the principles under which, technically speaking, revivalism functions. What gets to be communicated is the engineering power of pneuma, which, ideally, is less conducive to presence as to a kind of impropriety whereby songs, slogans, recitations, and gestures are owned by all and by no one in particular. In being interested in the underlying operations, for Charismatics it matters little where the organic, the mechanical, and the spirit begin or end. One is always in the middle, what Charismatics sometimes refer to as being within the third person (Holy Spirit). The relevance of the aerial (pneuma) in Charismatic theology (as opposed to the earthbound liberation theology) resides precisely in absorbing all causality—which a theory of mediation implies—into acting as such.[5]

In a special forum on the notion of mediation, Charles Hirschkind (2011) calls attention to the at once parochial and universalistic uses of mediation in the study of religion and media or religion more broadly. Despite how encompassing the term *religious mediation* is, Hirschkind rightly questions its adequacy in the study of other religious traditions, where such concepts, at least in their dominant framing, may not apply. In his own study on the practice of listening to recorded sermons among Muslims in urban Cairo, Hirschkind (2006) distinguishes how listening to sermons on cassettes does not merely mediate a religious message, for that would imply a relation of noncontiguity between the ethical sphere of the sermon and the act of proper listening. He proposes a more intimate connection of sound and power not to be rendered as either mediation or immediacy, as mediation's other, but as learned techniques. To give shape and "flesh to the ear" (Hirschkind 2006: 25) is to act on the ability of listening itself. In Hirschkind's analysis, therefore, it is precisely the irrelevance of mediation in the process of ethical formation that warrants the proper function of listening as a virtuous, constitutive act.

In view of the aforementioned tension between Catholicism and (in many respects, Protestant-derived) Pentecostalism internal to Brazil's Charismatic Catholicism, neither mediation nor immediacy will be adequate notions for understanding the operations in question, or, indeed, the concept of operation as such. As Christianized a reading as the pairing mediation-immediacy may be, *it is not Christological enough.* A Christological reading, as pursued in this study, owes little to the logical frames that normally accommodate that coupling. This is due to the particularly disjunctive temporality that characterizes Charismatics' *ongoing* acts.[6] Featured in a gerund as these are, these goings-on affect the very idea of presence. For Charismatics to incarnate is not to bring into presence. Neither is presence a problem in light of the possibility of nonpresence as is the case elsewhere (Engelke 2007). Rather, to incarnate is to give flesh, and to give flesh is to operate. It is to communicate the operations through which the *coming to pass* of the present itself is possible. It is to show, in the most technocratic sense, what in the sacred is at work. Presence, one could say, is the exhibition of a mediality in the flesh.

Charismatic operations hinge entirely on acts, not on figurative content; on practice, not on proposition. As we will see throughout, but particularly in part II, such is the crux of why Catholic Charismatics in Brazil must find aesthetic and doctrinal support in the tradition of the Byzantine from Eastern Orthodoxy, a tradition where, as several chapters will show, even the concepts of (real) presence, materiality, and immateriality fit awkwardly when it comes to grasping what in Charismatic doctrine is essential, notably, the operon underpinning incarnation as logos.

The present argument reflects on, and to some extent stages, a particular theatrical political form. This form is alternative to the one indebted to the structure of empathy. As an established referent of Aristotelian dramaturgy behind modern Western epistemes, empathic identification has long sustained a privileged acquaintance among sociohistorical analyses, the concrete, and the empirical, thus equating, in turn, the abstract with the nonconcrete, nonempirical, and noncorporeal. The structure of empathy likewise undergirds the centrality of terms like mediation and immediacy acquired in recent anthropological analysis. These notions highlight the role of practice in producing displacement and transformation. Yet the empathic structure that supports it implies a politics of grounds that ousts the full scope of the theory of performativity that interests me. Through empathy we get to learn how actions happen on grounds but not as much about how grounds themselves partake in actions as an intrinsic feature of the performative. Mediation helps us understand how citationality occurs in a space-time interval through repetition, but we do not understand enough about how the notion of the interval itself is transformed in that very cultural process.

To incarnate, then, means to step outside such an empathic framework. Indeed, it is this epistemic legacy born of empathic identification that Charismatics suspend in the ordinary practice of the disciplining gym. Instead of relating to the world (and to the theatrical) through a problematic of empathic identification, their practice draws on the powers of speech and acting to constitute the subject who acts as inseparable from the grounds that enable it. Instead of pursuing a form of presence in light of "the unity of action," as the structure of mediation and related empathic identification would require, Charismatics adhere to the performance of certain acts—such as re-citation—that stretch and extend the here of presence to an elsewhere. The result is a simultaneous here-else.

What is most required from religious practice is the ability to expose the principles of articulation as such, not unlike a gymnast whose acts show the entire economy, the operational network of muscles and joints. Put differently, what is important to retain is how this forming of the subject is the function of a highly pragmatic form of abstraction, the prime function of which is to expose the medial principles—Charismatics call them pneuma, spirit, flow, third—recognizable in their power to articulate, to bring formerly separate worlds into contact. It is a stretching of sorts, not a dramaturgy where meanings or even sensory experiences might be conveyed.

Given the crucial reconstruction of the narrative frame in which it operates, this study adopts the typologies it describes. Instead of framing critique as a problem of empathic identification, the chapters build on the economy of "articulations" that compose an act, a scene, a gesture, a word game. This approach makes the writing at times crude, jolting, and obtrusive (at points, even unsteady), but that should rejoin my ambition to take thought and language to the gym: less by way of revealing meaningful bodies than of exposing the articulations that allow Charismatics to speak of bodies, acts, and speech in terms of rule, logic, play, principle—in short, operations. The style of narration ought to reflect an effort to train myself in a form of writing that absorbs the content into its form. This double bind was challenging as it required a simultaneous doing and undoing of proficiency in standard academic writing. The task was to unground myself in a largely earthbound discipline through leaps and connections so as to bring the Charismatic gymnasium—and its pneumatic worlds—into full view.

ıııııııııııııııııııııııııııııııı

With the aim of showing how particular reformulations and practices have been taking place within Brazilian Catholicism through the example of the Catholic Charismatic Renewal, I focus on two key structuring sites of description and analysis. These are divided into two parts. The first part of the book is dedicated to the Canção Nova Community, a global media network compound situated outside São Paulo. In these first three chapters, the argument evolves from an overarching perspective of the place to the most particular, yet without refraining from showing the oscillations between one and the other.

Chapter 1 analyzes the constitutive circuits of pneuma involved in the making of the Canção Nova Community. Through the reenactment of the biblical Acts of the Apostles in the current age of global media, Canção Nova fashions itself not as a community that communicates but as a community that *is* communication. The community is its ability to communicate its own operations. This tautological arrangement has tremendous power as it transforms a noun into a verb: *being* community and *doing* communication coincide. In coinciding it implodes the borders of all containment, spatial and temporal, so as to institute the temporal logic of a gerund—an ongoing middle—through which power is deployed. This gerund is the temporality that ties the ongoing breath to the expanding life of the media community itself, linking a theological understanding of laboring operations in view of a certain orthodoxy.

Chapter 2, dedicated to confession, focuses on the linguistic tropes of the physiological human body explored in a show of public confession at Canção Nova. Specifically, it explores how the function of rhythm in language and movement helps to reveal the technical articulations that structure the possibility of the circulation of pollution or sin between bodies across space and time. If in chapter 1 my examination identifies the circulations that tie and entangle the different nodes and joints of the community, chapter 2 investigates that work of circulation in bodies in performance. Both chapters posit circulation as the being in relation.

Chapter 3 then zooms in for a close-up of the dramaturgy of *Adoration Hour* on the Canção Nova TV channel. The chapter describes and analyzes the economy of operations behind a one-hour mise-en-scène exposure of the

Eucharist on TV in real-time transmission. Given the technical ability of television to show at a distance, that is, to be at the same time both *here*, in front of the spectator, and *there*, on the scene, the Eucharist can neither fully be here nor entirely be there. It is a stretchable here-else. But how will the claims for the mystery of real presence be realizable in light of such a split? How do the postulates of real time and real presence meet on the TV screen?

Together these three chapters offer an analysis of the different entanglements, exercises, and techniques in and of material production within which sovereignty is incarnated. All three chapters also come back to the overarching argument that the exposure of operational techniques suspends all representation in order to direct the flow of the images coming to pass. The chapters show how this coming to pass of the image (as incarnation, as flesh, as opus) unfolds according to a synthesis not just of the Trinitarian apparatus but also of the Catholic Pentecostal tensions that set and allow Catholic Charismatics to adapt and utilize elements from Eastern or Byzantine Christendom.

These same aspects are taken up again in part II, but even more explicitly. Starting with chapter 4, the book concentrates on the multiple sites associated with a single personality, the media-savvy lover of sports and Charismatic Padre Marcelo Rossi. Emerging as a priest in the iconoclastic atmosphere of the Guerra Santa, Padre Marcelo (as he is commonly known) popularized the Charismatic movement. Through skillful adaptations of what seem like incommensurable elements—medieval Byzantine prayer, aerobics, and techno music—Padre Marcelo has orchestrated a powerful regime of prayer that has become incorporated into the daily habits of millions of Brazilians, ranging from the very devout to the casual fan. Exploring the granular effect of aroused skin through the power of song, this chapter is a precursor to the *béton brut* affectivities that will become apparent in the next chapter dedicated to architecture. From bodybuilding as what gives form to spirit through choreographed breath, we move on to a building that draws on a certain conception of the body, indeed, of the body as conception.

Chapter 5, then, analyzes how the Byzantine icon of Theotókos came to be an architectonic model for a new sacred space: the stylized ferroconcrete megasanctuary Santuário Mãe de Deus (Mother of God Sanctuary) in São Paulo. The chapter tells how, unable to pay off the prohibitive expenses of building a space, Padre Marcelo transforms such limits into a theology of Marian conception. To come to the church, to participate in his "aerobics of Jesus," becomes in itself a mode of contributing to the outgrowth of the sanctuary. First dedicating the sanctuary to the Byzantine Virgin of Theotókos, at a later point Padre Marcelo would withdraw from such referential worlds and turn Theotókos itself into a model for the administration (*oikonomia*) of a territory. This he does when Brazil is being torn apart by the shock and scandal of Operation Car Wash. Circular and self-adaptive, as in a topological feedback structure, the icon of Theotókos will be a lesson in orthodox theology as much as in civil engineering. It will be theology in the flesh, whereby the construction of a massive space is administrated around emergence, self-referentiality, and self-transformation.

Chapter 6 focuses on the monobloc chair (the white, lightweight, stackable, plastic, ubiquitous, and anonymous chair) as an object to think the relation between pneuma and design. The chapter analyzes the popularity of the chair as an icon of neoliberalism among Catholic Charismatics. It highlights how the conceptual and aesthetic properties of the chair encode unexpected relations among politics, plasticity, and theology in a religious tradition such as Roman Catholicism that has long valued noble materials, weight, and gravity.

A short epilogue reflects on the value of theology in ethnographic analyses.

An afterword recapitulates how the logics and operational mechanisms this book sets out to expose—the "how" of the Charismatic gymnasium—can be thought as a *dispositif* for thinking Brazil's contemporary political system under Jair Bolsonaro. In the interval that Guerra Santa opened up in the "body of the nation" during the 1990s, there appeared a shift in political dynamism that finds its apotheotic—and ultimately, I suspect, sacrificial—governmental expression in Bolsonarismo.

||||||||||||||||||||||||||||||||||

My interest in researching Brazil's Catholic Charismatic movement has been primarily guided by the desire to expose the form of an idea, the technical operations that attend it, and the conceptual work behind the spiritual and political constitution of an important religious phenomenon. While this book is certainly not a description of Brazil's political life, it does constitute a serious attempt to come up with the rhythmic mechanisms—the operational logics—that subtend a particular era. In laying bare the principles through which Charismatics operate, I hope to induce a particular mode of critique, the kind that Janet Roitman (2013: 36) calls an "unveiling of latencies." And yet, this nonrecognizability perhaps is precisely the point. In insisting on attaching critical function to positionality, in reaction to the legacy of appropriation and capture under colonialism, contemporary critique and political resistance fail to consider how the "Right" operates today on entirely different grounds and under very different parameters and temporal horizons. Much like the "gymnast" in the case of Charismatic Catholicism or the "Cossack dancer" (see the afterword) in Bolsonarismo, our critical function must now adjust itself to mechanisms of movement and fluidity. At stake is a form of power that draws energy and political shape not from moving toward a specific goal but by running, like an athlete in training, after itself. Such power goes nowhere in particular and yet, precisely, makes this lack of motion without telos its own inevitable end. My hope with this book is to inch our way into a breach and thereby lay bare some of those operational mechanisms and vocabularies intrinsic to a power formation of our time.

PART I

....

And just as lungs are passed between persons and districts, so are news and gossip. In this way one can receive news from remote districts, even those at the very edge of the world, without needing to leave home, although I myself enjoy traveling.

—TED CHIANG, *Exhalation*

PART I

1. THE MEDIA ACTS OF THE APOSTLES

....

Let us now launch the nets.
—PADRE JONAS speaking to his community

In the early months of 1978 in the state of São Paulo a youth group gathering for an event called Seminar in the Spirit in the small town of Areias witnessed an extraordinary event. A priest named Jonas Abib asked the group, "Which of you would be ready to leave everything behind—family, career, hobbies— in order to fulfill a mission God has placed in my heart?"[1] The story goes that exactly twelve people raised their hands as they "were moved by an incredible force." Then Padre Jonas added three points: first, the mission would involve working with communication; second, it was addressed to youth; and third, the community would be called Comunidade Canção Nova (New Song Community). This chapter is about the making of Canção Nova Community, a thriving global media network of Catholic Pentecostalism based in Brazil.

Communities have been analyzed in terms of a social construction organized around the management of symbols, events, or aspirations, which together create a sense of bonding and belonging. Anthony Cohen's (1985) *The Symbolic Construction of Community* suggests that communities can be understood as meaningful constructs that ground the cultural inscription of identity. In so arguing, Cohen implies the existence of a predetermined plane of reference against which construction happens. Benedict Anderson's (1983) notion of "imagined communities" provides a more flexible model for grasping the complex dynamics of community making. Still, imagining in this framework remains dependent on a point of origin or foundation on which communities imagine themselves. We do not have a sense, here, of how the ground through which imagination evolves is itself already constituted by those imaginings (leaving aside, for the moment, that communities may not be reducible to processes of imagination alone). In what follows, I develop a more circular and interactive approach to community by looking at the bodily and processual mechanisms that signal the communal as always brought about and implicated through its own making. Instead of subscribing to the idea of community as a bounded entity that communicates a particular identity it constructs or imagines, the goal here is to expose the ongoing mechanics or technological existence of a community *as* communication. Rather than conceiving of it as a containable entity awaiting signification or as an assemblage of discrete bodies that instrumentally communicate, I examine the communal as constituted by communicative processes. In short, this chapter argues that communities not only communicate, but they *are* communication.

More specifically, relying on the Christian notion of *pneuma*, I invite the reader to ponder the concept of community through the breathing body. Based on the biblical narrative of Pentecost that tells how the Holy Spirit came down on the apostolic community "in the form of a rushing mighty wind" (Acts 2:2), this chapter explores how inspirited breath sets the force or mechanism through which the community as communication unfolds.[2] I then consider the motile expressions of breath, that is, the aspect of reciprocation between inside and outside that is inherent to respiration. Attending to the cycle of breathing in and out closely leads me to question the modern separation between inner life and outer expression. The breath cycle, as I note, disallows any prolonged closure or any external point where the boundaries of the community might be clearly drawn. What becomes relevant instead are the processes and dynamics by which bodies are implicated and distributed in the broader natural, human, and technological landscape by means of circulation and a self-regulated balance between input and output.

I owe my understanding of a breathing body in this discussion to the efforts of the figure with whom I started this chapter, Padre Jonas, the media-savvy Brazilian Catholic Charismatic who promoted an expanded middle in an era of strong political polarization between right- and left-wing party ideologies. While the 1970s were rich in calls for social mobilization in Brazil, Latin America, and around the world, Padre Jonas's engagement with movement was primarily vestibular and kinetic. He chose not to be *part* of a social religious movement but to *be* movement. This entailed a leap over the walls of ideological positioning and landing in a space of affective and sensory modalities. This chapter thus proposes to analyze a particular figuration of power through movement on a level with operations, one that ties the body to the landscape to the mystical to the technological.

While the analogy between anatomy and community is not new, I examine it through the distinctly sensory modality of proprioception. Akin to kinesthesia, proprioception is the primary sense responsible for the perception of motion. Sometimes considered a sixth sense, it refers to the internal mechanism that enables a body in motion to maintain equilibrium through awareness of the relation of the joints and other body parts to one another. In the same way that proprioceptive awareness keeps track of and controls circulation among different parts of the body, this chapter shows how Canção Nova has evolved and maintains itself as a whole community through a circuitry and transmissibility that it has established between different community stations. Here nature, body, architecture, media technology, and economics all enter a relational field of inter- and intrareferentiality in ways that engage with and actively configure electronic technology. My overall goal, following the empiricism of Canção Nova's members (in the aforementioned double sense of membership and limbs) and followers at large, is to highlight a structural analogy between the influx of sensory information in the body and the regime of circularity that connects the important joints of the community.

In sum, the purpose of this chapter is threefold: first, to foreground the Canção Nova media community as a sensuous community in motion or a community-in-the-making; second, to reflect on how such a community-in-the-making instantiates the very mechanics of communication it puts to use; and third, to disclose the constitutive relation between an aesthetic economic regime of transparency and Catholic Pentecostal practices of embodied charisma. In line with recent scholarly interest in the relations between the aesthetic and the political, the notion of aesthetics as applied here reasserts the political power of the sensorial in organizing the dimensions of experience (Rancière 2005; Hirschkind 2006; Verrips 2006; Meyer 2009). In order to grasp the processual making of community, it is advisable to take seriously the discursive practices through which communities produce themselves. In the case of Canção Nova—and the Catholic Charismatic movement more generally— this entails two basic reforms: a new valorization of movement above positionality, and the rise of a politics of the middle and an attendant disclosure of the rules of operations therein.

Unlocking the Paths

In 1969, the same year the Catholic Charismatic Renewal (CCR) arrived in Brazil from the United States, Padre Jonas Abib (of Lebanese origin and recently ordained under the Silesians) entered a sanatorium in Campos do Jordão, in the state of São Paulo, to be treated for a serious lung disease. His pulmonary illness kept him from participating in the activities of his parish in the region of the Paraiba Valley. An ambitious and restless person, he rebelled against his chronic fatigue, just as he did against his superiors, who, unable to make sense of his agitation, kept shuffling him to various parishes in the valley. In the sanatorium Padre Jonas started to compose songs, and he would go on to assemble a choir of fellow pneumonic patients. He spun tales about the breath of Pentecost. He recited biblical Acts, Acts 2 in particular, in its laudations to the wind of the Holy Spirit. He taught the patients to engage with words and the powers of recitation as a method to clear their respiratory systems. Sculpted and directed through the power of prayer and song, the parable of Pentecost became a kind of filling station for air that presented as able to connect, as if through a network of pipes, spirituality to the natural and the natural to the mechanical.

Padre Jonas recited Joshua 1:1–27, the parable about the blasting of the walls of Jericho by Jacob's seven ram horns. In the 1970s and 1980s Charismatics were sometimes seen staging what they called the "tumbling of the walls of Jericho" in public spaces within São Paulo. They would set up tents in the vicinity of a cathedral or significant building within the city and go on a seven-day vigil of singing, clapping, and dancing. As in the parable of Pentecost, that of the "walls of Jericho" was to draw on the powers of pneuma to transform walls by making them less rigid and more permeable—more membrane-like. This is also the script that Padre Jonas re-enacted while at the sanatorium. Lapping their tongues, Abib's choral group, so the legend goes, shook the walls of the place. The workers at the facility read into this bizarre event the expression of an ultimate force that was asking for the release of Abib. As he explains in one of his books, "In the next month we had a youth meeting at the sanatorium. Then, not without reason, the doctor called my superior, and told him that if he would want me to be cured, he had to let me out. That is what my superior did: he sent me off to Lorena" (Abib 1999: 14).

While in Lorena, one of the valley's districts, Padre Jonas Abib met American Father Haroldo Rahm during an early Seminar in the Spirit. During that event in 1971 Padre Jonas was baptized in the Spirit. He was filled with the grace of the Spirit of Pentecost; above all, that meant he would rise up to put grace to use. For grace, in the Charismatic sense, is not owned by an individual but in effect involves abandonment to a disowning pragmatism, one that is made possible (and therefore recognizable by fellow anointed Charismatics) by an assimilation of grace (*kharis*) to artifice, and to equipment. To be gracious was then, and is still now, to plumb the world of operations and to put them to use.

Many locate the origins of Canção Nova in that baptismal moment. Then, and only then, did the pneumonia of Padre Jonas start to heal. With an effusion from heaven his unyielding lungs began to inflate, his chest expanded, his engrained fatigue mysteriously disappeared. After that, Padre Jonas spent seven years moving around the green valley in order to baptize individuals and proclaim his experience of healing to weekly prayer groups he helped organize. Since he always carried a Bible with him, the locals called him the Padre Da'Bib(lia) (the Bible Priest). After seven years of meandering around the valley in service, the body of Padre Jonas fused with the local landscape, each becoming inextricably associated with the other. By his breathing in and out, the story goes, his body dissolved and was distributed in the valley, just as the entire ecological landscape became embedded in him. And this is why, when people said, as many did indeed, that they were ready to leave everything behind and follow him, he would correct them by paraphrasing the Apostle Paul, that inasmuch as his body was no longer his but one with the world, whoever followed him was following a certain "third." More, given that such an embodiment of an ecological third (he called it "Spirit") communicated the potentialities of a practice honed through years of erratic wandering, they were, above all, following their future-anterior selves. Errancy was for Padre Jonas Abib a form of applying the ways of the Spirit who bloweth where it listeth (John 3:8). To a wandering in space he related a conception of time, one that owed little to sequence but much to the resonance between the now and the ancient.

During his spiritual wanderings Padre Jonas wanted to assimilate all of the surroundings into himself, to steep the local morphology, natural and artificial, into his lungs, like a reservoir or dispenser, and mold his instinct accordingly. To do that he found the element of air, as pneuma, to be the great medium and articulator of otherwise insurmountable disparities. Pneuma would align what others viewed as incommensurable—the mystical and the technological, the natural and the artificial, the sacred and the profane—with abstract breathable minimums. Thus reduced, these could be easily smuggled across borders, in time as well as in space, in view of a global expression of Catholicism. Such was the lesson Padre Jonas drew from the Apostle Paul, the great gymnasiarch of an unfolding antiquity in times of mass media.

A site where meteorological and spatial science, ufology and mystical happenings combine, Vale do Paraiba proved hospitable to Padre Jonas's prophetic outpouring. Just a few miles from Lorena is the national sanctuary of Our Lady of Aparecida, named after Brazil's patron saint. The valley is also known for its many shrines, tales, and mystical phenomena that add to the sense of a site that is ripe for miraculous encounter. Padre Jonas, however, was adamant in stressing that his authority would not be circumscribed by either law (*letra*) or place (*lugar*). Rather, his addresses called for a radical decentralization in order to make room for air as spirit (pneuma), boundless yet effectively balanced in its passing. The words he spoke thus suspended all circumscription for the sake of force and passing. The regulation of this force necessitated the creation of a new space, the middle—or better, the midst—from which prophetic speech and modern media technology might connect and circulate anew, in the process reenacting an old parable, that of the Acts of the Apostles. And so one day, during one of the youth meetings, Padre Jonas felt a thrust in his chest and a vertiginous urge to speak up. As words came out of his mouth, he realized that the call he was about to issue had been building up inside him for years. Voicing it out expelled the last residue of his phlegmatic past along with the outline for a new project under the pneumatic intervention of the Holy Spirit. Padre Jonas's airways were finally unblocked. He could breathe, and on his knees he went.

Channeling Proprioception

The rise of Canção Nova was thus underway. Unlike the American Jesuit Eduardo Dougherty, who founded the Associação Senhor Jesus media station in the town of Valinhos, São Paulo, Padre Jonas lacked financial resources, marketing expertise, and technical equipment, as well as experience with televangelism. The only thing he had, he likes to say, was his faith and his twelve followers. Such lack, however, was precisely what allowed him to stick closely to the message of the Pentecost and, more specifically, to the aesthetic economy of charisma. Having no capital to launch his call, Padre Jonas focused on his charismatically unlocked body in order to tune into his immediate surroundings.

Drawing on his breathing body—the at once abstract and concrete operations of breath—meant entering into negotiation with a new theory of ends. For Padre Jonas, the movements of breath are to be thought of as the operational matrix for the building up of an entire apostolic and religious edifice, a global media religious net-work he and his fishermen of souls call a "New Song" (Canção Nova). This new edifice, as we will see, owes little to the Aristotelian sense of plot or narrative, with its emphasis on linearity and final outcomes. With a gradual rejection of eschatology, it would favor a dramaturgy that acknowledges pragmatic, technical, and equipment conditions. Networking is, after all, the working of a net: an entangled system of knots and loops.

It is said, printed, and recorded in dozens of Canção Nova media productions that from the first moment, nobody in the community knew what the next step would be. The group was primarily an assemblage of individuals baptized in the Spirit. In a vivid reenactment of the apostolic community, they gathered in stables, in tents, and often in the open air in the green valley of the Paraiba River. Words fluttered out of the priest's mouth in ways that, his followers maintain today, "intoxicated our hearts."[3] It was as if the air that formed his words had the power to carry his listeners into another time, and yet his language was relevant to the present. One oft-cited example tells how he recalled Jesus addressing the apostles, exclaiming, "It is now time to launch the nets."[4] Phrases like this do not just disappear in the instance of their saying but linger in the air, like hibernating particles, awaiting future iterations. "It was as though Padre Jonas wanted us to repeat words so they would become the collective property of Canção Nova," said Nelsinho, one of the early apostles of the community.[5]

In reciting certain phrases, the community members would be in deeper contact with the infrastructure through which Canção Nova functions. Here, as in other moments of Charismatic practice, what was vital was the ability to erase the sense of origins and of calculative ends as a form of redemptive dramaturgy. As we will see in subsequent chapters, Canção Nova has its own physical stages, the stages for the shows and spectacles it mounts on a weekly basis, as well as the stage of the entire space, today ramified in a complex global network. It is a mise en abyme: a stage within a stage within a stage. And it is so precisely because the art of staging would never be dissociated from the infrastructural conditions that make it possible. By placing the most prosaic routines and ordinary acts of the community under the spotlights of the amphitheater, it is as though each gesture becomes an aerial protagonist involved in the "making of" Canção Nova. A theatrics of unfolding was thus foregrounded from early on, one that would take steps to abolish all referentiality in its stage form.

At other times Padre Jonas echoed Saint Matthew in his call "to evangelize through the roofs"; he talked about the poverty of birds just like Saint Francis had, and he repeated Saint Paul's prophecy on the Second Coming or the Rapture, saying, "We who are left alive will be carried off together with them in the clouds to meet the Lord in the air" (Thess. 4:15–17). In the words of Nelsinho:

> The history of Canção Nova has been made from body-to-body with the people. We had no real place. . . . Padre Jonas would walk around with a tape recorder and a bag filled with tapes. He would put on classical music and would ask: Who is God for you? Then, we would start crying, we were touched by the words of the padre. That prepared the sermon. Then the padre would make us travel, he had that kind of language. He worked with our imagination. There and then, the padre was DAVI [the audiovisual headquarters].[6]

Then as now, his followers maintain, everything occurred as if time and space existed alongside the dynamics of "breathing in and through the spirit," beyond which there was only uncertainty, the "unknown." Yet by perceiving time as unfolding with each singular breath—that is, by living ever more intensely in the present—they opened up to the universal. Each singular breath worked as an actualization of creative possibility. The more one inspired, the more one became inspired, and the more one's creative potential thereby grew.

In the Charismatic sense, to be virtuous (i.e., to be gifted) is an opening up to virtuality. It is argued that breath-induced virtue stands for the ability to open up to relations with the outside. The outside is implicated in the inside (and vice versa) through the dynamic rhythms of breath, meaning that any relation is always and necessarily tautological, a self-relation. In this process the body alternates its objective concreteness with the more abstract dynamism of transience and flow. Breath (pneuma) is at once a thing and its circuitous movement, a noun and a verb. It is a paradoxical process wherein the actual physical activity involved in the contraction and expansion of breath also becomes, by virtue of that very mechanism, the least material regime of corporeality.

To be economical, in this regime, would mean working on being balanced but in ways that have nothing to do with the usual sense of calculative ends—nothing is treated as linear and instrumental. Rather, the economic administration of Canção Nova would draw lessons from the inner ear or vestibular signals that regulate and prevent imbalances. Thanks to the pneumatic sense of mystery—and sense of play—Canção Nova would hone the role of input and muscle strength in maintaining a bearing through pace, posture, and a certain agility too.

The body, its articulations, its rhythms, and its balancing skills thus became a barometer connecting the center of Canção Nova to a wider global order. The more Padre Jonas became aware of the proprioceptive fluencies occurring in his body, the more distributed and co-implicated he became in the physical, human, and technological landscapes. Just as the physical landscape permeated the body and the body was recalibrated to suit the local environment, so the collective and the community inhabited the individual. This process of nondistinction between discrete elements in articulated motion had—and continues to have—huge political force. It defines the operational field in which the Charismatic gymnast works out a particular sense of self-perception less as an isolated entity but as a complex system of articulations. To work out the articulations becomes a way of addressing the middle—the joints, nodes, and junctures—and of testing the balance of any act on the slimmest foundations that characterize the Charismatic gymnasium.

The Media Acts of the Apostles

"The Acts of the Apostles," Padre Jonas frequently exhorts, "is the Acts of the Apostles."[7] Often used as a statement of prepositional logic or, alternatively, as a rhetorical strategy, the redundant and symmetrical nature of a tautology makes it good to breathe: one inhales while thinking "the Acts of the Apostles," then exhales while thinking "the Acts of the Apostles." Word-bearing tautological symmetries such as this help structure breath, the "art of mechanical reproducibility" that since at least the founding moment of Padre Jonas's prophecy has organized the life of Canção Nova. Such a practice follows the reformations of Catholic prayer techniques introduced by the CCR that characteristically use words and rhythm to structure breath. Bearing in mind media's contemporary efforts to convey a sense of live transmission and directness, Canção Nova's adoption of breath as a dynamic principle allows it to instantiate liveliness at the core of the technological, one modulating the other.

Guiding these practices is the aspiration to act according to the teachings of Saint Paul, for whom communication is inalienably associated with the living body (i.e., a body that communicates). As Manfred Schneider (2001: 202–3) notes, Paul was "the media specialist of the Apostles" who "radicalized the difference inaugurated by Jesus and his reporters: namely, that God's power, and the medium of his revelation, consisted in spirit." As one of the main protagonists of the Book of Acts, Paul spoke and lived according to the idea that the body was at once the medium and the message, the singular and the universal. For Paul the body was not an instrument of communication but was itself communication.

In the story of Pentecost as per Acts 2:2, charismata, gifts, and virtues—composing Paul's "media theory"—fall on the apostolic community in the "form of a rushing wind." Pneuma is this *rushing wind*. Yet, contrary to other works on pneuma focused on *prana*, the Sanskrit word for "breath," or *qi* in Chinese culture, Charismatics do not relate to it as an abstract principle anterior to experience, what the phenomenologist Maurice Merleau-Ponty ([1945] 1962) called the realm of the "pre-objective" (see Csordas 1990, 1994, 1995). On the contrary, anteriority or causality is precisely what is tentatively abolished in the Charismatic model of practice in general and of communication specifically. This abolishment of causality is paramount if we are to understand how Charismatics' indexical power in communication is a symptom of a semiotic displacement. As chapter 2 shows through the myth of original sin, this symptomatology associated with the abolishment of anteriority translates into somatic manifestations that displace the referential qualities of the index to self-referential gestures involving hand and fingers.[8]

Emerging at a moment when new configurations of publicness appear desirable, Charismatics aspire to rupture with existing logics of conventional language. In the context of resistance to military intervention and in defense of the oppressed as epitomized in the influential pedagogy of Paulo Freire in the 1970s, Charismatics (who are Catholics but do not wish to be confused with evangelicals) also understood or intuited that those models of linguistic function were under new pressures. These pressures came from different sides simultaneously but most expressively from two interdepending aspects: on the one hand, the burgeoning technological potentials internal to mass media and, on the other, the desire to embrace the figure of the crowd. This double pressure from new forms of media and publics—mass media and the crowd—came to influence the relation Charismatics entertained with language. It affected both its old function and the subject of individuation it presupposed. Specifically, the political ideal, so preponderant in Brazil's traditional Catholic circuits, "to give voice" (as in grassroots ecclesiastic communities) becomes a manifestation of voice itself. This incarnated presence of voice in the figure of the crowd is nowhere as spectacularly manifest as in the collective phenomenon of glossolalia, but it also manifests through other spiritual gifts.

However, this linkage between language and pneumatic gifts also leaves in sight an incongruence within the communicative model in question. As Rosalind Morris (2013) explains, the model of the new public, the public of the technological network, or what she refers to as *öffentlichkeit*, has the power to unsettle the analogy between language and exchange. For Claude Lévi-Strauss, as for Marcel Mauss, to give is to enact the excess that is also the necessary horizon for a future reciprocity. Such a reciprocity to come is what enables a circulation between parts, but it is one where "corporeal individuation" is maintained as intrinsic to intersubjective communication (Morris 2013: 98).

And yet, as the next section will show, while Charismatics at Canção Nova aspire to overcome corporeal individualism, they do so without sacrificing the possibility of exchange. Relying on charitable donations (*kharis*), Charismatics cannot disallow the language of reciprocity that undergirds the problem of a contractual individuation between parts. In other words, ideally Charismatics want to keep a form of exchange between parts that is nonetheless compatible with the dissolution of the individual. As we will see, the way to maintain this *nonetheless*—not as an obstacle but as conducive—is by coupling the event of exchange with the pneumatic gift such that what is foregrounded is not the exchange of gifts but the (spirit-endowed) ability to circulate as such. In short, circulation itself, not the gift, is what circulates. By drawing attention to the process of circulation proper, Charismatics perform a double function: on the one hand, they draw attention to the wholesome totality formed by the circulation of Spirit; on the other hand, they implode that totality with a logic of self-referentiality. The result is a paradoxically fluid totalitarianism.

In their practices, Charismatics describe charismata as tools or devices, yet not in the instrumental sense of these terms, for that would involve a separation between user and thing as well as between cause and effect. Rather, charismata are tools in the flesh, artifice incarnated in the form of potentials and abilities whose prime function and being—both—are to circulate. Thus the ability to prophesy, to discern, to cure, to liberate, to be charitable, to speak in tongues, and so forth, all these and other preternatural abilities are seen as pneuma *as it is put-to-use*, the being-at-work of Charismatic practice. Charismatics are acts—hence the reason charismata are neither solely abstract nor solely concrete but *abstract in their concreteness*. They are, one could say, gifts on the run.

That is why "To act according to Acts" is never simply like acting on a stage. To say that Charismatics act on a stage would suggest the kind of communicative model just discarded. When Padre Jonas encourages his members— and later, associates—to live according to the Acts of the Apostles, he is not suggesting a theater (or theory) of representation. He is not asking that individuals step into someone else's shoes, as a theory of empathic identification would have it. The good apostle at Canção Nova is not the good actor, in the sense of player and character crystalizing in a thespian play. A proper spirit-endowed Act, in the fire of anointment, stages its own reentry in scene, not to represent well what was "before" but to make "re-entry" itself apparent. Indeed, it is the act of reappearing on a stage that produces it as such, as though each "re-turning" added a loop to the interlocking of the net. This approach has the effect of displacing the idea of theater as dramaturgy of the extreme—what Austin's theory of theater called extraordinary—while giving center stage to the extremities.[9] Again, as chapter 2 shows, choreographed hand and finger gestures work the ethical body through the extremities, the limbs, the members.

In considering comparative traditions of theater and the differentials regarding how actions relate to grounds, the theatrical form of Canção Nova brings to mind Brechtian theater or even Antonin Artaud's (1958: 133) "affective athleticism." For Bertolt Brecht the theater condition is a conditioning, a verbed noun, a *nouning*. Distinctive from Aristotelian acting in its pursuit of the tragic event in a linear structure, Brechtian theater spins around the act of acting—the plotting—in ways that unveil the parts involved, like pieces and cogs in a machine: the entire economy of articulations behind a certain praxis. Unlike Aristotelian theater, in which the transformative process happens by means of a displacement whereby the actor identifies with the psychic structure of a character and acts *as though* it were his or her own, Brecht's theater disallows any identificatory process, folding all ends into a big middle: the middle of acting the very grounds where acting takes place (de Abreu 2020b). What might be defined as spatial displacement (what Stephen Greenblatt [1983: 224–25] calls "psychic mobility") in Aristotelean and Renaissance theater, might in Brecht be better thought of as a rhythm of disclosure.

Brecht, a modernist, pushed to counter the protocols of modern political theater. But he did so by appealing to a baroque sensibility, the kind of theater that informed the political structure of the Counter-Reformation in seventeenth-century Europe and the Americas. And it is in the name of a kind of Counter-Reformation that Catholic Charismatic revivalism pitched itself in the last quarter of the twentieth century and well into the present, not just in Brazil and other parts of Latin America but also in places like the United States, the Philippines, and Europe. Only this time the logics of staging and the political typologies directing it differ from those invigorating Brecht's time or the baroque tradition to which it referred. The elements and stakes are different today. Charismatic theatrical form, on the one hand, interfaces with the protocols and (interruptive) temporalities and logics of mass media technologies and, on the other, valorizes a flow or a spirit of neoliberalism that rejects the sense of an end so as to accommodate orders of built-in uncertainty, flexibility, adaptability, and so on.

Not that Charismatics don't have their model actors to act on. That much we saw already through Padre Jonas Abib's evocations of saints like Paul, Luke, Francis, or Loyola, their deeds holy exhalations to his lungs that the Canção Nova Community would, in turn, like a "new song," air out into the world. Apostle Paul is no doubt the great exemplary player in Charismatic political theater. (And so, in a more understated way, is Luke, who spoke of the enthusiasm of abilities [Luke 23:46].) Paul is a reference precisely inasmuch as Charismatics consider him Christianity's great articulator of times, spaces, and elements. As a habitué of the Greek gymnasium at Corinth, Paul is seen by Charismatics as the Trinitarian acrobat, the great fitter and bender of three personas into one. He is the apostle cited above all, the apostle under whose auspices theater and gym meet in the electronic amphitheaters of Canção Nova. He is seen as the great gymnasiarch of the Aeropagite. Paul's call for direct and transparent communication is a shaft whereon Charismatics exercise their muscular virtuosity. This they do by stretching such a maxim in a range of directions, with different inflections and to different degrees.

In the spirit of the restoration theology of the Counter-Reformation, Paul is the media theorist from whom to draw great lessons of governance. He is the light of grace that moves through time, the elastic that, through the miracle of leaps and bends, will reach all the sides and interweave these into a dense latticework, like the wires on which evangelization hinges within Canção Nova or like the nets of fishermen that rely on strong yet bendable strings and loops in order to better enmesh the topological motion of fish.

The know-how of a well-honed craft of netting shapes the pattern of oratory at Canção Nova. As crafters of a handmade fishing net will know, the strongest net is also the most malleable, the kind that can be thrown into the air, and circle around itself, so as to descend on an area of turbulence like a school of fish. Rhetoric here is not a function for what Barbara Johnson (1986: 29) describes as "the ability to have language say one thing in order to mean another." Rather language says one thing and the other simultaneously, or better even, language is the transitive space created from the flux between one thing and the other: tropes, themes, clichés, platitudes, aphorisms, anything that can compact language into brute nuggets of sound and meaning poised to be taken elsewhere. To transport through a rhythm, rather than persuade, is the prime function of language for which effect stylistic devices are deployed: metalepsis (the duplication and piling up of images and themes in setting a rhythm of going from one thing to the next), alliteration (the use of the same letter or sound at the beginning of closely connected words), and transumption (the transit of references from one level to another, close to what we today call quotation). Ideally, such linguistic operations form a Tower of Babel: a crude, inchoate structure with weak foundations, threatening to collapse under its own weight and yet, by virtue of that weakening transience and elusiveness, all the more reverberating, all the freer to travel. The process that starts from diachronic narrative often ends up looped into a synchronic catachrestic mixture of "tongues."

In early May 2001, for example, I attended a sermon at Canção Nova by Padre Léo who was then a permanent member of the community (*membro de comunidade de vida*). That day's sermon on Apostle Paul was anchored on two words: *direct* and *transparent*. The sermon would constantly come back to those words as a way to energize digression and reconnection. Moving between how he went about his morning, to something he heard on the radio news, to a biblical passage by Apostle John, to the frailty but determination of Pope John Paul II, to a story on the stoicism of Saint Francis who while cleaning his face rose to say, "This is for me. And what do you have for the church?," to his love for mathematics and the celibacy of prime numbers as a young deacon, to his distaste for *caldo de mócoto* (a Brazilian dish made from cow's feet) and more and more, he crisscrossed, with catachrestic *abusio*, his narrative all the while, at each turn of the thread, bringing up one (*direct*) or the other (*transparent*) word. And in the rhythm of cyclical renewal of those words— *direto, transparente, direto, transparente, . . .* gradually, like a ghost appearing out of semantic satiation, *diparent, transrecto, diparecto*—there was Apostle Paul landing, as it were, in the middle. Not Paul as characterizable but Paul as an abstraction. Paul the orator, Paul the weaver, Paul the "mass builder," Paul the tent maker, Paul the itinerant, Paul the trainer, Paul the manual, the knowhow. In short, Paul an emblem but not a person.

"Trust and work," Padre Léo said, opening his eyes. But there was more on his shoulder that today. Reduced to abstract minimums, the two words of the day—*direct* and *transparent*—could journey across new orders of signification. For example, *direct* and *transparent* are the terms Charismatics use in describing the live quality of Canção Nova's media programs (Ao vivo). *Direct* and *transparent*—this is how Charismatics describe the condition of being anointed by the Holy Spirit, as shown by the shared command that any person on the Charismatic stage invites the audience to "see through" them. The idea is that the sanctity of charisma, thanks to spiritual anointment, opens up the person for whatever circulates—what Charismatics call the "martyrium of transparency"—(a devotee once pointed out to me his preternaturally endowed "cross-ray vision," rather than the tilted X-ray vision). *Direct* and *transparent* also signaled an attempt to recover the lay forms of direct communication with saints typical of pre-reform popular Catholicism in Brazil prior to the advent of modern European Roman Catholicism during the latter part of the nineteenth century.[10] *Direct* and *transparent* also hinted at how Charismatics talk of an anointed person (*ungida*) whose proper practice—through prayer, contemplation, and baptismal experiencing—will allow them to *see through* time and space, instead of just "seeing."[11] *Direct* and *transparent* framed, consequently and perhaps above all, an epistemic problematic. In conceiving the Holy Spirit as a kind of caustic reagent that allows one to "see through" (experience = Apostle Paul = tent maker = breath flexibility), instead of "seeing" (knowledge = Apostle Peter = the rock = ideology = rigidity), Padre Léo at Canção Nova, and Charismatics in general, advanced an alternative to modern protocols of critique.[12] Last but not least, Pauline doctrines of "directness" and "transparency" connected to Brazil's economic and political moment as it entered the last quarter of the millennium: the exaltation of a universal malleable spirit, of pneuma, which, in coordination with an imminent neoliberal ethos, defined subjectivity and even citizenship in light of its possible fractal extensions, its ability to be fit in responding to emerging circumstances. Thus presented, form was not just opposed to meaning. Rather it explored meaning in order to weaken it and, with it thus weakened, better cruise it and transit, across leaps, into the near and the afar. A good sermon at Canção Nova is a mastery in techniques of weaving jagged threads. Like a fisherman crafting his fishing net, the orator opens up temporary apertures through which evolving threads pass, time and again.

Launching the Nets: Canção Nova

[Laércio intertwines the fingers of his hands] You have to think of Canção Nova as a network, which is also the work-of-a-net. . . . You see? It connects people and it catches people. Think of Our Lady of Aparecida, the saint that was found in a fishing net. Think of the apostles, they were fishermen . . . and now look at that antenna, does it not look like a net? And think of the INPE, the Aerospace Institute over there, what are they doing? Netting *[enredando]*! . . . Their work is to catch things in the air. That antenna also catches things in the air, it connects but it also catches, converts, transforms. Look at my hands now, what is the best way for me to make my hands stronger? It is by interlacing them. Look . . . your mind, if you listen, my mind is weaving these thoughts and when you see how things are so beautifully related, how can you doubt that there is a greater mind behind all reality?[13]

Canção Nova is situated in Cachoeira Paulista, halfway between São Paulo and Rio de Janeiro in the valley of the Paraiba River, a strip of flatlands that border the beautiful Serra da Mantiqueira and Serra do Mar, not far from the Atlantic Ocean. It has a total population of nearly thirty thousand and an average annual temperature of 26 degrees Celsius. Historically grounding its economy in livestock and agriculture, there has since the 1990s been a significant change in the town's population and infrastructure. From a predominantly residential and rural town, Cachoeira Paulista has developed a substantial commercial economy. Just outside the Canção Nova Community's grounds, there are a good number of hostels, cafés, and restaurants that cater to the weekly surge of travelers. Local residents have made space in their private condominiums to house last-minute pilgrims. Religious merchants set up their stalls around the community's limits.

A trip through the region provides a fair idea of the dominance of Catholicism, expressed in the many cathedrals and numerous unofficial chapels that were built by lay believers back in colonial days. The event for which the valley is renowned, however, is the great miracle of Aparecida, after which the national basilica and sanctuary were built. The legend tells how in 1717 three fishermen found the statue of Our Lady of Conception on the edge of the Paraiba River. Devotion to the image grew exponentially, and in 1929 Our Lady of Aparecida was crowned the official patron saint of Brazil. Since then, every year on October 12 thousands of pilgrims travel from all around Brazil and Latin America to the Sanctuary of Our Lady. The proximity of Canção Nova to the national sanctuary adds to the reputation of the valley as a privileged spot for religious tourism.

Today Canção Nova broadcasts on AM, FM, and shortwave radio; owns four television stations and 263 retransmitter antennas; is connected to 146 cable TV companies reaching Western Europe, North Africa, and Latin America; and operates the first web-based Catholic television station in the world.[14] TV Canção Nova broadcasts in UHF twenty-four hours a day, transmitting 80 percent of its programs live. The main base of the Canção Nova Community covers twenty thousand square meters and has many subdivisions: the housing complex where its three hundred communitarian members live and thousands circulate every week; the offices of Radio Canção Nova and TV Canção Nova; an audiovisual department called DAVI; a gigantic market area called Fundação John Paul II, which sells Canção Nova's audiotapes, video sermons, CDs, books, magazines, and clothes; various broadcasting studios; two small chapels; a specific area for intercession and exorcism; and a monastery for the Poor Clares of Assisi, a medieval monastic order (see chapter 3). Apart from the motherhouse, Canção Nova runs nineteen filial houses, called *casas de missão* (mission houses), which are distributed all over Brazil (four are in the state of São Paulo) as well as in the United States, Portugal, Italy, and Israel.[15] In 2005 Canção Nova inaugurated a gigantic hall with a capacity of seventy thousand. On weekends and on both religious and nonreligious holidays (such as Carnival), organized excursions arrive in Canção Nova from all parts of Brazil and neighboring countries to participate in religious camping, Seminars in the Holy Spirit (Seminários no Espírito Santo), and public confessional shows.

As a community, Canção Nova has fashioned, as it were, a town within a town. In addition to dormitories and the refectory, it has a primary school for the children of the community, a theological school for lay and vocational members, a hotel, a camping area, a medical and dental facility, and even a hairdresser. In the back of the complex is a big vegetable garden for the community, which extends out of sight toward the mountains. Although Canção Nova is always open to visitors, it charges an entrance fee of 10 reais during shows, which normally run from Thursday to Sunday. Participants are invited to bring a tent and camp in the large lanes of the site.

In general, Cachoeira Paulista is known for its many natural fluvial systems. Since Brazil is one of the highest users of hydroelectric energy worldwide, electricity supplies are greatly dependent on the amount of precipitation provided by seasonal rains. Canção Nova uses its watery surroundings to foster the relationship between spirituality and electricity, between the energizing power of the "flame of Pentecost" and a technological and electronic universe. These overlaps rely on the emblematic descriptions used by Catholic Charismatics to account for the richly somatic experiences of contact with the spirit. They often use electricity-derived terms, such as *warm voltages*, *radiances*, and *impulses*, and refer to practices of *infusion* and *diffusion*, *circuitry*, and the *conductivity* of spiritual charisma.

Similar juxtapositions among water, electricity, and spirituality became particularly salient during my fieldwork in 2001, when the so-called Lei do Apagão (Switch-Off Law) was declared. A national energy-saving regimen, the law was a response to the exceptional droughts of the previous years. The darkening of homes, hospitals, institutions, streets, and media stations galvanized a major campaign to find alternative resources to keep the country operating, reilluminate the unlit alleys and dimmed public monuments, and restore energy to defrosted fridges and other devices. As the government went on a frantic search for alternative forms of energy, Canção Nova mined all sorts of metaphors to further conflate the Holy Spirit with media's electric power. The Holy Spirit was compared to an "electricity generator" that "infuses energies"; the bodies of believers were associated with "antennas of retransmission"; and crowds were described in terms of their "good contact" (de Abreu 2005). Not infrequently, visitors to Canção Nova said they had come to "charge their batteries," "obtain good signals," "make good contact," or "galvanize the world."

In time, the circuit of analogies between weather, electricity, and spirituality also came to encompass Canção Nova's physical proximity to the National Institute for Space Research and the Center for Weather Forecast and Climatic Studies. The Aerospace Institute of Cachoeira Paulista is a national center that, among other functions, conducts research on atmospheric science, technical spatial engineering for remote sensing in the detection and control of geostationary satellites and satellite images as well as astronomical events. The institute has also developed a special program connected to the rainforest, housing a highly sophisticated monitoring system that produces images in real time of deforestation of the rainforest as well as of pollution levels in the main urban centers of Brazil. This proximity of science and mystical occurrence in the town of Cachoeira Paulista and the Paraiba Valley of which it is a part facilitates, and to some extent organizes, the desired fluidity within the Canção Nova Community, thus producing a ring of concentric orders of influence from the larger to the smaller scale.

Paraiba do Sul River Valley is a large territory that stretches into three different provinces of Brazil: São Paulo, Rio de Janeiro, and Minas Gerais. The Valley of Paraiba shows marks of the slave trade and the African diaspora in the Brazilian landscape. Its geographical position as a connector between regions, along with its rich natural resources, made it the hub for the Brazilian coffee plantations that would flourish in the first quarter of the nineteenth century. Religious elements from the settled African populations came into contact and enacted a thriving cult of popular saints and practices, in turn inflected by the explosive baroque and rococo statuary of the seventeenth century mainly coming from Minas Gerais. All these elements made the Paraiba Valley a site of intense interlocking trends, economic prosperity, and ghostly apparitions. It is therefore no surprise that the Catholic Church opted to locate its national sanctuary dedicated to Our Lady of Aparecida in the region. Since the 1950s the region has become largely industrialized, tapping into its colonial mercantile spirit, now served by a connecting system of roads, hydroelectric works, and a long and sinuous riverbed, the navigation of which is idyllically hampered by waterfalls.

Such is the setting of Cachoeira Paulista, where Canção Nova is located. Here pneuma is seen as the prime source of energy, one that sustains "the flow" of the Charismatic movement as a whole drawn out into prayer, sermons, utterances, gestures, clairvoyance, good and bad signals, hymns, prophecies, words of discernment, glossolalia. Pneuma's common associations with air and wind are then easily converted into other conductive elements moving from the archaic fire (as in the fire of Pentecost) to the more contemporary electricity. In essence, pneuma is motion, or better, what moves by setting in motion. These elemental identifications are provisional, part of a continuing movement of crossing into each other as varieties of the same principle of unction or anointment. Perhaps for that reason the dominant element in Charismatic practice is oil, as the stuff that facilitates the transition between all other emblematic substances of Spirit. The specificities of those elements are lost in the local parlance in favor of an idea that equates pneuma above all to life, play, the provisional. What matters is not one or the other element as much as "the play element" locals allow in making contact between the Holy Spirit and the Canção Nova Community. What is of concern is that this relation itself be conducive to a certain spirit of circulation, from the recessions of the member's body to the editorial backrooms where artifice too—if not especially—is a manifestation of spirit.

Of Oil and Anointment

Ideas of rejuvenation and renewal form an integral part of CCR's imaginary of an agile and aerated body. These attributes are projected on and embodied by the thousands of youngsters who come to Canção Nova, significant numbers of them from the upper-middle-class, well-educated youth sector. Most travel from within the state of São Paulo—but some visit from the states of Rio de Janeiro and Minas Gerais—in excursions organized by online university networks, where the CCR has always had a major presence. Events at Canção Nova are organized according to certain themes, such as "marriage and sexuality," "youth camping," "cure and deliverance," and "seminars in the spirit," many of which show a clear orientation toward young people. Religious megafestivals, such as the PHN show (the topic of chapter 2), use songs, prayer, and gestures to structure the breath and move the body to confess, demonstrating the restorative powers of the Holy Spirit. Whatever the practice, all these activities are reduced to one practical aim: the ability to skillfully manage the flow of pneuma.

For Charismatics, pneuma is the very protean principle of adaptability. It is renewable business and the business of renewal—hence the name Catholic Charismatic Renewal. Consistently, however, Charismatics talk of the condition of being anointed or under the effect of the unction of the Holy Spirit. Oil itself is connected to chrism and thus to charisma and to charismata, the gifts of the Spirit. In the early 1970s oil, fire, and electricity conjoined in the rhetoric of the baptism in the Holy Spirit amid prayer groups, which through the agency of certain key players had a strong orientation toward electronic technological innovation. Charismatic practice evolved out of the imperative "to improve on the body's potential to retain oil or chrism."[16] The gifts endowed by the spirit during baptism were manifested as an oily, fragrant substance; this is the reason Charismatics refer to one another as "anointed." An anointed body, according to this premise, can more easily articulate and adapt to the startling playfulness of Spirit and thus bring fitness to the members and offices called "secretarias" of the Charismatic movement.

With the background of the great oil crisis of 1973, which almost pushed the national oil company Petrobras to bankruptcy, Charismatics (whose sensibility orients them to express how an era is being animated by a certain spirit) were prolific in connecting the spiritual language of oil and unction inherited from Paul's teachings—and other such spiritual gymnasiarchs such as John of the Cross and Ignatius of Loyola—and the energy crisis affecting Brazil and the world. Early prayer groups in the 1970s were suffused by the oil-tempered language of pumping up, massaging, and balming the world, starting with one's body—not to be understood as the mere supporter or container of spirit but as its very articulation.[17] Frequently described as an "immersion in the spirit," baptism marks the moment when an individual supposedly attains a higher level of proprioceptive awareness. During prayer, practitioners are called to concentrate on the body internally and to redirect "oil" to points of tension, closure, or ill feeling in the body. The idea is to expand the degrees of freedom in the body, that is, to raise the level of joint mobility and at the same time to enter into a relation of permeability with the outside world. As in the biblical parable of Pentecost, the body, heretofore blocked and stiffened, starts to open up to the surrounding environment. The aerobic style of Charismatic celebrations increases such porosity. Through bodily engagement in prayer exercises, which people learn with the help of recorded technologies, respiration, transpiration, and transparency interrelate.

The communitarian spaces in Canção Nova likewise materialize an aesthetics of seeing through, of transparency. Voids, meshes, and permeable structures like tents have a distinct presence in Catholic Charismatic architecture, and Canção Nova is a powerful emblem of that design (de Abreu 2005). Metal grids in particular are used to intersect the walls of Canção Nova's spaces of celebration. As prefabricated structures, these spaces adapt traditional church furnishings to gym-like arenas. The wired metal fence that encircles the entire camp adds another layer to the open-ended and reticulated architectures of the place since those on both sides are able to see through to the other. For that reason, in Canção Nova one is never exactly outside or inside—to enter its ambit is to enter the province of the middle.[18] Space is delimited by a boundary that is at once everywhere and nowhere, its beginnings and endings, outsides and insides interconnected in ways that preclude any foundation on which a community, imagined or constructed, might be solidly delimited.

Vernacular Tactics

In the early days of the movement, Padre Jonas was presented with an immediate conundrum: how to tap into the alienation of a broad swath of upper-middle-class Catholics shut out of Brazilian Catholic liberationists' messaging (its "option for the poor") while navigating the critiques of televangelism proffered by his peers. As touched on in the introduction, the highly fraught Guerra Santa controversy of the mid-1990s left little room for error in making overtures to the televangelical medium. Padre Jonas's response to the heightened sensitivity of this moment was to eschew the overtly normative ideological content heretofore pioneered by the American evangelical Catholic Father Dougherty. His project would instead advance by retreating from instrumental calculative logics in order to better attune to the latent potential of the near future, preparing him to act once he had discerned the appropriate moment. His was a politics of ecology: staying in tune with his environment, to what was in the air, and carefully navigating the ever-emergent televangelical media landscape.

The only viable Catholic entry into the space of televangelism prior to this moment was via Father Dougherty, who introduced the Charismatic movement to Brazil in 1969. His plans were to implement Catholic revivalism by articulating its emphasis on enthusiasm to the protocols of televangelism according to US-based marketing, technology, and funding models. In the early 1980s he was chosen to be the entrepreneur responsible for applying the ideas developed by two groundbreaking global media projects in Brazil: the Lumen Project (financed by corporate institutions from Holland) and Evangelization 2000 (financed by Catholics in the United States). Receiving a donation of US$100,000 and new electronic equipment, Father Dougherty further extended his organization and the production center TV Century XXI (Carranza 2002: 246–65), subsequently hiring a team of professionals in the field of communication—unconcerned about their religious affiliations—and a well-known Catholic marketing expert. He had solid funds, something Padre Jonas did not.

The response to these developments among installed Brazilian Catholics was primarily one of consternation. The legendary liberation theology activist Paulo Evaristo, who presided over the archdiocese of São Paulo, strongly condemned Father Dougherty's attempt to "market Christianity"; meanwhile São Paulo's main broadsheet, *Estado de São Paulo*, denounced Dougherty's brand of CCR as part of a political maneuver by the Vatican and conservative elites to eradicate communism and liberation theology from the face of the earth (Carranza 2002). One reason for such vehement resistance to the importation of Catholic televangelism to Brazil was that it unsettled the assumption that televangelism was a strictly Protestant phenomenon. The medium of television itself, furthermore, threatened the church's heretofore near-total grasp of sacred means, a move very much aligned with the CCR's broader impetus.[19]

In search of a media platform that would shake loose from these prior associations with non-Brazilian origins, Padre Jonas eventually pursued a diverse set of strategies. Working to dissociate Catholic televangelism within the country from Father Dougherty's looming presence, he traced his own spiritual genealogy to Father Rahm, who was well known for his dedication to social work among the marginalized in Brazil. By stressing his bond to Father Rahm, Padre Jonas was paving the road to linking televangelism with social work, effectively undermining the image of both Pentecostals and Catholic conservatives as indifferent to social welfare. Gradually Padre Jonas managed to create an image among local people that included a possible reconciliation among social causes, televangelism, and Brazilian Catholicism, while distancing himself from the media network of his close competitor and most powerful rival in Valinhos-Campinas within the state of São Paulo.

Unlike his US counterpart, Padre Jonas discerned that freedom of action would not be found outside the local political setting but within it, vernacularly. The pro-technology policies of the ruling regime at the time of the CCR's arrival in Brazil seemed to offer particularly favorable grounds from which to launch a new Catholic global media crusade. These policies provided the conservative allies of Catholicism with the opportunity not only to counter the surge of US-based Protestant televangelism that was spreading throughout Latin America but also to break through the deep-seated prejudice against televangelism lodged in the progressive ethos of the Catholic Church of Brazil. The ability to compromise would henceforth become internal to the doctrine of elasticity, what would further and strengthen the space of the entrepreneurial third: spirit. Canção Nova would exist on the edge, a place where, so it goes today, no one could know for sure what lay ahead, which is why constant vigilance for emerging, unexpected events would be needed and swiftly adapted to by fit Charismatics.

Especially in the early years, Padre Jonas carefully avoided any remarks that could be read as directly aggressing against countermovements. First, he stayed away from direct confrontation with the main competing forces; second, he gradually moved within the church structure toward the murkier zone of a decentered center. He would take one step at a time, he would move diagonally, and, as fit, push and pull things in new directions. Rather than attack, for example, liberation theology's investment in ideology, Padre Jonas would praise liberation theology as "a fruit of the will of the spirit" (which also implied its gradual decline).[20] He supported and became associated with Toca de Assis (the Cave of Assisi), a hybrid liberation theology Charismatic-born neo-Franciscan urban movement—also known as Toqueiros—whose choreographies and songs, once in the style of Florida-based pop band Backstreet Boys, combined with disowning asceticism and caring for the poor, has attracted a large number of young individuals to this arm of Brazil's Charismatic movement.[21] All the while Padre Jonas pronounced his radical noninvolvement in politics. By withdrawing from the larger political conflicts, salient in the 1970s and 1980s as Brazil was immersed in a military dictatorship, so as to live with his community of disowned Charismatics, Padre Jonas created an aura of radicalism around him and his community. Some described him as a "prophet in the times of mass media."[22]

Pushed for resources that would rival those harnessed by Dougherty and others working with US televangelical productions, Padre Jonas would first contact local industries in search of funds. According to a much-recited narrative on the Canção Nova media system that circulated within the Charismatic movement, during a prayer retreat in 1990 he realized that he was "deviating from the divine path." The prospect of having Canção Nova's existence dependent on external publicity seemed incompatible with the principle of charisma underpinning the pneumatic experience of Pentecost or the *forma vivendi* of Saint Francis. Reliance on outside revenues risked broaching the opacities of mediation and of financial transactions associated with the conventional mechanisms of advertising and the pecuniary, not to mention the attendant dangers of unlinking the economics of the media platform from its embedded social networks. As a result, Padre Jonas declared that from then on Canção Nova would live exclusively on two sources: revenues from its own media productions and charity. Three months later he created a donors' organization, the Audio Club (Clube do Ouvinte). But for that he had to make clear what the rules of membership were.

The Audio Club

Since 1991 Canção Nova has transmitted a live TV and radio program called *Wednesday Mass of the Audio Club*, a weekly event meant to be a ceremony exclusively dedicated to the donors and *arrecadadores* (money gatherers) of Canção Nova. On November 7, 2001, I attended Mass in the camp. The ceremony was conducted in a hangar with a capacity of about a hundred people. On a smaller scale, the building had the same feature described earlier: a wall of rugged ironwork. The space's built-in openness kept it cool. A well-known member of Canção Nova, Padre Edmilson, conducted the ceremony, and the ritual opened with the sound of an organ accompanying the voice of a young female singer. The priest warmly welcomed the audience and asked everyone to tune in to Canção Nova as one "tunes in to the Holy Spirit." Padre Edmilson acted like a phone operator, switching the flow of spiritual energy from one element to another:

I am placing my hands on you [*gesturing toward the TV camera*]. Yes, Jesus reaches my brother. . . . Now I want you to touch your brother standing next to you with your left arm, while your right hand touches where it hurts. Cure, Lord. Liberate, my God [*closes his eyes while the audience prays in tongues*]. The Lord is touching a right leg, the Lord is touching a leprous [person]. Lord, a man is now placing inside you a problem with his stomach, this difficult vital organ, and I ask my Lord also for other causes that are not physical diseases but the others . . . emotional, adulterous, impossible causes. You who are the God of the impossible, look at the faith of your people, visit now, Lord. There is a man who is not a Catholic, he is an evangelical, and the Lord is touching [him], he will be among us soon. Thank you, Lord. And now a right leg. . . . Thank you, Lord, because now you are touching someone with ear pain. Visit now, my Lord [*pause*]. Now, my brothers, change your left arm for your right arm and touch the person on your right. If until this moment the words were lacking, now they will be released. You who had a dry, stuck tongue, now your tongue is free. Thank you, Lord. This is now a living church, not a dead one, because the Lord is the same yesterday and tomorrow, and we have been obedient with all the members of the Audio Club, all members of CN [Canção Nova].[23]

At one point Padre Edmilson interrupted the flow of incoming prophecies and healings and started reading printouts of emails that were on the altar table. The emails had been sent by viewers who had witnessed a miracle foretold by the priest. This process of sending and receiving spiritual messages has been intensified by and associated with terms that pertain to technological interactivity.

Padre Edmilson, you told [us] that we should put the hands where it hurts and that by doing so a person who has a problem with the ears was being cured. I am cured and the pain is gone. I thank the Lord.

Padre Edmilson, when you spoke about a man being cured of a stomach problem, I touched the screen with my left hand having my right hand on my stomach. My pain is gone thanks to the Lord.

The reading of emails was then interrupted by a surge of new revelations Padre Edmilson was receiving from the Holy Spirit:

Yes, Lord, a man is now being cured from a cancer on one of his testicles. Thank you, Lord, for this listener and another who recovered his right vision. My Lord, thank you. . . . Cure miasma, intoxication, cure a heartburn, a tumor on the spine. A forearm needed a prosthesis but today watching the *Mass of the Audio Club*, he is cured. Let us applaud Jesus, our Lord!

Exploring the semantic porosity of charisma to designate at once charity and grace, Padre Edmilson stages the possibilities of cure and citation for the TV cameras in a scene that is at once theatrical and scriptural. The Holy Spirit is passing through and curing its members as these connect by a long cord across distance and time (as sometimes those to be cured have already died). There is something pre-post about this circuit in its simultaneous addressing of something to come through what is already left. The voice of Padre Edmilson plays a key role in the interchange of flows between inner and outer, between producer(s) and audience(s). Far from being mere spectators, audience members are actively engaged in the framing of communal prayer. Padre Edmilson sanctions the cures received from the Spirit by reading the testimonies that arrive at his altar table via electronic means, "Hallelujahs" and "Amens" all the while adding rhythm to the readings. As the circuit speeds up, a swelling vocalization arises, dramatized by the roaring, unintelligible sounds of speaking in tongues. The laying-on of hands suggests a community of connected bodies integrated into a moving circle of light.

The body of the medium does not attempt to pursue communication between two worlds. Rather, the body—like space and like the TV medium—is employed as a medium of energy circulation and transmission. In other words, everything in the setting—body, space, media—participates in this movement of transmissibility. The laying-on of hands aims to restore harmony in the body, compensating for some emotional, physical, or spiritual lack. Placing and alternating hands on oneself and another individual, as Padre Edmilson asks his audiences to do, further reinforces the contact established between one's personal body and the collective, with the priest working all the while as a kind of power source, an on-off switch. The body of the believer and potential donor extend and identify with the technological while inscribing the transactions of charisma, which ultimately manifest in the form of donations. Insofar as charity is, according to Saint Paul, the highest charisma—the gift that overflows itself—"donations" do not refer to a disembodied act of giving but to a condition of being gifted, an aspect that goes through the praising body.[24] The act of giving here becomes, then, a sign more of dispossession than possession. As Charismatics put it, "One exists in charity." Or, to recall Mauss (1967), to give is to give oneself, hence to further propel the circulation of the "gift."

Technological Self-Awareness

One would expect that in order to sustain its own mystification in religious as well as economic terms, Canção Nova would erase its technological traces. Yet, quite the opposite takes place. Far from concealing, the Canção Nova Community constantly takes viewers into the backrooms to see the normally invisible offstage scenery, heightening viewers' awareness of the "live" transmissions of its material workings. Donors are given full access to flows of capital, encouraged to track the financial balance of transactions in real time as Canção Nova incessantly reveals the percentage levels in the race to 100 percent monthly donations.[25] The daily airing of these financial inflows and outflows closely resembles the mercurial depictions of weather radar, effectively contributing to an aesthetic logic of "economic transparency" (Morris 2000b; Taussig 2003). As we move toward the last days of the month, the emotional investment rises. The "generous downpour" of money, especially toward the end of the month, is often related to the highly concentrated cloud formed by intensive collective prayer; prayer, after all, is thought to be effected through breathing, thus directly impacting the surrounding atmosphere. This conflation of the material, dynamic life of the body with the immaterial, volatile aspects of the virtual through breathwork effectively juxtaposes means and ends according to the logics of the global market; through an aesthetics of transparency and its self-referential nature, control over capital flow as well as copyrighted properties is seamlessly maintained.

Unlike Father Dougherty, whose programs include commercials from other religious entities, Canção Nova is totally self-referential in matters of publicity. It publicizes nothing but itself. By overtly showing the means of technology—by turning the camera on the camera and on the community itself—those means reenter the scene of visibility; mediation, in other words, performs its own denial in favor of affective directness.

To refer to it as affective directness, however, is not to see it as mediation's trick in rejoining immediacy. At stake here is an action—an operation—that is neither mediation nor immediacy, the two-pronged logic used by existing social theories of religion and media (de Vries 2001; Stolow 2005; Meyer 2011; Witte 2009). Rather, it is the very withdrawal from these through a process of recursion of the image, as it were, looking back onto itself. In turning back on itself, like a topological feedback, the image (that is, what is offered to the senses) is the possibility of a circuit, a reviving of the cut, in the image's coming to pass. Mediation may be part of it, but it is not—cannot be—incarnational.[26]

A more elusive operation is at work at Canção Nova. If Padre Jonas withdraws from all publicity and from the help of external propaganda, it is not because he does not value the corporate model or, for that matter, the powers of the pecuniary, but rather because he sees in that disavowal precisely the possibility to summon a form of administration that is deeply indebted to a particular theological doctrine. In a period of major economic reforms for the country, Padre Jonas drew economic praxis out of an orthodox doctrine of incarnation—a mechanism defined as the ability to withdraw in the moment of appearing (kenosis)—and in this way rectified the theological status of the enterprise. In withdrawing from contact with outside agents of publicity, Canção Nova's TV cameras must turn onto themselves, in a kind of tautological self-embrace. The more the machinic and the artificial are exposed in Canção Nova's internal circuit, the more the principle of incarnation comes into sharp view as a model of dramaturgy.

Canção Nova was able to turn the value of money into an immanent aspect of its administration by grace. Such became the mode of operating that Canção Nova prided itself on enacting in place of marketing. In effect, however, what Canção Nova did to the market is what the neoliberal market, in the decade prior to and into the new millennium, was doing to the Brazilian state. It suspended referentiality to a higher order so as to invigorate a strategic vulnerability, the kind that would allow uncertainty and irregularity—congenial with the capricious Holy Spirit as *bloweth where it listeth*—to be an asset rather than a hindrance in governance. Self-referential and self-reflective, Canção Nova calls on values like charity, benevolence, and solidarity as part of its Charismatic "anti-institutional" rhetoric. And yet, as Andrea Muehlebach (2009, 2012) well shows, this type of anti-institutional discourse, the moral declination that posits "grace as illegal" (in the sense Paul put it, as existing outside the law, the letter), has been—and goes on being—favorable to the complexio oppositorum of the neoliberal state. In its active presence through withdrawal—what I am calling incarnational partaking here—from society and from offering welfare protection of its citizens, the state commands the markets and individuals to be up to more flexible demands. A rhythm more than a definable location, state power makes itself present through withdrawal. It's an operation. Acting thus, the state may call on the good sense of individuals to be generous and charitable: graceful citizens.

Canção Nova thus mimetically assimilates the figure of the market in the very moment of disavowing it. This is possible without contradiction because the market itself has no fixed position against which a contradiction could be raised. Rather, the market, much like Canção Nova, is an atmospheric enterprise.[27] In showing the TV cameras themselves showing, the drama of unity of action is split into a dynamic rhythm of leave-take proper to its political theater. In the name of reenacting the Acts of the Apostles, Canção Nova Community highlights its convoluted architecture of time, a reticulated construction that in its continuous growth seems to exceed grounds that would make sense of things even to itself. In this self-referential world of a "mediality without end," it is possible to imagine why terms like "adaptability" are relevant, or why members of the community, to this day, keep on stressing the positive uncertainty of the path ahead. Every step of the way at Canção Nova is an ethical lunging in proprioception.

Summary

This chapter has been an examination of the question of community as a system of communication. Rather than analyzing how a community uses media in order to instrumentally imagine itself, I have tried to identify the production of mechanisms that allow the community to identify with the act of communication. In other words, I have chosen to think of communication as a form of community processing. I have analyzed how the Pentecostal or Pauline notion of embodied pneuma provides Canção Nova with a kind of religious media theory, and have explored how that theory becomes articulated with an economic regime of transparency that is premised on the body's aptitude to perceive and regulate movement. Once perceived through the mechanics of breathing and circulation, there is no exterior position from which the community can be clearly defined. What matters instead are the cycles and reciprocations between in and out and the need to maintain the proprioceptive-like balance between them.

Mindful of how the majority of Brazilians demonized mass media, Padre Jonas knew that before he could start using mass media to convert people, the mass media had to be converted, their demons expelled, the air recycled. And for that he had to start with his most unassailably intimate being: his own wavering body. Instead of joining the forces operating in the polarized political context of Brazilian society, he focused on the motor qualities of the body itself—the middle of his being—and from there, in dialogue with his immediate surroundings, he began to open the way toward a balanced, expanded circuiting. While allowing Father Dougherty the honor of being a pioneer, Padre Jonas used him as a windbreaker against the local critical mindset. Far from the major hindrance it first appeared, Padre Jonas's initial relative lack of means redirected him toward a form of intangible capital, charisma, which proved an effective agent under the new conditions of a global economy.

Having little means with which to effect successful outcomes in strictly economic terms, Padre Jonas offered instead a well-staged prophetic return of the apostolic community whose power lies in its capacity to perform its own making, ever in motion, ever incomplete: a community that exists in the process of being made. Rather than offering a set of palpable instruments or a well-defined scheme, he incorporated a sort of productive precariousness that allowed him to coalesce mediation within the technological while redirecting his own marketing procedures to an open relational field of flows. As an engine of circulation and self-regeneration, Canção Nova both structures and builds on the imaginary associated with breathing dynamics. In that sense, it is not a "power sphere" (as Jürgen Habermas uses the term) where discursive meanings are built in, but an atmosphere whose volatility preempts any attempt to clearly define the boundaries of a community-in-the-making.

2. CONFESSION, TECHNICALLY SPEAKING

....

> We want to be near to the void, but not in order to fall into it.
> —GEORGES BATAILLE, *The Accursed Share: The History of*
> *Eroticism and Sovereignty*

On the bus from São Paulo to Cachoeira Paulista, I noticed a group of young people singing songs from Dunga's latest record, *Água Humilde* (Humble Waters), with loud voices and exultant applause. Their destination, I assumed, was the PHN Generation's three-day camping weekend at Canção Nova Community. The PHN (Por hoje não) program offers a chance to be a young Catholic with a recognizable style, reflected in bright, trendy PHN T-shirts, caps, gadgets, and magazines. The young people on the bus took turns sharing a bunch of CDs, a digital camera, and a video camera, which would be used for recording this or that show or a talk by Father Roberto, the leader of the distinguished Toca de Assis, a neo-Franciscan group active in the megacities of the country. The ten-bead Byzantine rosaries around their wrists completed their ensembles. Since I was heading to Canção Nova to follow the events, which had been highly publicized on TV Canção Nova, I eventually approached them, asking about their enthusiasm and expectations. The group consisted of three women and two men between the ages of nineteen and twenty-three, all college students from Campinas. Except for one young man who was coming for the first time, all the others had previously participated in PHN events. All had parents who participated in a Charismatic prayer group. They themselves participated in university prayer groups and were active in other projects, such as the Coffee Shops of Jesus.[1] I asked them what being PHN Generation members meant to them. André, the oldest of the group, replied first.

> ANDRÉ: Don't know if you know, but PHN means "Por hoje não, por hoje
> não vou pecar" [For today no, for today I shall not sin]. . . . Dunga, the
> prophet of young people, created his concept especially for the young,

for everybody, yes, but especially for us. There is a hip-hop song which opens up his program on Tuesday nights, *Geração PHN*, a program where only teenagers go and have a chance to ask their questions, tell their testimonies. It is on every Tuesday at 22:30 live, broadcast from the TV station in São Paulo, and then it is repeated on Saturdays. The song goes like "*Pode parar, vamos todos parar, vamos todos parar de pecar* [You can stop, let us all stop, let us all stop sinning]." [*They all sing and clap and move.*] You never saw it? If you see it, you will understand what motivates us. PHN makes us aware of the minute temptations of every day. It is a devastating "no" to sin. Dunga saw in music a way to keep young people aware of the dangers of sin.

What is the PHN Generation? It is this new generation of young people, like us, who see the challenges of everyday choices between good and bad. A day has many hours, many more minutes, and even more seconds, and PHN needs to be constantly in our minds to keep us on the right track all the time! Why today [*hoje*]? The day is always today, every moment, every minute, and you know that in that same minute so many bad things are taking place, if not with you or in your house, then elsewhere, in class. . . . We PHNers are constantly aware of the temptation. Every day we are confronted with temptation, you know, the sex, drugs, and rock-and-roll thing . . . but just with the bath you take every day you have to allow yourself to say "No!" You cannot conform to the world. It is the struggle of the spirit with matter. . . . But, of course, sometimes it is hard to remember this on your own, so this is why I go to this PHN camp, to get new strength. To show my "no," for today.

MARIA JOSÉ: Do you often wear your PHN shirts, like now? I heard you singing. These are songs by Dunga, right?

MAURÍCIO: Yes, they are from his album *Humble Waters*. . . . We no longer watch MTV or hear MPB [Música popular brasileira] or go to other shows because in PHN we find a higher form of amusement that is much more radical. It has a much more radical message that really transforms . . . because, how to say it right, . . . as André said . . . it is a form of amusement based on a denial of evil but in a young and rebellious way as well. Because it is not an easy job to say that "No!" It is not easy. . . . PHN is necessary so that we understand that that "no" is not only in these moments of show but is taken to our everyday life at school, at home, in our parish, with our friends. It is our DNA. As

Dunga says, the day of today is unique. It never was and it will never be [again], so one has to concentrate on the minute, on the second, on the now and keep saying *"No!"* Accumulating noes. And at the end of the day ask: How many noes did I say today? . . . When we want to go out, there are the Bars of Jesus [Barzinhos de Jesus] organized by Charismatic groups in São Paulo. There we learn about new compositions, new songs, and choreographies to praise Jesus. It is really nice. . . . You are Portuguese, right? I hear it in your accent. How is the Charismatic Renewal in Portugal?

MJ: Well, it is starting to catch up, but I do not think it is as lively as it is here in Brazil.

ANDRÉ: Aah! Yes, Brazilians are very musical and like to be spontaneous, isn't it [so]? I heard that in Amsterdam they have these places built just for sin. The coffee shops, the houses for prostitutes. . . . Here it is out in the open.

||||||||||||||||||||||||||||||||

This chapter describes and analyzes how, through the rising influence of Charismatic Catholicism in Brazil, the modern system of confession has been adjusted to a new confessional program: the PHN festival. These shifts are delineated by four main points: first, the substitution of a primarily verbal regime with a bodily one; second, a transition from the private realm to a public, socially framed performance; third, a transference of the postulate of "original sin" from a foundational belief to the middle ground of embodied practice; and fourth, a change in the conception of the confessional self to whom the circulation of sin has become more important than self-authorizing. I show how these key shifts provide the formal structure for confession among young Charismatics in Brazil.

The PHN festival is characteristically marked by interruption and repetition in order to progressively attune the rhythms of the body to those of mechanical media, thereby rendering visible what is otherwise normally kept invisible: technique itself. Addressed particularly to the youth, the three-day festival presents itself as an alternative to the private confessional. It is a practical manual for young people to wage war on sin. In this context, language, gesture, sound, breathing, sensation all join to bring out in confession what Charismatics call the voice of "the third." This displacement of the confessional self into the spaces of the third—the third person, the Holy Spirit—breaks away from traditional conventions in its reliance on a prior self. To confess from the perspective of the third means saying nothing specific.

To confess, rather, is to expose the spiritual dispositive—the articulations—that confer on the body the adaptive ability to repeatedly *unsin*. Confession involves rendering explicit the physical techniques that acknowledge sin as a condition of possibility and, in turn, work preventively on the body—like an antibody whose very presence speaks to the possibility of infection. Posed as practical and processual, the PHN confessional subject is never contained by the tense indicative of a *there* in the sense of concordance of self to itself. To be in the person of the third ideally means to be in passing, to be untimely to oneself, as in the gerund of continuous coming to pass (Weber 2004; Sánchez 2001). The resultant emphasis on this gerund-like quality unsettles and probes the logics of causality intrinsic to the postulate of original sin underwriting Western logics of confession: if the subject is ongoing, not quite there—but only in passing—within the space of practice, then who or what speaks if not the apparatus of a medium, the doing of confession as such?

Happening at least once a month, the PHN festival attracts hundreds of young people, many of them college students educated in the natural sciences. They come to Canção Nova not so much to confess past deeds but to, as they put it, "regenerate" or "upgrade" their bodies to better levels of resistance to sin. Paradoxically, the exercise of avoidance also trains the body to be a prime channel for making visible the circulation of sin. The challenge PHN poses to modern confession lies in how the practical body is at once a controller of and a conduit for danger. In the very act of exposing the sins that are always already circulating in the world, Charismatics train the body for nonsin. The more one physically works out, the more fluidly one behaves during the PHN shows, the better able one is to bear witness to the reality of pollution. This is because in these shows sin is not perceived as something that ought to be captured and exorcised (though in extremis that will indeed be the case) but as a call for movement and for circulation.

At stake is how the body internalizes the very structure it wishes to combat. Sin is unbounded, and therefore, the body must internalize that very condition of unboundedness. It must get rid of bounded artifacts in order to mobilize a certain linguistic body, we will see, around a particular "semiotic ideology," to use Webb Keane's (2007: 17) term, one that will institute the terms of that desirable unboundedness. To practice is to expose sin, while turning that exposure into a sign of how a moral body should circulate. In PHN, then, individuals are drawn not so much to confess as to perform that *a confession is taking place*. What is valued is the circulation that asserts the passing of sin. Unlike more familiar iterations of the modern confessional, accountability (in the sense of an individuated account that absolves sin through narrative disclosure) threatens the circuit proper. Ultimately it is the body that fails to partake in the passing, the body that wants to claim sin as singularly owned—"as my sin alone"—which becomes likewise a target of an individualized treatment.[2]

Among the ailments explored for the perfecting of confessional techniques are the evils of addiction and masturbation (often the two as one), alongside other techniques of nonreproductive sex. Scholars have studied the implications of nonreproductive sexualities in relation to questions of nationalism, muscular politics, and sovereignty (Bataille [1976] 1993; Sedgwick 1985; Butler 1997b; Berlant 1991; Alter 1993, 2006; Povinelli 2006). This chapter aligns with those efforts in exploring the implications of condemning the nonreproductive in a setting governed by the law of reproducibility. I draw attention to the techniques of displacement that swerve between gendered categories and a greater nongendered referent to which Charismatics submit. For while Charismatics invest in "ungendering" power relations as part of an effort to displace authorial subjectivity into the spaces of the third where it flows, such displacement is nothing but the expression of a radical compromise that ultimately forecloses the very openness it puts forth. The logic here is one that needs our attention because it posits a form of totality where it is precisely the preterition of the norm or law for flow or grace that ultimately fulfills the former. Much like in the circular play that builds up the theatrical architecture of PHN, as this chapter describes it, where the beginning of each line is also where a line ends, so the evoking of a third, ungendered being reiterates precisely what will be denied to it. The semiotics of semen, conventionally attached to masculinity, may in the process be rendered in terms of anonymity but only to forward "graces" that are distinctly patriarchal. What follows is a three-day festival whose theatricality is marked by three key facets: rapping, masturbation (or its negation), and resurrection.

Friday: Rapping

When the bus arrived at Canção Nova, there were already a couple hundred people, mostly young, roaming the green fields, which spread toward the beautiful Serra da Mantiqueira. Punctuating the lanes were hundreds of colorful tents and young men and women fusing into bigger groups. Some who had arrived the day before were clustered in circles around a guitar player, singing and rehearsing PHN songs. Many others were in the audiovisual hangar named Fundação John Paul II (John Paul II Foundation), where they could acquire all sorts of PHN paraphernalia: CDs, videos, audiotapes, shirts, jackets, bags, books, and other Canção Nova media products. Others lined up at the coffee shop or joined friends around a table, heightening their expectations about the festival through a variety of gestures—for example, circles in the air like in a cowboy lasso or the much-loved V-ing of the hand through the use of the middle and index fingers—codes that helped to ground and shape the social.

By 2:00 P.M. the main hangar of Canção Nova, baptized Palco do Senhor (Stage of the Lord), was packed with young people. The space resembled a gymnasium with different levels of seating around a central area where people also stood. Toward the rear of the hangar was a tower with equipment for live TV coverage. The gymnasium effect was reinforced by the uniform appearance of hundreds of PHN T-shirts and sweatshirts, purchased from Canção Nova's sales department, which many wore as though they had come for a sports match. The backdrop of the stage was a giant poster with graffiti-style letters spelling PHN. On the stage floor multicolored cables provided electric power to microphones, the organ, electric guitars, and amps. As the inner aisles and the middle area filled up, people remained on the outside but could still follow the show, as the scaffolding that creates the hangar intentionally allows those on the outside to see into and through the building. People greeted each other, absorbing the optimism that would bring them closer to the scene, which their past experiences helped to anticipate.

The electronic organ located in the back of the stage released a familiar tune. It was the melody to the PHN refrain I had heard on the bus, an audio signal sent out in anticipation of Dunga's imminent appearance. At a quarter past two, Canção Nova's spiritual leader, Padre Jonas Abib, appeared from behind the red curtain, holding a microphone, to welcome the few thousand young people to the campus. A guitarist, organist, drummer, and two backup singers formed the ensemble onstage. After a song of praise, Padre Jonas introduced the agenda for the following three days: the first two would be dedicated to combating addiction and the compulsion to sin, the last to liberation and prayer.

At that point, Dunga showed up onstage, sending a wave of euphoria across the audience. The excitement came to a peak when the sound of the PHN track started to play, and everyone started to sing along. Dressed in a

PHN hoodie, Dunga choreographed the young crowd: "Pode parar, pode parar de pecar [You may stop, stop sinning]. . . . Por hoje! [For today!] E . . . pode parar! Pode parar! [And . . . you may stop! You may stop!]." Dunga went on using parataxis in order to intensify the song around the same refrain. Parataxis, the linguistic technique in which phrases are placed side by side to induce a rhythm, is an important device of the confessional because of the structural equivalences it elicits in symmetry-based actions, like breathing, clapping, or swaying. Paratactical speech constitutes a key metrical signature. It is the way language folds into the body and makes it organically sound. Alongside the tautological phrases mentioned in chapter 1, such as "To stop sinning is to stop sinning," "The Acts of the Apostles is the Acts of the Apostles," and, a favorite in PHN, "Today is today," citations from the Bible such as "If I perish, I perish" (Esther 4:15) are often evoked at PHN shows. The prime aim of these figures of speech is to stimulate a circuit that prompts the body not to individualize but to reduplicate or extend itself. As with parataxis, the emphatic function of tautology aims to emphasize the semiotic potentials of the "speaking body" such that the voice does not sing about a particular object but, rather, *voice sings itself.* To sing itself means to aspire to say nothing in particular but simply to mark the possibility of passage to a simultaneous elsewhere: an else-here.

PHN confession hones the perception of relationality, such as the relation between language and space. Is a proposition like a solid object that occupies a particular position, or does it evoke the space of the limitless and the boundless? In his *Tractatus Logico-Philosophicus*, Ludwig Wittgenstein ([1922] 2001) associates tautology with the latter, what he calls a "logical space." A "tautology," he writes, "leaves open to reality the whole—the infinite whole—of logical space." This logic of space affects its relation to signification. "In a tautology," he continues, "the conditions of agreement with the world—the representational relations—cancel one another, so that it does not stand in any representational relation to reality" (Wittgenstein 2001: 54).[3] In a tautology (*tautos* means "same"), a statement becomes true by means of saying it twice. This implosion of meaning through redundancy is the necessary tactic to align speech to act and to have language objectify its own praxis—what, according to theories of performativity, constitutes a speech act. Rhythmically twofold, tautology presents reality in terms of an *it is what it is.* In that it poses a form of totality, *it* taking the entire space.

At the same time, however, precisely because of the repetition in tautology (as in PHN's "Today is today—not any other day"), the latter defines itself not merely in terms of what *it is* but also in terms of the potential extensions such repetition allows. As a result, tautology not only establishes sameness, but in so doing it also enacts a potential displacement or differentiation elicited by the repetition intrinsic to itself. Accordingly, what is reductive about tautology (it is what it is) is also what potentiates (its possible extensions). Tautology posits an instance of Judith Butler's (1997a, 1997b) theory of performativity regarding "the social iterability of the utterance," or what she calls "ex-citable speech," or, still, what Benjamin (1968, 1998b) in his work on Brecht's epic theater defined as the "ability" to say again: to re-cite (see also Weber 2008). The duplet in tautological speech, the twice-being of its operation, turns the *it* (present indicative) of it into an ongoing (present participle) open-ended temporal frame (de Abreu 2020b).

One hour after the start of the show, the atmosphere inside the hangar was cheerful. Dunga moved on with the objective of calling attention to the formal components of sound. In order to work out the "heart of a/the new song" (*o coração a/da canção nova*) so that the song "comes to life," in order to modulate the passage from semantics to rhythm, Dunga said, music "has to incarnate [*tem que incarnar*] or else [it] is not music." Molding his intervention on rapping techniques, he truncated the song into ever-smaller vocal nuggets. Verses were divided into units, into sentences, into words, into syllables, letters, sounds. Reduced to a minimum, sounds were typed into the flesh of the singer. With the microphone close to his mouth, Dunga moved melody into rhythm and sometimes rhyme. One moment raising his voice, then suddenly suspending it, the sounds exposed their exchangeability through additions, delays, intermissions, iambs, syllabic redoubling, and cadenced inflections. The goal was to organize sonic building blocks and to hone awareness of the manifold possibilities of recombining these; a song can always be divided and recomposed.

For Charismatics tautology must not be merely propositional but experienced bodily. Specifically for PHN, the symmetrical doubling in the tautological statement mimics the mechanisms of breathing through which, physiologically, speech is possible in the first place. Tautology, one could say, is good to breathe with. If it were propositional, a tautology would implode the borders of its being. It would be a perfect circle, a perfect mirroring between two static clauses. In being brought to the level of the experiential body, however, the latter is able to draw form (pneuma) out of a repetition. If incorporated into song and then sung, it is harder for the circle to close. Then it is easier to sustain a practice whose temporal hallmark is the gerund. The challenge of revivalist Catholicism is how to circle without encircling, how to advance the middle while staying in it. Avoid full closure at all costs.

Having disassembled the PHN track into isolated units of sound, Dunga ordered the song to stop: "Pode parar! [You stop!]." But he was being playful because the track begins with *pode parar*. A caesura was inserted where beginning and end met in the word/sound *stop*. The command to "stooopp" singing was in tension with the lyrical content of the song that had triggered the singing to start. The word *stop* split the verse, producing an incisive indecision at the heart of the song between cessation and the incitation to continue singing. It created tension between syntactical threshold and phonological limit, both announcing and delaying the event of the song coming to an end. These sets of disjunctions, like a rudimentary enjambment, produced a dynamic circularity where, as Daniel Heller-Roazen (2002: 94) puts it, "the beginning of the text became pregnant with anticipation of its ending," only to reenter its nonteleological cycle.

Song makes one aware of the messianic qualities of time, the time that time takes to come to an end (Agamben 2005b). In that interval of the time that remained, Dunga's song had no beginning or end. It ran in circles while expanding by means of that repetitive circling. *Stop* pulled time in both directions, into the past and into the future. It exposed the split or interval of breath itself as what articulates the circularity of time into *pre-* and *post-*. What ought to have referred to an end—an actual stop—became a big middle for the ongoing. Reenacted time and again, *stop* became the sonic signature of a temporal smudge, a vortexed middle with blurred edges. It was a work in progress.

The singing went on until it stopped definitively, and when it did the end was not definite but its potential extension. The end was more middle than before. In its circular operation, the word *stop* in the song not only departed its referential world as represented in the lyrics ("Stop sinning") but became punctuation that played on the rhythmic structure of the song. Attention was thus drawn to the circularity of text as it affects the medium of circulation as such. This was circulation through stops, later through spasms and gags.

It was Lent, so Dunga chose a verse he found appropriate for the season, 2 Corinthians 6:2: "In a favorable time I listened to you, and in a day of salvation I have helped you. Behold, now is the favorable time; behold, now is the day of salvation." He combined his reading of the Bible with a news event that had just been heard on Canção Nova's own broadcast: drug-trafficking killings in a São Paulo favela the previous Tuesday. To wage war against what he called "the sin of addiction" (*o pecado do vício*), he quoted himself quoting the Bible: "Now is the 'favorable time, behold' to harvest, not take away, life"; it was time to get "addicted to the spirit," not yield to "evil vice." "So tell me now, what is vice?" he asked. "Also those at home," he added, as he faced the TV camera. He read another verse, this time from Matthew 15:22: "And a Canaanite woman from that region came out and began to cry out, saying: 'Have mercy on me, Lord, Son of David; my daughter is cruelly demon-possessed.' You young person out there, you know what vice [*vício*] is the opposite of? . . . of? . . . of virtue!! [*virtude*]. Amen, son of David." He then used his index and middle fingers of both hands to make two *V* signs. "In victory," he said, "by the way, also in victory, right?" "The spirit wants this *V* [vice = violence = left-hand fingers] to be defeated by this *V* [virtue = victory = right-hand fingers]." He asked those present to do the same, to *V* their fingers and use the *V* on the right, as if scissors, to cut the *V* of the left. He asked them to stretch their arms, hands, and fingers and take the *V*-as-scissors as far as possible in space. He then commanded that the brother or sister on the left cut the *V* of the left hand of the person on the right, then of the person in front of them, then of the one behind them. It was as though through such gestures the assumed interiority of subjects, as posited by modern ideas of the confessional, ceased to make sense. Rather than being contained by a subject, the hands seemed to draw the body to an elsewhere. In what was an electronic-infused environment, hands and fingers pointed at, indeed performed, digitality avant la lettre.[4]

Dunga continued, "The spirit that breathes in these words [from Matthew] wants this PHN to be a moment to declare a stomping war on addiction [the *V* on the left], not just [a] war on drugs, but also vice, use, abuse, misuse [*mau uso*] of your body. . . . The Holy Spirit wants this PHN to be a devastating 'no' to addiction. Let us work out this 'no' in us." And at this point they went on ten times saying "no," one after another, alternating with clapping: No! *Clap!* No! *Clap!* No! After the tenth "no," Dunga returned to the PHN refrain: "Pode parar" (You may stop). He asked them to not stop singing but to stop sinning. "It is not easy, but you can do it. You just have to continue to stop! [*pause*] Stop! [*Pare!*]"[5]

The band onstage played songs from Dunga's new CD, *Água Humilde*. From one track to another, the throng sang along, danced, and applauded relentlessly for twenty minutes. The collective knew the melodies, the lyrics, the choreography, the protocols, even the hypnotic drone they were about to get into. At close range I was able to see conflicts in coordination, but from a distance the audience gave the impression of moving like a *some-one* to the accompanying melodic and prosodic songs. As before, nonetheless, the function of the show was to alter the text and the script: it was to crumble the text by the power of repetition, to widen the interval between the written word and its delivery, to bring the song to the edge of time as well as to the extremities of the body and let it hover at its crest.

More pivotal than the plot during Dunga's performance was highlighting the songs' improvising possibilities. Yet the levels of improvisation tend to remain within the range of possibilities opened up by the powers of incantation. That is, improvising is less about adding something wholly new than about exposing the internal elasticity of the song, so that moments in the song are amenable to citation. Accordingly, what is emphasized is primarily the song's quotable potential. Rather than song expressing the internal life of a subject, song ought to expose its articulations—that is, its ability to be displaced to other moments, to make itself available for future echoes, and ultimately to confound the here and now of its singing with the possibility of a here-else. Singing is thus all about exposing the conditions that give it being, the operations of its own reproducibility. In practice, this translated into making a song into an infinite entity whose potentials were manifold. One single verse was at once too short but also boundless, since the role of singing was to travel deeper and deeper into its basic constitution where, ultimately, pneuma exposed the principle of its supposed operatic presence (that is, in passing). Such was the diaphragmatic horizon of a PHN song, beat by beat converging toward and utterly untoward and retarding *tata-rum-ta-rum-mara*.

Making the songs citable—and excitable—transformed the status of authorship (Derrida 1988; Butler 1997b).[6] Onstage, Dunga insisted on the idea that the author of the songs was not himself but the Holy Spirit, "the one creator who gives us the ability to breathe." Such a displacement of authorship becomes here a condition for the proper exposure of the song's quotable potentials. By allowing itself to be citable, the song is unmoored from an origin and can do its transformative work in the very act of its utterance. It is therefore important to convey not that a person is singing but that a song is being sung. Dunga's function was not to perform *for* an audience but precisely to highlight the power of song to blur the contours between his performance and the crowd, between the stage and its auditorium extensions. Crucially, though, this blurring was not meant to suggest a capacity to walk in the shoes of the audience, which as an exercise would appeal to a sense of empathy. What was at stake was a suspension of the kind of subject positioning that empathy requires. It was, rather, the sense of having the origin (Dunga) appearing in pragmatic adjacency into the space of the song. It meant, technically speaking, having the origin entering the space of the middle/milieu. The overall purpose of the show was not to define a telos, an integrated narrative, but to expose a rhythm associated with the song's pliability. In such an arrangement, song coincided with the act of its singing, the to-and-fro of its being. If the song's originator became anonymous, it was to make more visible the song's own conditioning operations and the milieu in which it circulated.

Understanding the centrality of displacement here is crucial since it in turn structures the logic through which sin and confession were experienced by the PHN Generation. As just mentioned, the function of the author figure, or originator, was to disappear behind the song—to martyr authorship—so as to highlight the infrastructure that made singing possible. Later we will see how this withdrawal owes little to an effort to externalize God, to highlight the extreme of a transcendent. In effect, much like the phasmid (from phantom) or stick-insect in relation to the branch it mimetically assimilates, God gets "middled."[7] In this work of camouflage in the collective environment of PHN, there was no motivation for the kind of dramaturgies of introspection and repentance typical of the modern confessional. Rather, that journey into selfhood was seen as precisely one of the temptations to avoid in PHN confessionals. This is because the ability of a body to regulate flows that were *already* in the world was more important than the possibility of creating or generating these anew. More significant than attaching sinful content to the singularity of the perpetrator or acting under redemptive exculpation and expiation was the harnessing of a space of circulation that was already to some degree underway. Christian metanoia (conversion) became reinterpreted through a model of circulation that both hinged and aligned the body to a media environment and, finally, to a mode of relationality marked by substitution.

At the core of such ongoing circulation lay a model of communication that aimed to overcome the context of the modern confessional, premised as it is on what Michael Warner (2002: 90) calls a "localized exchange" of a speech act involving speaker and addressee.[8] In the tradition in question it targeted the confinement of sin to the absolute private realm under the seal of the *sigillum confessionis sacramentalis*, which de facto prohibits all circulation. Making sins public thus became a means to acknowledge the logic of circulation that, in Warner's terms, ultimately constituted the public as such. Sins were at a far remove from being heard and even seen, sensed instead as passing impulses, manifestations. Bearing witness to, publicizing (in the sense of making public), or, more emically, "martyring" sin, all actively worked to shape a public in circulation, indeed public because in circulation.

And yet at key points Dunga would recuperate his position as leader. After a period of sing-alongs and dancing, he returned to the position of preacher. Where earlier he had endeavored to become one with the crowd, in the final moments of the day, the first of three, he climbed back onto his pulpit and called for what he described as the "decisive moment" (*momento decisivo*) of the "journey." The organ held a long fermata. Holding tightly to his microphone, he started crooning, leaving long pauses between phrases:

> Libere agora corpo [Free the body from sin]
> Deixe chocalhar pela musica e pela palavra [Shaken by the music and the
>   word]
> Deixe a musica entrar . . . agora [By letting the music come in . . . now]
> Deixe [Let . . .]
> Penetrar carne e coração [Enter flesh and heart]
> Vibre e trema [Vibrate and tremble]
> Para que os frutos podres caiam [So may the rotten fruits fall down]
> Aliviando, vivificando o Espírito [Relieving, enlivening the Spirit]
> Ó confessore. [Oh confessor.]

With the organ moaning in the background, an elongated vibrating sob, the atmosphere in the hangar went quiet. Like the silence that precedes lightning, the air felt filled with static. Here and there incipient eruptions of praying in tongues died out before taking off again. It lingered like a long suspension, a moment of inactivity to recover from all the dancing, clapping, and singing; a breather. The silence drew attention to the mass of body heat in the hangar. Feverish, atonic, eerie. And then, with no clear physical signal, a joined vocal sound rushed wildly through the arena. It was not coordinated language but a jumble of voices coming together and apart. A rumbling sound coiled through the hangar much like the twists and turns of starlings. Hands started digging into pockets, wallets, and bags. From all sides hundreds of objects were being sent through the air in the direction of the stage: cigarettes, condoms, lighters, hashish, erotic calendars, matches, lipsticks, and anything else the audience associated with sin. It was a massively coordinated deletion, expulsion, ejection. The noise of excitement was fierce. The mass of youths started to jump, pointing toward the stage, expressing a commotion of denial, loudly shouting, "NO! NO! NO!" All across the room youngsters screamed their heads off. With the organ still on, like a steady drone, the atmosphere of the ritual performance of a sermon had turned into a mass public confession adjusted to the temperament of a wild and rowdy pop show. In cool acknowledgment of what was happening, Dunga raised his hand in a *V* (for victory) and asked the audience to offer "big applause to Jesus."

Saturday: Auto-Affection

The next day at 9:30 A.M. Dunga again appeared onstage and received a roaring ovation. The PHN hymn followed, welcoming everyone with the usual euphoria. Then Dunga spoke to the young crowd:

> Silence, please. I bet you slept really well in your tents after yesterday, not *tend*ations [he is making a pun between *tent* and *temptation*, which in Portuguese is *tenda*, thus, *tendação*], right? Aha! So please, bring your hands together now in prayer, palm against palm, finger against finger, press, press, press. . . . Tell [me], as you press palm against palm, why is today so special? Because today is unique, so unique that, even if those present have been here before or shall be tomorrow, if you are not here today, you will never be here today: *Por hoje não! Hoje não!* [For today no! Today no!] Say it. [*The audience repeats the phrase.*] With your hands together, pray with me. [*The organ plays.*] Lord, help me to be chaste. Today. Help my eyes, my ears, my hands stay away from easy temptations. Today. Temptations that offend God as much as they harm me, my health, and the body of my community. Say it: *Por hoje, não. Diga com toda a força pressionado as palmas de suas mãos* [For today, no. Say it with all your might while pressing your palms]. . . . And now I want to go back to the moment where we finished our meeting [*encontro*] yesterday. . . . I want to start today where we "stopped" yesterday . . . by . . . applauding Jesus. We start today where we "stopped" yesterday. So let us applaud again, and again, and again. That's it [*Isso*]. *Por hoje não, não. . . . Pode parar, por hoje* [You may not stop it. For today you stop. Not for today]. Applaud, my brother, my sister, applaud until your palms are red, blue, yellow, dark, bruised, all the colors of the rainbow, applaud without stopping [*sem parar*], like you are no longer sure those are your own hands. Let us applaud your applauding. You are good in the applause. Let's applaud some more. That's it.

Applauding is pressing hand against hand. It is steering the air between palms. Clapping sounds bear witness to the gesture that produced them. Rhythm sets the desirable aperture or time threshold of the applause. It is what Henri Lefebvre (2013) in his work on rhythmanalysis defined as musical measure.[9] If repeated enough times, clapping becomes automated, intuitively marching into its future. Repetitive clapping leads to variances within a group. It flocks into new tempos, steering new trajectories and resonances. Charismatics like saying that claps are extensions of the heartbeat. At other times they are likened to the sound of the flapping wings of the Holy Spirit. The link between ovation and ovum, or egg, is another relationship that little by little becomes apparent in the PHN ritual and the labors of palming on account of the PHN's obsession with the conduits of semen. The repetitive movement involved in the meeting of palms, of hand touching hand (and of feeling itself feeling), pumps the blood to circulate. Like the movement and filtration of bodily toxins, this circulation, powered by the continuous panning, screens out the passing presence of sin.

Sins, at the PHN festival, were not called on to be owned and expiated. Rather sins were like orphan entities, the offspring of labor alone. If this idea were a gesture, it would be like screwing a lightbulb into a lamp through repeated rotation of the hand, where awareness gradually moves to the circuit between motion and energy. Inserting a lightbulb means bringing light onto something, yet the act itself points to a labor-intensive obscurity in the very gesture of bringing light forth. Because no one should own sin but simply conduct it, it is important to withhold an idea of reception. Rather, the value of sin is in its conduciveness. Above all, sin illuminates.

To be sure, it is not that PHNers have no sense of personalized guilt. Yet, that owning of guilt is precisely what must be sacrificed for the circulating of spirit. The scene in question corresponds to what Eve Sedgwick (1993: 38–39) describes as "a tympanically responsive transmitter," that is, the labor of ignorance needed just to not stop desire. As Sedgwick explains, this process must be calibrated to a halfway station, as the success of that labor of ignorance paradoxically requires the subject in question to know that he or she could be tempted or manipulated into owning what should be circulating.[10] What is at stake here, in other words, is a particular understanding of accountability, one that does not presuppose an authorial origin but on the contrary relays accountability to the middle of a process or praxis where there will be acts ("tendencies" in Sedgwick's words [1993]) but no actual perpetrators. Ideally, sins are called on but as polyphonic indexes that *a* circulation is at work, beneath verbalization and personal accountability. Sins are passing, and in that passing they abstract themselves from the confining frames of ownable flesh. Sins become abstracted and estranged from their authors while each body is a potential host—or what philosopher Michel Serres (2007) would call a "parasite" in the sense of a "thermal exciter"—a stage for the dramaturgy of an outpouring.

What mattered in the PHN festival was to bear witness to the existence of sin as such and, paradoxically, turn that recognition of an inevitable reality into an exercise of prevention, to fold past and future into the internal process of an ongoing action. What's there to reform, therefore, is not just the sense of personal accountability that absolves and acquits. Indeed reflection happened only retroactively among participants and remained absent from the event. Rather, what is reformed is the very (pr)axis between sin and act. Rather than eluded, sin is the pedagogical mechanism that must be rendered visible— somatically applied for—so as to operationalize it toward its own negation.

For PHNers at Canção Nova, the way to show that the operations of confession had been effectively absorbed by the body was to somatize sin as in the act of a passing. These somatizations included a feeling of dizziness, nausea, levitation from the ground, weight loss, sense of aging, disequilibrium, arms involuntarily stretched forward or backward, tingling extremities, loss of balance, paroxysms, pain in the ear (the vestibular bone), electric tingling, numb extremities (e.g., hands and fingers), perspiration, heart palpitations, dry throat, uncontrolled muscle movement like jaw clenching, fast REM, low or high blood pressure, an irrepressible desire to laugh or cry (often both), visions, arousal, howling, barking, screaming, and, quite frequently, an experience of personal derealization sometimes accompanied by a disconnect in perception, prophetic visions, or revelations. These somatic manifestations made sense only to the extent that they made apparent the passing of "information" between bodies. What this information conveyed was a self-referring occurrence. It informed that circulation was happening.

Clapping worked as a basic rhythm, an elementary structure of the body's percussion to which all could return as a kind of commons. The charismatic gymnasium, as I am calling it, primes the ability to be in sync as a kind of love, and Paul, of all apostles, claimed the power of oratory to recruit the primeval, in a blind rebellion to the law, and in ways that link the archaic to a technological beat. This does not mean that all rhythms were equally effective during the PHN confession show. Occasionally there were dissonances that called for some form of reparative intervention. One telling example of this, if more frequent among adults' meetings than at a youth camp like the PHN festival, were eruptions by one person in the audience, whose clapping had fallen into a kind of disarray, out of sync with the others. At these moments clapping no longer worked as a technique of fusion with the collective milieu but became the opposite: it became a way of calling attention to oneself; it individualized. There was always the possibility that a somatic manifestation would harden around a particular person with the effect of, perhaps under the guise of satanism, weakening or interrupting the "coming to pass" of things. When this happened, the person (as the *I* pronoun) was helped by those nearby, those who were in the flow of the third person interceded in a practice Charismatics call the "laying on of hands" (*intercessão das mãos*). Those who were seated close to the individualized person would come to "charge" that person and rescue him or her back into the flow. If that did not work, then the person whose body was "way too closed" (*corpo demasiado fechado*) would receive special attention from a lay Charismatic or a priest of the community. On these occasions the person was asked to leave the hangar (away from the TV cameras) and was taken to a place apart for a deeper intercession by someone from the Canção Nova Community. During the Masses of cure and deliverance (*missas de cura e libertação*), where adults were usually a majority, a whole tent would be set up to attend to such cases of "blockage" (*emprisionamento*) or "blackout."[11] The PHN Generation shows, on the other hand, being frequented mostly by young people, needed those parallel spaces only "for the very special cases," as put to me by a Charismatic "liberator of spirits" I met at the site, implying that these blockages were rarer among younger people.

Somatic manifestations per se were welcome as long as they did not become too attached to a particular body. It was only when the circuit stopped and soma had the power to individualize and circumscribe that sin became an issue. For example, intense burning, itching, or a dry throat are inscriptions of the figure of circulation. The problem is not with the inscription; the problem is when the inscription also becomes a circumscription, when it freezes a "first" person out of the flow of "the third." One is therefore in a setting where confession happens not on account of a circumscribable, blamable self, and indeed the impetus toward this circumscription is to be avoided at all costs. This is because, as mentioned, the prime goal of PHN is not to confess something that happened to or by way of a subject but rather to make confession internal to the training process of avoiding sin in the future. Such is, essentially, what differentiates individualization from incarnation.

This self-referential logic is not only a methodology toward an object but one that turns the object it targets into its mode of operation. Referring to the thousands of anonymous letters sent to the studio of Canção Nova by young people on a weekly basis—many of which are read on his weekly PHN talk show—Dunga rebuked the audience with a studied, cool flair:

> Oh! Masturbation is not sinful? How come? [*Como não é pecado?*] Have you ever seen someone masturbating by looking at a lamppost? Aah! Post, you are so sexy! Of course not! One masturbates in order to take pleasure from the body. . . . But it is true you have to put it out. But your body does it for you. Your body puts it out. The grace that you have to ask from God is that you may have a nocturnal emission without erotic dream[s], with no pornography. I used to pray to the Lord, in front of the Holy Sacrament: Lord, may I this night have nocturnal emission with no erotic dream. Lord, I do not want to masturbate because if I masturbate, I will think about that woman, will buy that magazine, listen to pornographic music [*pornofónico*], see pornographic movies [*pornocénico*], excited to the point that I will go, all alone, into my room and masturbate. One has to fight. It is not simply going there to the confessional or to a confessor of some sort. [*He impersonates the confessor:*] "Ah! Take it easy! Masturbation is not a sin!" Of course it is sin, you philistine! Yes, because it involves thoughts and sentiments that do not please God.

In his formidable work on language performativity among Catholic Charismatics in North America, Thomas Csordas (1990: 18) observes that the practice of raising hands in praise or in clapping is a strategy that Charismatics employ to keep "hands out." In the PHN meetings, however, gestures are not just strategies of diversion or recreational sublimation. Gestures themselves are transformative in ways that tie the physiological to the ethical. Specifically, PHN exercises function as contrivances for the rhythmic entrainment of the circadian system. The primary aim of rhythmic entrainment is to regulate and induce the body to release a nocturnal emission. The idea is that the circadian timekeeping system will respond to the temporal feedback arising from the vocal and physical exercises performed at the PHN show. Dunga, who often identified his life trajectory with that of St. Augustine (like him, a late converter to Christianity and a "great coach of souls" [*treinador de almas*]), held the patristic Christian view that nocturnal emissions do not pollute the will because they are not voluntary. Yet it was also this very involuntary aspect of sleep—as opposed to wakefulness—that PHN sought to combat through disciplinary exercises so as to make the emissions while sleeping into a form of action or activity and not just a residual side effect. At stake is the unsettling of a classic distinction to be found in Aristotle's important treatise on ethics between *energeia* and potential (*hexis*), where sleep, a state of potential, is seen as an inferior state with respect to *energeia*—but an unsettling that nonetheless also presumes that very hierarchy suggested by Aristotle between wakefulness and sleep.[12]

Masturbation, on the contrary, is harmful to the soul and to the body. It is like copulating with a demon, a *succubus nefastus*, both slothful and voluntary. One goal of the PHN camp was to find a biological-moral concordance between bodily performance and biological response. Rhythm through gestures, word-bearing air, studied concordances between lungs and heart, all were important in regulating the relation of the body to itself. Respiration, particularly, as it involves self-relation was emblematic. This is to the extent that too much taking in of breath, or hyperventilation, could be associated with self-copulation.[13] To counter this possibility, well-built symmetry of song and prayer—in particular, the prayer of the heart according to the Byzantine rosary (as described in chapter 4)—was used in regulating the balance between inspiration and expiration. The aim, moreover, was to take such a balanced economy of air (pneuma) into the deep recessions of one's body so that one no longer acts but is acted on. At stake is an active participation in one's withdrawal.

Similarly, what was condemnable was not the night emission but voluntary autoeroticism. In contrast, nocturnal emissions were taught to be the necessary valve of natural sexual release as compared to the artifices of film, image, word, or sound. The experience of that discharge, Dunga explained, must be so natural that not even dreaming would be tolerable. Far from sublimated, wet dreaming was attributed to a conscious act of the imagination in absorbing sounds or images that would likely stir and goad the body into emission. Unlike Sigmund Freud's classic construal, in which wet dreaming functions as a kind of relieving hallucination for what is repressed while simultaneously protecting sleep, Charismatics see wet dreaming as an active extension, even an occasion, that expands on the artifices of pornographic films and images, which are explored in practices of autoeroticism. Dismissed altogether was the theory of the repressed, which could all too quickly become associated with theories that endorse the cathartic benefits of wet dreaming. Favored, rather, was a theory of action that might dig deeper than the dominion of dreams into the imageless crude mechanics of human biology.

As already mentioned, the relation to confession in PHN is not one of hermeneutical debunking of past deeds and expiation. It is a laboring of the limbs and members, a modifier of physiological rhythms that aims to cut beneath the conscious and even the unconscious thoughts and dreams to become one with the circadian hormone profile. In other words, one does not come to PHN to confess but to work on sin's preclusion, a preclusion that involves its practical acknowledgment. The logic, in sum, was the following: Bodies engage in exercise. By engaging in exercise, bodies acknowledge what people already know, that there is sin in the world; sin is within us. Indeed, it is us. As sin circulates, however, there is transformation that shows sin is passing. Yet the actions that expose sin also work to preventively exercise and thus exorcise it. Bodies show—perform—the very thing they want to avoid.[14] To confess, one could say, is to potentialize the "autoimmune community": a kind of protection that incorporates the logic of the thing it condemns and for which *it*, therefore, must protect against protection itself: *sin*.[15]

What Charismatics condemn about sacramental verbal confession is the effortless relation between deeds and words, the affirmation of the origin through introspective reflection, the logic of containment that turns the self into a recipient rather than a transmitter of spirit. It is more urgent, Charismatics explain, to work on the conditions (on the possibility of sinning or not sinning) that are *already* in the body. It is because the body itself embodies the contradiction between good and bad—because the body is also an antibody— that it becomes the foundation for an ethical exercise. In that work of prevention, by exercising the biological and moral conditions for not sinning, one also flirts with danger (Asad 1993), for the very means of prevention of sin that favor biological reproduction also challenge selfhood. As I have indicated, the entire PHN apparatus promoted circulation, which in turn involved a form of self-estrangement. Participants became "peopled by others" (Jacqueline Rose quoted in Napolitano 2015: 48). In that sense, PHNers adopted the very relational logics of the masturbatory subject who needs to numb the self in order to inflame otherness. The PHN philosophy of practice is about making explicit what one wants to overcome. It is an exercise of autoimmunity that turns the immunological paradox of protection through controlled exposure to danger into its proper theme of performance.

At the hangar, the clapping went on for minutes, gathering and then eventually fast-forwarding to its own ending. Dunga asked that people raise their warmed-up hands (*levante agora suas mãos fogosas*) and make contact with the Holy Spirit: to feel the fervor in their hands, at the tips of their fingers, and then to imagine their bodies as antennas or transmitters as though they were extensions of (the work of) Canção Nova. With the sound of the organ in the background, Dunga started to orate. He asked those present to make a human circuit by giving their hands to one another: "With the heart we feel, with the mind we think, with the mouth we eat, with the feet we walk, and with the hands we do things. As you are holding the hand of the person next to you, invite the spirit to pass, let it pass, without haste, without forcing. It is passing now. Feel it through your reheated hands, your fingers. What is it that you feel? What is that?" He commanded that each feel the hand in their hand, as though the axis of personhood was shifting to that connection, that uncanny copresence, on the right side and on the left. In bringing the extremities to a center, through that hand-in-hand contact, each person became a quasi person, the being of circulation itself.

As the day wound down, Dunga sang a ballad, backed up by two men and a woman, which was followed by a new round of applause. This was the exercise through which inscriptions of sin appeared on the surface of the collective (rather than on the individual), exposing the labor of protection and autoimmunity of the body toward sins to come as they passed. In this logic the principle of original sin withered in relevance. The purpose was not to wash the origin by revisiting it or by conjuring a clean state but rather to regulate what was always already in the world. Such a self was not autonomous but replicative and not discrete but indiscrete. It was self as medium, self as other than self, self as third. This idea became powerfully manifest when Dunga asked PHNers to perform the human wave or "Olla" (after the Mexican World Cup), one favorite theatrical element of Charismatic events. Following the stretched-out hand of Dunga, which drew circles in the air like it was the hand of a clock, the wave traveled through the crowds, producing, in its coming to pass, the effect of an all-encompassing oscillating body. The choreography of coordinated standing up, raising arms, and sitting down, round and round, exposed key elements of a PHN show: the partaking in a circulation by virtue of which elements ("information," "sin," "Spirit") are transported and transformed.

And yet the nullification of an agentive, accountable self also raised anxieties about unhampered excesses, about too much fluidity of the sign. There was a need to prevent it from becoming too erratic and uncontainable. A balance had to be sought between, on the one hand, a prodding of corporeal fluidity through excitability and, on the other, the risk of endless signification. It was in view of this contradictory demand that Charismatics—and the PHN festival most particularly—evinced a sustained and focused concern about matters of displaced sexuality, especially masturbation. This was not simply because autoeroticism is a theme that has long figured in Christian thought, but because it offered Charismatics a primordial structure through which to think the relation between self and alterity. It was precisely the parallel logic underwriting masturbation and what Charismatics collectively strove for—the act of displacing authorship by inhabiting the space of a nonself—that made it such a valued theme for the structuring of the exercise. Given the focus on working out the body to counter the temptations of nonreproductive sex, the thing that had to be expelled had to structurally resemble the methodology via which expulsion was possible. The logic of self-relation internal to autoeroticism hinged entirely on the fact that evil must be fought at its own game (Mondzain 2009). On the second day of the PHN festival, thus conceived, self-relation was both anathema and remedy. And that ambivalence allowed the possibility of engendering a third space as a system of thought and manifestation.

The command to exercise entailed a productive paradox. On the one hand, it enforced the idea that one's body is not one's own—it is the product of a collectively performed, entrained rhythm, thus undermining recourse to techniques of a supplementary nature, including masturbation, coitus interruptus, and the use of contraceptives, which would trouble and obstruct reproductive sex. On the other hand, PHN exercising fought such supplementary dangers with logics to be found in the physiological mechanisms of the body and that were compatible with the work of technical reproducibility. What mattered most was the alternating motion between two *hands*, as though they were not opposites at all but more like the hands of a clock steering time and space into being: circling without encircling.

Sunday: Resurrection

It was the third day of the PHN camp. The group of the previous days had mostly been made up of eighteen- to thirty-five-year-olds. On the third day, however, people of all ages came for the morning Mass. Afterward there were sermons and songs of praise. The hip-hop-style PHN banner was still in place, but on this third day onstage there was also a Byzantine icon of Theotókos, the Mother of God. It was the first time I had thought of hip-hop and Byzantine iconography together, but dissonance was by then a familiar pattern. There was a portable altar at the center of the stage. A procession of five novices headed by a priest carrying the holy monstrance entered Rincão do Meu Senhor (Hangar of My Lord), the principal hangar of Canção Nova, through the main entrance. The procession also included a priest swinging a thurible, the metal censer used in worship services. Following convention, the acolyte held the censer with the right hand at the height of the breast. The censer was then raised up to the height of the eyes and, with the left hand, given an outward motion, in a double swing, first slightly ascending toward the altar and then toward the celebrants, then again toward the altar. One, two, three, four. Cardinality, not ordinality, ruled on this last day of PHN.

The morning sun was coming through the latticed hangar, but two large candles were burning on each side of the altar. The number of people had almost doubled compared with the previous days, and many followed the Mass on TV screens set in the passageway to the site. The ceremony was much more solemn and rigid than the earlier performances. The vests of the priests, the altar, and the props of the missal and the Holy Eucharist added the kind of institutional weight and authority absent from the previous days (and not always welcomed by Charismatics). These institutional aspects seemed incongruent with all that could be associated with the "third," that is, Spirit. Yet, this stages another instance of the complexio oppositorum, in which the tension of opposites bodies forth the both/and quality of a self-immunized *corpus ecclesia*: institution and grace, Peter and Paul, tradition and dissonance.

Historically speaking, it is the fate of most Catholic movements to slowly and incrementally readjust their settings, ideas, and techniques to the canon, which often inspired the need for change in the first place. This is the feature that makes Catholicism the most "elastic" of all religions, as Carl Schmitt ([1923] 1996: 6) notes.[16] But tensions and friction can become apparent. These are themselves not always viewed as problematic, so long as the adaptations are executed with the balance and compromise that will outpour grace, sanction what could otherwise appear subversive. After all, tensions and conflicts define what in Catholicism is most appreciated as a sign of its heterogeneity and ability to encompass (that is, to include) the extreme of extremes.[17] Extremity is fine as long as its edges meet the point in the circle where it all begins again, in a roundabout way.

The Mass was celebrated with the introductory rites, praise, and three readings. The liturgy of the Eucharist turned attention to the preparation of the altar and gifts. As the congregation stood, the priest gave the exhortation to pray: "Pray, brethren, that my sacrifice and yours may be acceptable to God, the Almighty Father." The congregation responded, "May the Lord accept the sacrifice at your hands, for the praise and glory of his name, for our good, and the good of all his holy church." With the Eucharist transubstantiated, silence fell on the hangar, a silence that had the power to integrate the mass of people as the host disintegrated in their mouths. The next minutes descended into an even deeper quietness. It seemed as though celebrants were holding their breath, inwardly. The air felt powerfully loaded, wired. And then, much like what had happened on the first day, the silence was canceled. With the cleric facing the crowd from the altar, a raucous, rumbling speaking in tongues started sweeping across the arena, blasting through spaces of silence, enclosing the throng from all sides, independent of their speakers.[18]

Three rows down from my seat, a young woman started to shake. She tilted her body sideways as though she was about to faint. Those standing next to her first prayed for her, reaching out their hands, but she did not show signs of calming. Instead, her shaking became more expressive, and she fell to the floor in what looked like an epileptic seizure. She was lifted and taken away by two women, who took her outside to one of the benches; at this distance, the sounds of praise had lost their corporeal reality. As the doctor of the community and two other women approached to assist the one who had fallen, she said she felt better, "only dizzy," and assured everyone that this had happened before without consequence. One of the original helpers told the newcomers that she had received an electric shock when touching the woman as they walked together out of the hangar. It surprised me to see how the one who had "seized" reassured the members of the community about her condition rather than the other way around. So deep in her lungs had this woman gone that her body shook like it was an extension of her speech: *estoummbem* (I'mmm all right).

When do the features called on become too much for their own good? When does too much circulation lead to being read as stuck? The woman who had fallen would seem to embody in that moment all that PHN had been trying to achieve throughout the long hours of performed singing and moving: a voice in tune with the raw material of confession, a voice that spoke for all and nobody in particular, a sibilant (too-darkened speech?) that interrupted itself in pace with the body from which it spurted. This was speech threatening to turn the body inside out. But it was equally the case that the very state of things that could be rendered as the culmination of an idealized achievement—the singing of the body electric[19]—had to be contained and divested of its power. It itself had to be interrupted. And so, like a bad connector, she had to be restored and reintegrated in the circuit.

Desirable as circulation is at PHN confessional shows, there are regulatory censors for something like too much expenditure, a point in which circulation becomes a sign of the devil's capacity for mimetic appropriation. And while, as we saw, mimesis is the way to go at Canção Nova—evil, we saw, is fought at its own game—the opposite can also happen. Mimetic appropriation by the devil must keep a Charismatic hypervigilant against excess, which must be driven out and dealt with off-camera. It is precisely the exposure of a consciousness of excess, of too much circulation, that allows Catholic Charismatics to interpose a distinction between themselves and other groups, such as Pentecostal evangelicals, which they are accused by some of resembling too much. Obsession with the devil, the casting off of spirits, and exorcism are features that Catholics and liberals alike have long condemned about Pentecostal televangelism. If Catholic Charismatics wish to anchor their confessional regimes in the labors of the Holy Spirit, the third person, they must not descend into a public display of ousting, the argument goes.

The difference between the PHN confessional and evangelicals, as I was told by Canção Nova members and by Dunga, lies in the very conceptual treatment of the third person.[20] As Charismatics at Canção Nova insist, the third person is not a nonperson. When evangelicals cast out devils on TV, they annihilate the person. There on the camera, they suggest, is the figure not of the first, the second, or even the third person, but of something like "a fourth squared person," the devil itself, that in being feverishly externalized by exorcism has taken hold of the whole space. The actual withdrawal of an individual who is out of sync with the circuit of confession by human regulators of the show (sometimes by participants) is therefore a measure that invests in removing "evil in excess" as much as, if not more than, in making that gesture of removal itself into a display of differentiation vis-à-vis other Christian (non-Catholic) denominations. In these circumstances what is being declined is not just a first or second pronominal but the conjugation of an all-encompassing third that nonetheless must not be as reducible to a *them*. And so, "We are not *them*," Padre Edmilson (who celebrates weekly at Canção Nova) told me as we walked through the vegetable garden of the compound.

The off-camera element is important not only because it distinguishes Charismatics from evangelicals ("They have limits, whereas the latter not") but also because it allows Charismatics to subscribe to the idea that the visceral and providential economy of the third not only is not compatible with artifice in the making of live TV but requires making visible the editorial operations behind the picture. Since the 1990s when Charismatics at Canção Nova decided not to use the external referent of publicity or propaganda (means to an end) but only what was "in the bosom of Mary"—by which they mean the entire administrative economy of the place (*oikonomia*) from technical machines to the land—that technique is no falsehood. Quite the contrary, the exposure of artifice is precisely what elevates the "image" to the proper sense of life: "as image," as Charismatics put it.

And so, rather than assessed or, to use an emic term, "discerned" by the surrounding practitioners as a successful example of the circulating third, the young woman who had fallen out of sync was seen as *presa* (stuck), *fechada* (closed), or *carregada* (loaded). The very signals associated with circulation— the blurring of contours between self and other through prayer in tongues, the trembling of the members—all should have made her a hero of confession in PHN terms. But instead the degree of her externalizing ran in direct proportion to a radical closure; indeed it was so externalizing that it became counterintuitive to the relational space of the third. At the same time, if a "person" is taken away, it is only so he or she can again enter a circuit in process. This reentry speaks volumes, for it is how the community expresses both fortitude and flexibility, limits and openness, as the essentials of renewal. These are aspects that Catholic Charismatics in Brazil must keep in the balance, as evidenced when I asked whether their emphasis on spirit and charisma could lead to a rupture with the church, only to hear from followers and leaders alike, in terms that excessive reiteration has made impersonal, that "to stretch to the limit is to know the limits of stretching." The problematic in Charismatic Catholicism, members will remind us, is not one of rupture but of transfiguration.

Importantly, by having a confessional show that culminates in a babble of tongues, in the idiom of a speech that suspends all referentiality other than the conditions of its reference, PHN powerfully dramatizes the locution of the middle voice.[21] This middle voice posits a field of anonymity and generic ipseity through a regulated rhythm. Yet at the same time it is at the crest of this work toward anonymity that a totalizing system of being is reinstituted. The tautological absolute Jacques Lacan identifies as "the I who says I am the one who I am" erupts through the very scene that has just transpired in the effort of suspending all specificity. This is the tautological I, moreover, that recurs in language as well as in images. From PHN graffito to "the bosom of Mary, Mother of God" (*o ventre de Maria, Mãe de Deus*), at the end of the third day, we find ourselves back in the totalizing and patriarchal One, paradoxically, made possible by a labor-induced radical openness.

Such is the oxymoron that the holy third engenders in the body of Mary—an organic yet mechanized uterus where, for Catholic Charismatics, the generative tension between Catholicism and Pentecostalism takes place. By the third day when the mechanisms of influx are at their peak, it becomes apparent how servile such a compromise is to the patriarchy. Calls on chastity become the tools for the reinstitution of a doctrine over the female body who is, and must remain, at once virgin and mother, origin and reproducibility. If all goes according to program, by the third day, the looping of the thread of the net is closed. Until the next PHN confession festival.

Summary

Inasmuch as circulation confirms the circumstances under which it functions, it must also expose the disciplined rhythms that structure and endow it with a certain percussive order. While interruption and break are the necessary devices to align the body to its mechanical rhythms, there is always the risk of turning flicker into seizure and capture. Spasms, tics, and convulsions are good as long as they do not become spastic; that which initially moves toward seizure must not cave to it (paradoxically so seizure through nonseizure is possible). PHN pulls the center of action away from the self and into the exercise. The ability to displace the self onto a third, to a middle space, to affect by way of being affected, to translate and make explicit the spirit or third person that flows in the sanctioned limits—that is what is technically required to have the sacred manifest.

Instead of confessing their deeds, young people are asked to act on the circumstances under which sin functions. Confession here is a practice plan toward automation, prevention, and the multiplication of life, not a cathartic discharge. What might readily be interpreted as cathartic in intent—the collective purge of sin-impregnated objects occurring on the first day, for instance—deviates from standard understandings of the term in that it was not meant to be a gesture through which a truthful self would be externalized, nor was it about acknowledging how sin dwells in the deep recesses of our selves. Rather, what PHNers were ridding themselves of was the confessional itself, that is, the sacramental contract according to which a truth told, through the private and verbal mediation of a priest, is rewarded with absolution.

Many priests in Brazil disparaged the idea that a format of mediatized public confession, like that of the PHN, could replace the traditional sacrament of confession. It was a debate that led to hundreds of theological meetings and conventions, missives between clerical offices, and studies and publications within and outside Brazil. When questioned, Charismatics emphasize that their intention is not to replace the traditional confessional but to call attention to the fact that there is no better way to fight sin than by addressing it directly. And by "directly" they mean turning the act of confession itself into a disciplinary exercise of preventive work.

More relevant than delineating the space of repentance and personal salvation was training Catholic youths to become exemplary imitators, agents of citation, mosaic and copying, through which sin enters and exits a scene. The ceremonial purging was, in other words, a staging of the framework and practice that exposes both the incontrovertible nature of sin, transgression, and temptation and also the desire to overcome it. Such an emphasis on how sin works in the world (not simply how it exists as a human condition but how it itself *conditions* human actions) requires a certain sacrifice of the self for the sake of circulation as medium. It is integral to the zealotic components of entrainment that bodies might expose the human archive of iniquity only to realize how replicative sins are, how the same sins arise time and again in the flow of come-and-go that each moment both enacts and dissipates.

Whatever sin one may have committed, it could have always been committed by someone else. And that possibility, that conditional or otherwise, is what is ultimately at stake. What is to be humiliated is not a subject—the sinner—but sin itself, yielding to endless citation and dissemination. In its resulting depersonalization, the coherence of a subject who would claim proprietorship over sin dissolves. This concentrated and disciplined humiliation of sin through expropriation and proprietary displacement helps explain why the Canção Nova TV camera filming the PHN event moved across the space, oscillating from right to left, as if to make manifest the fungibility of sin, effectively aligning the filming's mechanical function of circulation and reproducibility with its ongoing transference, crossing, and displacement.

Speaking in tongues became the climax of the PHN confessional. One wonders what—or even who—is confessing in this context. As Michel de Certeau (1996) argues, glossolalia reopens the surface of discourse to the noises of otherness. Marking its identity as a language that withdraws from (a definite) signification, the spoken "I" folds within itself other selves, other tongues. "To speak with tongues," Daniel Heller-Roazen (2002: 93) writes, "is to speak without definite meaning and without even speaking oneself. It is in every sense, simply to speak."[22] This self-referential nature of glossolalic speech—a speaking that speaks—is what Charismatics foreground as an alternative to "real presence." This is covered more in chapter 3.

For young PHNers, highlighting their commitment to reproductive sex via the condemnation of any form of nonreproductive sexual encounter involved a particular conception of the subject on which sin, confession, and salvation depended. More still, it exposed anxieties regarding how to control fluidity when the latter becomes attached to a ritually fashioned anonymous subject and thus is no longer moored to and containable by the possessive individual. This chapter addressed this paradox as a distinctive tension in the problematics of confession among Catholic Charismatics in Brazil. As in other moments of this book, my intent is to dwell in the tensions and extensions that paradoxes enable—rather than obstruct—in the formation of a politics of pneuma. In chapter 3 I analyze how such extensions unfurl at the core of Christianity's deepest mystery: the Eucharist.

3. OUTSTANDING ELASTICITY

....

Such a full desire for emptiness.
—GEORGES BATAILLE, *The Accursed Share:*
The History of Eroticism and Sovereignty

"A monastery of Poor Clares in Canção Nova?" I asked, not believing my ears. The initial procession had just entered the alley by the left rear of the building. The priest leading the procession walked down the aisle, raising the holy monstrance. "That's right!" said the woman I had befriended, adding, "They came here because of a moment like now, a Thursday just like today, when Canção Nova was offering contemplation of the Holy Eucharist." Perplexed and excited, I wondered: Could it be that a confined world such as a monastery of the Poor Clares of Assisi existed inside a Pentecostal global media campus, the older religious order known for its embrace of silence embedded within the noise of such a highly mediatized religious expression? Founded during the thirteenth-century lifetime of Saint Francis, the Poor Clares are recognized for their rigorous disciplinary rhythms, which are organized around the Liturgy of the Hours. Apart from their vows of chastity, poverty, silence, and confinement, the members of this order are known for watching day and night over the Holy Eucharist; this is why they are also known as the Sisters of Perpetual Adoration. In line with other early and mid-medieval religious orders, the Poor Clares transferred the silence that others had previously searched for in the desert to the interior world of the monastery; the cloister became the designated area for exercising the soul to go elsewhere.

"Look at meeee," heaved the voices in celebration. The host was now placed at the center of the altar. It would stand there for a full hour—the so-called *Adoration Hour*—for contemplation.[1] *Adoration Hour* was a test of attention and endurance during which miracles, such as healing, prophecy, and discernment, poured out. I left the building through a long passageway, along which several TV screens showed a close-up of the Holy Eucharist, and

I rushed to the spot on the Canção Nova campus where I had been told the monastery stood. I rang a bell placed by the front door and waited by a second door after reading the words "Do Not Enter." An abbess came out and advised me to move toward a dark cubicle near the hallway. Minutes later a young nun walked out of the entry connecting that cell to the world indoors, introducing herself as Sister Rita. Only then did I realize, as I fumbled with what to do with my tape recorder, that our conversation would have to happen with locked iron gates separating us. I was indeed inside a monastic home, itself inside a Catholic Pentecostal global multimedia network.

MARIA JOSÉ: I must admit that I'm surprised to find you here, a Poor Clare . . . [in] a monastery, in such a place as Canção Nova.

SISTER RITA: It started with the inspiration of one of our nuns, in the town of Santa Catarina. She was also called Clara, just like Saint Clare. Because of her immobility . . . her family offered a TV set to the nursing facility of the monastery so that she and the nurse could follow the Mass. One day, on a Thursday just like today, on the screen was the Holiest. . . . So she was looking at the exposed Jesus on the TV screen when she received a revelation. This revelation was that a monastery must be built in Canção Nova Community. . . . The feeling was so strong that she confessed to the abbess of the monastery. She told her all that had happened. At first, she doubted whether in her condition the sisters would take her seriously. . . . She thought they would think she had gone mad. But then they prayed together, and it was discerned that they should contact Padre Jonas [the spiritual founder of Canção Nova]. They wrote him a letter and told him about the revelation. When Padre Jonas read the letter, he replied at once to the abbess: "Madre, this is nothing else but an answer to my prayers. I am just returning from Assisi in Italy where I visited Saint Clare's monastery and asked her to help our community, which is undergoing so much resistance and discredit." And so at that moment it became clear that Santa Clare played a role in mediating our presence here. . . .

MJ: But why Saint Clare?

SR: Saint Clare, don't you know . . . there was this episode in her life in the thirteenth century. . . . On a Christmas night she was bedridden, so she could not join the other sisters and Saint Francis for the Mass. The others went and left her behind, alone and sick in her cell. But when the sisters came back from the feast, and they were about to describe the event, Saint Clare told them, "There is no need to tell me anything. For I have seen and heard all through the walls of my cell." So, because of this episode, in 1958 [around the time television was invented], Pope Pius XII made her the patron saint of television. Saint Clare is the patron saint of television. That is why Padre Jonas went to Assisi.

I left the monastery in wonder. What entangled worlds flickered around the material signifier of the Eucharist? What of disputes over "real presence" revolving around an entity so utterly evanescent? Could an idea of a "here-else" be what precisely defines Eucharistic real presence in Sister Rita's narrative? Or is there something *else* at stake here that affects the very core of our inherited conceptions of presence, mediation, materiality, silence, seeing, singularity? Something that concerns the very idea of offering attention, or even attending—what, in tandem with the Poor Clares, TV Canção Nova calls *Adoration Hour*?

My surprise at learning about the Sisters of Adoration at Canção Nova alerted me to the larger sphere of influence in my own thought as, speaking to representatives of the Catholic Church in Brazil, I register their discomfort—disgust, even—when they hear about the monastery of Canção Nova (de Abreu 2013b). How could such a highly prestigious spiritual order exist alongside such a newly stylized media Pentecostalism? Was it not an essential contradiction in terms, the depth of the first against the flatness of the latter? Being one of the main faces of the Catholic Charismatic Renewal in Brazil, Canção Nova Media Community has always been largely contested by the church establishment. In the 1990s, after two decades of its existence in Brazil, Charismatic revivalism was seen by the more progressive allies of the church and various intellectual sympathizers as "a flat message making use of an equally flat medium." To include a medieval monastery of the sisters of Assisi within their media campus, however, was something of a conundrum, a profanation, if not an outright aberration.

In 1999, when the news had spread that a monastery of Poor Clares would be built inside Canção Nova, many in the establishment were vociferously opposed, highlighting the disciplinary chains that they thought of as incommensurate between the two traditions. The Poor Clares, the general narrative ran, were stewards of a much greater pristine spirituality than Canção Nova's prêt-à-porter spirit. With their strict conduct of expiation and recollection, the Poor Clares were deserving of a much "thicker body" than Canção Nova could ever possibly attain, with its "Put your hands in the air" kind of religiosity. In turn, Canção Nova and Charismatics more generally saw in those arguments signs that the establishment was, as usual, placing institutional criteria above pneuma and grace—and what is more, that tension in criteria confirmed how inseparable they in fact were as an overarching institution. For if there is one thing that more deeply (not flatly) characterizes Catholicism, so it went, it is its capacity to embrace worlds apart: its outstanding elasticity. Let, then, this moment of *Adoration Hour* be an illustration of that ability to elasticize, Charismatics proposed. May the holy attention offered to the Eucharist be nothing like the confirmation of what is simply there, fully present to itself, but of its stretchable potential to extend into an *alhures*, as here-else (Collu 2019; Ng 2020).

In this chapter I argue that the embedding of one of the oldest arms of the Catholic Church within Canção Nova establishes a line of coherence rather than just an aberration. This line of coherence can be traced through contested notions of vision, writ large, disputes that have a long history within Roman Catholicism, Protestantism, and Orthodox Christianity and are dynamically synthetized within Canção Nova's televised *Adoration Hour*. Rather than view *Adoration Hour* as incommensurable with the Sisters of Perpetual Adoration or Poor Clares, I will probe their areas of overlap and likeness by examining, first, the theorization behind the artifices of televising the Eucharist; second, the subject as spectator that is called on to react to a televised paradoxical presence or nonpresence, and the different modes of "viewing" therein entailed; and third, how Sister Rita articulates a notion of her own belonging within the Canção Nova order that departs from other priests' and church theologians' notions of grace, the miraculous, silence, and vision. As elsewhere in this book, it should be noted that for Charismatics it is never a matter of producing a rupture with the institutional but, on the contrary, a form of integrating pneumatic tension as the very condition that may strengthen the institutional qua corpus. Such are the rules of the gym according to Catholic Charismatics, all the more so when it comes to the Mass of the Eucharist. Amenable to homeomorphic deformation, the body of the Eucharist may expand, fold, and squeeze, but not break. The Eucharist, of all things living and sacred, withstands the tension of opposites.

Catholic Charismatics have long talked about the "militias of God" who keep vigil by hailing the powers of the Holy Spirit, which extends to all times and places. During the 1990s the meanings of being attentive and vigilant were changing in Brazil. It was a time when, after the military years and in preparation for what would be popularly known as "the shock of neoliberal capitalism," new orders of seeing and calculating in coordination with new inhabitations of time and space were being called on. As the country entered a new political and economic order characterized by compromise between Right and Left ideological camps attempting to shed the rigidity of the military years and take seriously the call for adaptable flexibility in order to open up to emerging global arenas, there was a sense that different levels of coordination between events and proprioceptive re-acting were necessary. Later we will learn how authoritarianism and flexibility were not two approaches that succeeded each other in time but were coexisting realities for more than twenty years, budding in the liberal-conservative presidency held by the two parties, the PSDB (Partido da Social Democracia Brasileira; Brazilian Social Democracy Party) and PT (Partido dos Trabalhadores; Workers' Party). In politics as in religion, debates between camps revolved in large part around the skill to embrace opposites within itself. This approach took time to shift into the social, its realization culminating only in the mandate of Jair Messias Bolsonaro.

Yet Charismatics have long postulated the dual presence of totality (father) and limberness (son) as organizing aspects of their pneumatic Trinitarian economy. The role of the spirit, as third, is precisely to draw reality from that tension. For this revivalist Catholic faction this was the feature to cultivate and so was the centralist government in power. That Charismatics saw this as being the case was in itself not only a sign of how attentive they were to the spirit of the times but how this very attentiveness to what's in the air was in itself considered a sign of spiritual anointing.

In his work on "holy attention," David Marno (2016: 10) notes that the word *attention* entered English through the Latin word *attendere*, which means "stretching toward" or being under a certain tension. In Portuguese the kinship between "paying attention" and "stretching" is revealed in the link between *attender* (to attend) and *tendão* (tendon). Marno describes how attention oscillates between transitive and intransitive modes; that is, the exercise involved in attaining an ideal state of attention implies a circularity by which one pays attention in order to become properly attentive. What this circularity makes evident is how "stretching toward" is hardly to be understood as a means to an end but rather as an action that aims to expose the specific structure or medium through which stretching itself is possible. Far from aspiring to additions and accretions, then, to stretch, indeed to extend, involves a constant return to a zero point, a point of self-emptying that exposes the exercising of attention as such.

This chapter is therefore also a reflection on the mechanisms of production of attention created in the spaces of articulation between the monastery and TV Canção Nova. In 2000, when I first watched the program *Adoration Thursday*, filming technologies were still rather rudimentary at Canção Nova. The totality of the close-up reflected a purposeful aesthetic as much as the limitations of filming whereby the framing of the shot was reduced to basics like placing the camera on a tripod with the scene established at the eye level of the Eucharist. A few years later Canção Nova would adjust the frame of the shot to the new languages of television production, which favor multiframing and zooming in or even juxtaposing views. These technical and technological adaptations reflect not just economic success and the possibility of incorporating more cutting-edge special effects into the process of filming but the co-optation of the Charismatic movement by the church hierarchy in Brazil. Most of what follows focuses on the earlier stages of television making at Canção Nova. The analysis is centered on the mise en abyme of televised exposure of the Eucharist through three key operations: first, in relation to a strategic emptying of the screen, then through the power of the voice, and finally, through the art of attention.

Three Operations of Attending

By the time I exited the monastery, most participants had already left Rincão do Meu Senhor, the hangar where the adoration of the Eucharist took place. Only a few technicians and the cameraman remained, unplugging the electronics and clearing out the space for the next event. I lingered and approached the cameraman to inquire about his work as the image maker. In talking about his work filming and editing the different events at the hangar or studios on a weekly basis, he pointed to the distinctiveness of the weekly *Adoration Thursdays* TV show, the requirements of which "are special." He explained: although technically prepared to film movement, the camera must be absolutely still for an hour. "So still," he emphasized, "that a person will not be able to tell the difference from one instant to the next." "Like a photograph?" I asked. "No, it is not like in a photograph because the image must be *live*," he said, widening his eyes to emphasize the word. He then went on to describe the most striking interchange between seeing powers. The eye of "the TV camera zooms in to the eye of the monstrance" and lingers there with such intensity that "one would imagine [observing] an exchange of entranced looks between two people in love." "Not rivals?" I asked. He adjusted his thoughts and then said, "In order to lead the viewer to the divine path, rules must be followed." With the help of his fingers he explained that there are "three fundamental rules of operation to consider."

In the first instance, the relation between the camera and the monstrance (or receptacle of the host) is not one of capture: "It is not about capturing and projecting an image. No." That would institute a hierarchy between camera and object. "But how can one capture that which is . . . infinite?" *Capture* would imply that the filmed object is finite, thus violating the understanding of the Eucharist as boundless and therefore impossible to contain. So the camera does not capture but rather juxtaposes. *To juxtapose* implies adjusting the camera to the physical space of the Eucharist: zooming in. That is, rather than being a tool of capture, the camera mirrors its target. Constituent and constituted powers enter a relation of circularity. Their respective operations—seeing and seen, eyesight and image—intertwine and spiral. Maximized juxtaposition is thus the first rule.

The second rule is related to the first and is the rule of stillness. At this point the cameraman explained that, ideally, the screen should be one-dimensional to match the surface of the host. What one is, the other is too, striving for a perfect visual tautology. This conflation of entities, of camera and host, to the point of equivocation (a *con*fusion in *dif*fusion), entails a particular logic of showing. If the screen should be one with the host, it is so that the host may also work as a kind of screen. The host becomes its own parasite. It hosts itself, as it were. This means that, as such, the screen shows absolutely nothing. The self-referential logic in this, at once a simple and a complex operation, results in the idea that what is being shown is the showing of possibility itself: the technique of showing. One could say, in rather metaphysical terms, that there is a zeroing of the screen; there is simply gaze and a desire for more. As the cameraman explained, if the camera moves, if it tilts, it introduces perspective and angle, and that is not suitable. And it is not suitable because perspective and angle would reintroduce the idea of showing something *in particular*—precisely what the camera, according to the first rule and its aspiration to the universal, wants to repress. This it does by zooming in to perfect concurrence with its target. The relation between camera and monstrance must be one of null degree in perspective and no movement. "No particle must be left out," he stressed. A tilt of the camera could add motion (and motion can be good, but that comes later). Movement would also add perspective, dimensionality, whereas our realm is substance. It would be like introducing shadow to a Byzantine icon, which traditionally is shadowless so as to disavow finitude and angle. Stillness and juxtaposition thus cooperate in doing the following: the screen must show nothing in order to show the possibility of vision itself. The whiteness and stillness of the image become more than the product of a particular vision (the camera's). Rather, the operational effect itself becomes the cause or ground for future visibilities.

Now, the stillness of the image in the same continuous shot only works to highlight the imminent presence of its contrary: movement and reproducibility. That is why a third and last operational rule is added to the conditions of mystical presence at Canção Nova. This third rule relates to the imperative of notifying the viewer that despite all the appearances of juxtaposed stillness, the image is in movement. This operation introduces the absolute and necessary extreme opposite to the previous operations. At stake is the guarantee that no shot of the Eucharist will be the same as the next. This is the reason that at the top-right margin of the screen, one will read the word *LIVE*. It is a reminder that what appears to be the same—an image, *the* image—in essence is not; that what looks *still* is, in effect, *passing*; and that what would be otherwise mere sameness takes leave from *that* through the technical possibilities of live transmission. In sum, despite the stillness, we are *still* looking at a live recording, a still in motion, the wholeness of a vast movement.

These three chief operations—juxtaposition, stillness, liveness—of a TV show are the basic principles for *Adoration Thursday*. As we will see, the procedural requirements exist in close tension with a series of demands constituting the spectator as active practitioner in a way that challenges ordinary understandings of the visual sense as inadequate to pious contemplation.

Watching After

What is "so special" about *Adoration Thursday*, a female devotee named Nora Joaninha tells me as we sit in her living room while the Eucharist is on the TV screen, is that "one looks in order to hear [*a gente olha para ouvir*]." Such seeing through the ear is not synesthesia. It attests to the power of the voice that speaks through the nothingness "there" (*ali*), a kind of desert or negative space which the screen has become. Even though the medium in question is television, it is the voice, not the image, that speaks throughout the *Adoration Hour*. Off camera, the priest announces the many cures and miracles that happened that week. He reads and prays about the messages people sent to the studio in letters, emails, and phone calls:

A woman who could not bear children tells how the "Eucharistic waves" helped her and opened her womb as God did to Rachel in those times. Three months later, she was pregnant with a baby girl. Hallelujah, my Lord. A twenty-four-year-old man named Jerónimo Sayrne wrote how he saw an image of the Tower of Babel "inverting, rotating, inverting," the roof becoming the foundations and the foundations the roof. As he discerned it (for he had been recognized by his peers for having the gift of word and science), this inversion in architecture corresponded to a shift from Babel to Pentecost, the difference being that if in Babel they all spoke one common language and yet could not understand each other, at Pentecost they all spoke different languages and yet understood one another.

The voice-over described this vision as liberating the person from dyslexia. The person would no longer fight to understand writing, no longer had to conform to the rules of language. Rather the person "out there" would simply say the words God placed in his throat. The same goes for the person who had "serious stuttering. . . . Look at the screen now. Remember God chooses stutterers too, like Moses stuttered, to be leaders." Accompanied by the sound of an electronic organ in the background, murmuring in monotones between major and minor, the voice-over continued reporting and commenting on other testimonies. At one point the voice-over enumerated a sequence of cures and revelations; so torrentially did these arrive that the voice-over kept interrupting itself, interjecting "Hallelujah!" and "Amen!" as though to keep a grip on language as refrain, as phatic speech. Once again fluid, if furnished in rhythmic inventory, it continued:

And there is now this testimony [esta fala] from over there in the state of Maranhão that tells about a visitation of the Holy Spirit in a dream saying that there will be a cure for someone with an acute pain in the abdomen. And another person with kidney stones . . . and another shall be cured from a leg that walked shorter than the other . . . and a miasma and pain in the lower back, and for you who feel depressed, a testimony came through saying those words by Isaiah 35:8: A highway will be there, a roadway, and it will be called the highway of holiness. The unclean will not travel on it, but it will be for him who walks that way. And fools will not wander on it. You . . . walked and shall walk. Amen.

Three candles burned on Nora's windowsill, one in the name of the Father, another in the name of the Son, and the third in the name of the Holy

Spirit. Nora told me that she lights the candles around the same time, but the candle of the Holy Spirit always burned "ahead" (*vai na frente*) of the other two. It was an enigma to her, but she believed that candles burn according to concentration. She thought that during the *Adoration Hour*, as when we were meeting, the Holy Spirit burned "impetuously" (*impetuosamente*) because so many people in Brazil (and elsewhere) were expressing adoration, bearing witness, and praising. Nora discredited those who related to the TV screen as though it were a radio. She reasoned that because for a whole hour the image looked much the same, people (busy as they are, she knows) walked around the house and listened. To do so, however, was to miss out on the vocation to contemplate and guard the Holy Sacrament in line with the traditional teachings offered by the Poor Clares. Nora was responding to the appeals made by Canção Nova that people not turn their eyes away from the TV screen and actively contemplate the image of the Eucharist for the whole hour. Such is the ritual practice behind the program *Adoration Thursday*.

Emphasizing the value of attention, Charismatics at Canção Nova refer to one particular Bible passage to support the idea of a one-hour "perpetual adoration." The passage in Matthew describes how just hours before the crucifixion, Jesus requests of Peter in the Garden of Gethsemane that the apostles remain awake and "watch over his body for an hour," which they fail to do, instead falling asleep.[2] Thus Charismatics correct those who say they were "seeing" or "looking at" the Eucharist on the TV screen throughout the *Adoration Hour*. The right thing is to say, "I was watching it"—for it's live! This command to "watch over" exerts a pressure "to see" in a way that is more than "to look."[3] This is a seeing that "looks after." One not only gazes at the image but engages in an exchange of looks that combines care and vigilance. The *Adoration Hour* ritual thus stages the idea of a vulnerable body that must not be deserted by the gaze of contemplation but guarded, looked after.

The reminder of the apostles' failure to watch over Christ's body intensifies the necessity for vigilance among Canção Nova televiewers and participants, among those who attend and offer their attention. Nora described how she prepared to stay vigilant for the entire holy hour. If something else had to be done during that time, however, she would rather turn off the screen than turn her back on it, so that the "holiest is not left alone *there*." These very same words were used by Sister Rita when we spoke, as she commented on the appellation Sisters of Perpetual Adoration by which they are known. The label "perpetual adoration" points to a tradition, she explained, of contemplating the Holiest 24/7 that went back to the times of Saint Clare and her male counterpart, Francis of Assisi, to whom the Eucharist was at once a source of illumination, an object of contemplation, and a shield against the enemy.

Take a much-evoked "Eucharistic miracle" that tells how one night in the year 1244, Saint Clare was paying vigil in her cell when Arabian militias that had invaded the valley of Spoleto climbed up the walls of the monastery of Saint Damian in Assisi. Holding the monstrance in her hand, Saint Clare blinded the invaders with the intense light emitting from its center. And if Saint Clare is with Canção Nova, who can be against them, Charismatics asked every time debates about the sisters within reappeared. Vigil service is a practice that is long embedded in Christian rites, particularly so in the Eastern Orthodox Church. During the Counter-Reformation, the Tridentine calendar created under Pope Pius V (1545–63) reformed the list of vigils in the Book of Common Prayer. All-night vigils were regularly celebrated on the eve of Sunday and major religious feasts as part of the liturgy of the hours. Quite often, though, vigil service was used in a military sense, as a way of acknowledging the vicinity of the enemy or the vulnerability of a body, as in the scene in the Garden of Gethsemane, where guardians sleep as Jesus is taken away by the soldiers, or in the legend of Saint Clare against the Arabian invaders.

While vigil service is also practiced in traditional Western Catholicism, as for example in gatherings before funerals (a wake), Eastern Orthodox Catholicism associates the vigil with the strength drawn from numbers, endurance, and repetition (Largier 2007, 2014). The list of vigils is strongly connected to a regimen of prayer through verses, as in *stichera*, hymns defined by their tempo and specific melodic formulas, that, like arrows, pierce the veil of sleep, keeping the devout in a state of controlled vigilance against arising in the dark of the night. It is this tradition of disciplined wakefulness through number and repetition that Catholic Charismatics in Brazil want to recover in contemporary Brazil. Hence there is an extraordinary frequency of meetings, events, symposiums on a regional level across the country, the continent, and the world writ large. And what better than mass-media technologies to undergird the authority of repetition and endurance, both sustaining vigilance and offering the image that will wipe out and shield against all others that may surreptitiously raid the sublunary chambers while dreaming?

Adoration, in turn, is the image of a mediality. One contemplates the operations that allow one to see in the first place, yet the condition for such an allowance is that not for one second of time can the Eucharist not be illumed by the eyes it itself illuminates. A circularity and remote-operated technique must be in place so that the seer and the seen become one, much like in a vortex of time that ultimately opens the deep middle to a totalizing and all-encompassing one.

We saw in chapter 2 how PHN public confessions at Canção Nova aim to activate in the practitioner a certain wakefulness in sleep, the kind that polices unduly erogenous spurs under the belt of consciousness. The pneumatism that undergirds prayerful exercises at Canção Nova is a practice created to affect sleep's deep recession, such that even while sleeping the person is on guard. Likewise, vigilance toward whatever may come through the air is a repeated practice. That, too, we saw earlier. For Charismatics, the call to keep vigil relates to the spirit-endowed "gift of discernment," the cultivated sensibility in seeing through: a situation, a narrative, a person, a thing. As in the story of Saint Clare, physical obstacles like diseases and walls are not obstacles to true seeing but in effect the very constitutive limit to proper seeing through. By recovering the ability to see through a moment, it is possible to better attend to the *here* and *through* otherwise torn apart as here-else.

In times marked by a heightened sense of transition, such as the period before and during the turn of the past millennium, to be anointed by the Holy Spirit (to be Charismatic, to exude grace) denotes the ability to adapt to (the) times, not despite but because of the unforthcoming. And it is this different mode of viewing, rendered in terms of a seeing through that is more circular than teleological, that is more about middle than about ends, that allows Charismatics to connect, without the slightest consternation, the tele-visions of Saint Clare in her medieval cell to *Adoration Hour* on TV Canção Nova to even the psalmody of late capitalism in Brazil. At stake for viewers of the program is a deeper engagement with the concept of "liveness" as well as the need to protect what is "live." This heightened sensibility toward what is live is associated with a regime of seeing. A particular logic in the experience of TV "watching" becomes apparent. One does not watch something because it is on TV. Rather, what is on TV exists by means of being watched. Even as one watches *after* the screen, one watches *before* it too. One both sits *before* it and watches *after* it.

Visualizing Speech

Sitting before, however, is not enough. In addition to being before the screen, viewers of *Adoration Hour* focus on the voice in order to excite a seeing. As alluded to, at stake is a particular mode of seeing *through* the voice such that the white screen invites viewers to become themselves image producers. The ultimate point of making the Eucharist coincide with its filming is to maximize the potential of the public as producer. More than produced for a public, the image turns its public into image operators. The image as such is not there; it is only latent, a kind of desertion. The whiteness of its being is comparable to the white blankness of speaking in tongues as it will figure again through the replicative monobloc chair, the topic of chapter 6. It is the color of pneuma as such, and the principle of elasticity that subtends it in its desire to absorb all and nothing in particular.

The voice-over is what activates what is already latent and incipient in the TV screen's plenum space of whiteness. On the one hand, the voice-over ventriloquizes other voices, the voices of those who wrote to or called the studio to report their deliverances. In that sense, the voice-over is the organizer of a certain operatic flow. Yet the voice also adds commentary and adapts those incoming messages to fit a common formula. Far from personalized and unique, the descriptions of miracles are formulaic and overused. A good testimony is valued not in terms of its exceptionality but for the possibility of being cited, reproduced, copied. And the role of the voice is to modulate those testimonies as appropriable, standard, formulaic. Far from univocal, the powerful miracle is the one that is easily extendable to others, adaptable and malleable to other reiterations. "Yesterday her eye, tomorrow yours. This week the liver of someone from the northeast, next week from the southwest. . . . Canção Nova wants to connect you out there."

In the framework of enunciation, the voice-over constitutes in relation to its speaking both a near and a far. The voice-over is not telling a story with a beginning, middle, and end; it is not about causality and telos, nor about sequence, narrative, or representation. Rather the voice works on the possibility of taking content elsewhere, of transporting and relaying testimony to different places and different times. It does not simply require attention but performs it in the sense of a stretching toward itself. That is why the voice-over cares little about the particulars of a narrative. Instead, the function of the voice's language is to keep viewers infinitely in the middle, the middle that both hosts the gaze and is constituted as such—as Host—by means of being gazed upon. The operation in question is very much like the interface of a display whereby the whiteness of the Eucharist becomes the screen out of and onto which a layered repository of images of cure and liberation can be activated.

Language is rhythmic and elliptical. Each narrative is both itself and a bridge to *alhures*, the Portuguese word for the felt copresence of another moment, another place. It is both the flesh and the tendon that supports it, what connects and joins. It is not entirely speaking in tongues, for despite its fragmented structure, the voice never entirely departs the realm of semantics. It is still referencing a certain event, a cure, a prophecy, a revelation. At the same time, however, the task of the voice is to unsay or perhaps retard a saying, so that in this retarding the principles that ensure its transferability become apparent. The voice unspeaks itself. The host exhales a speech form that is both Franciscan and technological, impoverished and flexible: potentialized.

The voice wants not only attention. Above all, it wants to communicate the rules of attention. This is why sometimes the voice trembles, like a fluttering curtain, as it tries to stutter and suture two or more apparently unrelated *falas*: the old man who lost his right eye, the young man who is in a deep depression, the woman who lost all her patrimony in gambling, all become *hailed* as "the daaaark [*treavas*] . . . riiiising in radiance . . . and gggolden brightness . . . by the Eucharistic waves of Santa Clare." In the communication of a stammering through continuous rupture and interruption, break and hesitation, language gives up exteriority in favor of its operations. At the same time it makes public the hearing of that which arrives as testimony from elsewhere and the relaying and detouring involved in devolving such testimony back to the world. Language is thus in a constant state of self-martyrdom, predisposed to bear witness to its principle. It is apostolic in that very kenotic (emptying) sense. While never coming to glossolalia, the entire filming exhibits a deviant fluidity or delinquency, marked by what Michel de Certeau (1996: 29) calls "the quotations [and] . . . fragments of other voices that punctuate the order of sentences with breaks and surprises." It is a speaking that rides on heteronomy, close to the point where voice and image merge in a kind of distended aural homogeneity.

Rather than addressing someone specific out there, more than offering a semblance of meaningful statements, the voice-over thus bespeaks flow itself. Roberta, whom I met at a prayer group she coordinates in Sé, in the old center of São Paulo city, described her experience paying devotion during *Adoration Hour*: "You bring yourself to the place [*se põe no lugar de*] to hear the voice of the padre. Then as he speaks all the things the Holy Spirit is telling, you just feel the force of all those graces pouring, nothing but that and then. As it happened to me, in that moment that you no longer listen very well to what the padre is saying, that is the moment you are totally there, then the Holy Spirit offers a word [*dá uma fala*]."[4] At stake in this description is a mode of attention that produces not distraction but a kind of abstraction or emptying that allows something to reappear out of the flow of words being communicated by the voice. The role of the voice is to reduce language to its abstract minimums, to numb intended signification so as to potentialize its semantic stock, to the point that the same enunciation (*fala*) can be owned by two or more people who may share nothing else in common. To bring things somewhere, to host and teletransport, is what the voice must accomplish, so by the time it is heard the voice has become the great linkage of the crossing of gazes between the Eucharist and the television.

The voice mimetically performs the medium of television, which as Saint Clare apprehended in her thirteenth-century cell, involves a "seeing at a distance": a tele-vision. The mirroring entertained between Saint Clare in medieval Europe and a Poor Clare in a late twentieth-century convent in northern Brazil enters the space of mimetic resonance, which the voice also aspires to induce. The voice of *Adoration Hour* is like the invisible element, whirling within the substance and molding it into new visions. And just as there are key technical rules for visually transmitting the Eucharist, so voice adheres to a few directives.

During a meeting with one of the broadcasters of Radio Canção Nova, a young lay member who had some previous experience in radio told me of earlier arguments regarding whose is the right voice to be communicating the miracles during the program. The discussion had essentially to do with the tone and pitch of the voice of the communicator. In the beginning, someone had suggested that the voice should be as neutral and flat as possible so as not to distract from the preeminence of the Eucharist. A voice without prosody, he suggested, would exclude all reality beyond itself; it would have no signifying precedent, no externality. It would in that sense be one with the universal space of the Eucharist. But in prayer one afternoon Padre Jonas received "a word of science" (*uma palavra de ciência*) that said that speaking without tone is a prerogative only God retains. A voice without expression is like that spoken by the God of the desert to Moses or otherwise as "in tongues," sometimes also called among Charismatics the language of the angels (*fala dos anjos*). It has the force of a command and lacks all anteriority. It is its own cause: "I am what I am."

The voice *of Adoration Hour*, it was decided, would hence bear the human imprint of prosodic speech. It should have qualities of expression such as timbre, tonality, and pitch, not because these features would allow the voice to create something original and new but precisely because they would not. "The voice-over is a voice-over," to put it in the tautological terms Charismatics are so fond of. Its function is not to create ex nihilo but to aurally illustrate and add to what is believed to be *already* in the image. The voice-over neither is within the narrative of the image, nor is it entirely extradiegetic. It is *neither* internal *nor* external to the image but enters its worlds adjacently, as in the felt loquacity of slant rain in Fernando Pessoa's apt image. Its sole function is to be responsible for a rhythm, a balancing coherence in acknowledging the rushing breath of Spirit.

Yet if the voice must not totally coincide with its source either—for that coinciding would signal a lack of expression that belongs to God alone—there is also the risk of too much latitude between source and sound. It is, after all, the body of Christ that is at risk of becoming all too human. And that is no negligible point. Historically speaking, since the eighth century prayers of consecration of the host had been carefully restricted to a few men. This restriction was carried out by imbuing sacramental power in the words capable of producing the body of Christ. The words were endowed with an aura of secrecy accessible only to ordained priests. The restriction was meant to control who owned the power over such ritual techniques. But it was also a means of regulating the production, multiplication, and appearance of the body of Christ that would go into the hands and mouths of the laypeople. It was therefore important to create not just words of prayer restricted to a few but also a boundary of silence around these. For there was always the danger that a layperson, distractedly, might overhear the content of those words, the anaphoras, and reproduce them without restraint or not in the proper time or space. As put by a skeptical priest about the TV show, "The Eucharist is bread, but not all bread is Eucharistic."

Given these considerations, in the late 1990s the voice-over during *Adoration Thursday* was for a while a woman's voice, spoken by a laywoman who was a member of the community. Yet having a woman's voice speaking over the image of the Eucharist became problematic within the largely patriarchal structures of the Catholic Church. While Charismatics set out to challenge the existing structures through their lay basis (including, as I discuss later, the logic of real presence associated with the Eucharist), they did so with the view of reinforcing an orthodoxy that insisted on associating femininity with mystical—not institutional—power. Once the exposure of the Eucharist on TV became a topic of discussion among Catholics, Charismatic and non-

Charismatic, it also came under new institutional surveillance. And so, the hierarchy ended up insisting on the need to (at least) have a male voice doing the chanting.

And so, the voice became that of a priest (not just lay male or female but ordained male). It was a decision facilitated and supported by a change in the technique of filming dating from the early 2000s, one that started to value camera angle and variety in sequence shots outside the realm of the Eucharist alone and onto its physical support: the relic or monstrance and even the altar that supports it and, finally, the audiences that assist in situ at the Rincão do Meu Senhor filming of *Adoration Thursday*. Neither God nor layman, the priest takes up the task of balancing a double finality. The voice will be the referee of a certain economic balance between charisma and institution. It will be at once sound and censor, reporter and consecrator. It is a compromise that tests the very elasticity of the substance in question. No less.

Real Circulation

In the 1990s, particularly in the second half of the decade, Brazil was in search of a structure that could not only frame a sense of the everywhere but might exceed it. It meant resorting to all-embracing logics and geometries the prime referent of which was circulation. The value of circulation was best rendered in figures that circulate, yet do not encircle. What was real became what was able to circulate, and what circulated had to *be* real. This is how, in the following decades, coins and wafers—long joined in the history of Christianity and Catholicism—became united under the common sign of the *real*.

In July 1994, after a decade of failed stabilizations and under the presidency of "third-wayist" and founder of the PSDB Fernando Henriques Cardoso, Brazil embraced a new coin: the *real*. The market, it was declared as Cardoso stepped in, would no longer be the enemy of the Left but an ally upholding humanitarianism and personal emancipation. The new coin allowed the nation to articulate its neoliberal programmatic ambitions through the idiom of monetization and circulation. Money and the transferability of value were part of daily conversations and percolated throughout the entire media scene, which recursively absorbed that same principle into its makeup. This emphasis on circulation not only affected how to relate to image production in the explosion of electronic media and technological equipment but revived religious debates on the status of presence, mediation, and materiality. The introduction of the *real* coinage coincided with the rise of the social democratic PSDB under the new statesman in the mid-1990s, the party that together with PT and MDB (Movimento Democrático Brasileiro; Brazilian Democratic Movement) would become the tripartite structure of Brazil's politics. Ideological differences notwithstanding, all three parties understood, each at its own pace and in its own worldliness, that flexible compromise was a skill to be honed—which is why, paradoxically, it was important to sustain conflict in the political space. With evangelicals entering the scene as holders of capital, technical know-how, and influence, the left-wing PT, with which the majority of progressive Catholics and the liberal-minded identified, was forced to reorganize its constituencies. Meanwhile, the other two parties went on bending and absorbing whatever elements appeared in their way, Left and Right, fomenting a widespread capillary network with links to the Senate, to officeholders, to the media, and to evangelism, both Catholic and Protestant.

In the wake of this trend in politics, Pastor Sérgio Von Helder, who opens this book, assaulted a statue of Brazil's patron saint on real-time TV on a Catholic religious holiday in a gesture that shocked the nation. This was more than just a strictly religious dispute; at stake in this transgression was a rejection of the rigidity of statues in favor of the flexibility of structures. It is true that the bullying method adopted by the pastor was polemic, but the kick to the statue also enacted the perception that the times were ready for change. In this spirit the Catholic Charismatic Renewal, diverging from an influential left-wing ally within the church, sought to uphold a new economy of the image, doing so by way of engaging the highest mystery of the church: the problem of real presence. Like the evangelical Von Helder, who drew on the powers of real-time TV to make the statue look all the more arcane, Charismatics wanted to reform what real presence is; unlike the pastor, however, they were not prepared to disrespect overtly an icon of the Virgin, of whom they were in need, all the more so as to host the Holy Spirit, for they are *both* Catholic *and* Pentecostal. Rather, their efforts would involve a more subtle operation, which would draw on a Byzantine repertoire—the sanctioned expression of a compromise—by which to engage what in Christianity is most precious and pristine, even if so predisposed to squabble and disagreement.

Thank God, salvation and rescuing are veritable Christian things. What the Byzantinists did to the icon, Canção Nova would set out to do through its experiments in televising the Holy Eucharist. Born of a compromise between iconoclasts and iconophiles, the Byzantine icon incarnates operatic compromise in itself (Mondzain 2005). To please both sides, the icon must be *at once* there and not there. Both arriving and leaving, the icon disowns presence precisely so as to become prototypical. It must be in passing, and a passing (as practice) it must show in the flesh of its dynamic being. Much renunciation of presence must apply to the Eucharist for it to be real. The icon is a supreme bender of form that the Eucharist not only mirrors but, in the profoundest sense of the term, incarnates. The operations in question have nothing to do with presence, or with the mediation of a presence, or even with an emphasis on matter. Rather, what is real is circulation, a movement whose steady passing requires that the image be in constant oscillation between rise and fall, like the princes in the European baroque period of the seventeenth century or like political personalities in Brazil in the era of the PSL (Partido Social Liberal; Social Liberal Party).

Real coinage could therefore semantically meld with real flesh and these with vigilant bodies that adore and listen in order to see.[5] For in passing and because in passing, that which is visual earns the structure of sound: the *iara-rum-rara-hum* now as electronic image. Canção Nova's televised exposure of the Eucharist in the mid-1990s could thus stage in its convoluted loop the manifold: technological presence and mystical seeing through, past and present, the before and the after, a range of sensorial registers from visions to hearings, from haptic sensation to synesthetic cohabitation. But it could host the profane dwellings of power such as those under the aegis of the pecuniary and the market of a globalizing Brazil. Such is the degree of unbounded elasticity of the substance in question radiating out of *Adoration Hour*. So much can the host lodge in itself that proper justice to its eventfulness can be rendered only in the idiom of its opposite: as the luminous nothingness of a nonevent. This is why on the TV screen the nothing and the everything coincide and converge asymptotically.

The analogies between the two universes—of coins and wafers—have been acknowledged by historians and semioticians in the material world of circulating things. The host, like the coin, instantiated the possibility of circulation through the respective and often mutually imbricated channels of the sacred and the profane.[6] The mechanical manufacturing of hosts in the twelfth century highlighted not only the reproducible quality of the host but its distinction from other artifacts and icons where the trace of its making (brushstrokes, marks, chisel, wax, etc.) partook in the end product. Its monochromatic quality and its roundness, together with the imprinted imagery in the body of the wafer, worked to emphasize the consubstantial connection between form and content. The host ought to be pure mediality; its frame coincided with the infinity of its roundness. Its semiotics of presence was one of circulation and infinite passing, its fungible quality asserting personalization as much as depersonalization (Bedos-Rezak 2000, 2008; Travaini 2015).[7]

Charismatic experiments with depicting the momentous nonevent of the Eucharist in real time build on a long history of theorizing the line separating the mundane and sacred as they meet in the body of the host. When during the Reformation Protestants voiced their anti-Roman views by asking, as a certain medieval archbishop did, "What is all the rush to see nothing special?" they were missing the fact that nothing could exalt the Eucharist in higher terms than this undermining of specialness.[8] This form of diminishing relates to the famous strategic susceptibility of the Eucharist in making itself noticed. Thomas Aquinas spoke of the host as "a currency with a reputation for debasement," evoking the idea that the Eucharist facilitates its own humiliation (in Kumler 2011: 179). Indeed, one of the most effective ways to humiliate the Eucharist in medieval Europe was by pointing to its artifice, by exposing what it had separated from: bread. The sacredness of the host thus relied not simply on the ritual of consecration—in the sense of a separation from the realm of the mundane—but also on the ability to show how dangerously similar to its origin it was. In other words, its extraordinariness could be highlighted only by simultaneously withdrawing from it, by pointing to its fabricated reproducibility. The operations of presence associated with the Eucharist have had little to do with a passage from the profane into the sacred. What endowed the Eucharist with sacred power was the dramatization of coexisting opposites. It was precisely the withdrawal from presence that instituted real presence.[9]

Hence there is the need for hypervigilance. Quoting Philippians, Charismatics say that the paradox of the Eucharist ought to reflect the incarnational tenet according to the idea that Christ was "he who being in the form of God thought it no robbery to be equal with God. But emptied himself [*ekenosen*], taking the form of a servant, being made in the likeness of men, and in habit found as men." Likewise Charismatics are aware of and explore the problem of compatibility between presence and reproducibility, how it affects the relation between mass media and the Eucharist. Running a media network, Charismatics at Canção Nova draw on the long-standing idea that replication and serialization distinguish the ritual nature of the Eucharist. As the historian Aden Kumler (2011: 182–83) writes, "It was essential [in medieval] ritual performance that the host be [a] serially produced object: week after week, communicants received the same object in their mouths. In a given church, the priest's larger host always looked the same, and the smaller hosts distributed several times a year to the faithful were similar replicas to each other, infinitely substitutable—in practice and in dogma—once they had been consecrated."[10] This aspect of multiplication brings up the rationale by which great mystics felt compelled to account for their deeds and which, despite all the wonders, made their tales exemplary for others.[11] The fundamental conception of presence lay in the ability of the sign to circulate and to make such circulation its value.

Disputes in Tele-Vision

The exposure of the Eucharist and the pouring through the television of miraculous revelations, cures, and liberations from demonic influence, "like a petition to provoke new graces," received fierce criticism from key players in the church in Brazil.[12] Monsignor Arnaldo Beltrami, the president of the communications sector of the archdiocese of São Paulo, could hardly contain his sarcasm when I met him in March 2001:

> Yes, the church always had many movements running in parallel, but what we have here is one movement absorbing a completely different reality and moreover gaining prestige and depth by means of incorporating [that other reality] inside its own premises. . . . Look carefully. First, Clarissas [Poor Clares] are consecrated to silence; the Charismatics, you see, they like noise. . . . [*He puts his hands in the air imitating the Charismatics' mode of praise.*] They sing in bands, they own TVs, they dance, they speak in tongues, et cetera. Second, the Clarissas, they live in reclusion, [but] Charismatics are all for visibility—the show. They have the media and they have their tents, gyms, et cetera. Then you have the third vow, you have poverty. Clarissas live with very humble means, [but] Charismatics have money and special ways of making money, aha! . . . that resemble the techniques of the evangelicals. And then you have chastity, but the CCR is a lay movement so . . . they are very different. And most of all, they differ in their spiritual depth. Clarissas are an exemplary order in the Catholic history of mysticism. There may be some people involved in the Charismatic Renewal with serious intentions, but mostly, I am afraid, there is much loaf and little ferment in that bread or [*addressing me*] how the Portuguese say (they'd rather put it in wine terms, right?) . . . *é muita parra, pouca uva.*[13]

Similar to Monsignor Beltrami, Don Paulo Evaristo Arns, the legendary leader of liberation theology and polemic supervisor of the archdiocese of São Paulo, was unambiguously critical of the monastery at Canção Nova. His words and body language articulated uneasiness. After a preamble in which he criticized the Charismatic Renewal for its lack of political engagement with social inequality, he continued:

> São Francisco and Santa Clara were very close, not only in space and in time but also spiritually. . . . The Catholic Charismatics put a great emphasis on the spirit, thinking that to be spiritual is to talk about the spirit all the time. . . . When the sisters went to celebrate the Mass with São Francisco without Santa Clara, she may have had a vision, but it was a crystal vision, simple and unprompted. We are talking about a vision that arises from intense devotion and prayer while in silence and isolation, which has nothing to do with the phenomena being encouraged by the Charismatic movement.[14]

Here Don Arns articulates a fundamental delineation of sensory experience as either authentic or inauthentic, provoked or unprovoked, a demarcation more or less in keeping with the average subject's expectations. Was not I, after all, initially stunned by the incongruence I sensed between Sister Rita's (non)appearance behind a monastic latticed opening, only some yards away from satellite parabolic antennas, microphones, and TV cameras? In examining the intersection of the Charismatic movement and the electronic medium, then, perhaps we need to ask with aggressive simplicity, as Marie-José Mondzain (2010) does, "What does seeing an image mean?"

Debates on televised media and proper monastic practice prevalently emphasize the nature of seeing that is distinctive for each realm. The philosopher Jean-Luc Marion (2003), for example, has dedicated a long treatise to the powers of the "uncalled for" that, according to him, distinguish the vision of the mystic from the televised gaze. Marion makes a correlation between this distinction and that separating icon and idol. Mystic vision, he argues, happens without the least pressure on the divine through the use of artifice. What defines the miraculous is an unprovoked agreement between the divine and the interior attitude of the contemplator, who asks for nothing of the sort. Marion calls the icon a *voyant*, where miraculous vision may unfold out of the "crossing of gazes" between entities, whereas the idol is a *voyeur* who "governs" the image toward certain ends (Marion 2003: 91; see also Slatman 2001: 222).

Don Arns shares with Marion the importance of distinguishing between the uncalled-for nature of the mystic vision and the artificially contrived nature of television culture. According to Marion, the artificial vision forces a showing that is different from the miraculous, which falls unsought—that is, by grace—from an elsewhere. This is the kind of distinction that inspired scholars like Hent de Vries (2001) to recuperate a theological formulation that exposes telling affinities involving what Marion designates "miracles" and "artifice." What according to de Vries regulates this potential equivalence is the concept of mediation, a concept that has itself attained a quasi-sacramental status in the study of religion and media. Far from being opposed to or severed from each other, de Vries argues, miracles and special effects are structurally analogous terms in a concatenation brought up by mediation. In so arguing, the Schmittian idea according to which all significant concepts of modern theory are secularized theological concepts holds sway. But while it is true that Charismatic thought and practice adopt analogical relations—say, between mystic vision and television or between pneumatic flow and electricity—they do so in a way that diverges from the parameters framing prevalent theories on mediated presence.

Canção Nova Charismatics differ from both Beltrami's and Arns's comprehension of what visions means. In both Don Arns's and Monsignor Beltrami's accounts, in order to be mystically authentic a vision needs to be unprompted and uncalled for. Paradoxically, the condition of this unprompting is that it be preceded by intense devotion and by prayer of a specific kind (silent). In such an understanding, mystical vision is something only a few can attain. The discipline involved leads the mystic to enter into communion with the sacred *in* the image. The image is, accordingly, a referent toward which mediation tends. The movement in question is addressed to a model and proceeds from the invisible to the visible via the sacramental institution.

In Sister Rita's account, in contrast, there is nothing intrinsic to the image that some see while others do not. Instead, the power of the image lies in how it calls on the practiced vigilance of the seer to see nothing at all before seeing something through the voice. That highlights the sonic qualities of the Eucharist: it makes it sound evangelical. Thus, for Sister Rita, silence is not the absence of sound but a learned deafening to "bad sounds." Speaking in tongues, as she told me, is "another form of not speaking" (thus of being silent), a speech so bare that it folds into the other side of noise, much like the whiteness on the TV screen in *Adoration Hour* enfolds all possible visions.

Sister Rita shares with the members of Canção Nova an understanding of silence that is multidimensional, departing from that which would proscribe the realm of mystical experience in Arns's and Beltrami's perspectives. At Canção Nova, to see is to discern what allows one to see in the first place; the condition for such allowing is that, let us repeat it, not for one instant can the Eucharist not be illumed by the eyes it itself illuminates.

SISTER RITA: Our brothers and sisters were wondering about Irmãs Clarissas in Canção Nova. They did not accept us here. There was resistance, but we did not fear. So the madre [the abbess] had to talk to them and also guarantee the word of Padre Jonas Abib that the spirituality of the Poor Clares would be respected. This new madre, she wants to recruit other novices and postulants to come to Canção Nova. There are new candidates because before we were very few, but once the monastery becomes legalized, with everything straight on paper and so on, there will be more of us. . . . So we live our own charisma, and we respect the charisma of Canção Nova. . . . We maintain silence, obedience, and live secluded from the world outside.

MARIA JOSÉ: But can silence be there with all the singing around the corner, with the thousands of people who come here every week, [with] the TVs in every corner?

SR: Our madre says, "Silence is not the opposite of sound but the opposite of 'bad sounds.'" She teaches [us] to accept the music and prayers that come from Canção Nova as "good sounds." You must not think that just because we like silence that there is no music inside of us. We are the Ladies of Perpetual Adoration. Everything we do, our daily acts, are a form of prayer, a daily song. . . . Canção Nova means "a new song."

MJ: That is what people in Canção Nova say. . . .

SR: Every fifteen days there are camping events here at Canção Nova. Many young people come to participate in these events and feel attracted to come and visit us here. So we try to respect our daily rituals, the praying hours and so on, but the monastery and Canção Nova are together, opening up many new vocations.[15]

As our conversation continued, Sister Rita opened her book and began to read a poem composed by Pope Innocent IV (c. 1195–1254), inspired by the figure of Saint Clare:

Oh! Grandiosa veemência [Oh! how great the vehemence of the]
Do brilho desta claridade [Brilliance of this clarity]
No mundo foi esta luz cativa [On earth this light was indeed kept]
No interior de um claustro [Within cloistered walls]
Todavia, radiou seu brilho [Yet shed abroad its shining rays]
Cativa numa cela do convent [It was confined within a convent cell,]
Espallhou, contudo, sua luz para todo o mundo. [Yet spread itself
    through the wide world.]

Summary

The TV Eucharist on *Adoration Thursday* expands outside the sacramental field of a mediation. Elevated to the level of an eye-to-eye encounter, the relation between the Eucharist and the TV camera activates, more than mediates, the principle of the cause that gives being to the image: the Holy Spirit. What is rendered to the senses is as follows: *On the TV screen there is nothing to be seen other than the ghostly figuration of a possibility to see.* This is the logic that Canção Nova holds as incarnated presence. Its elasticity is attested in this capacity to make dynamic extreme opposites in a ternary land of the spirit of Pentecost that must never, nonetheless, relinquish its Catholic long arm.

While *contemplation* is a term that has been associated with the aesthetic engagement with a piece of art, as that which separates and positions the subject apart from an object and that confirms its aura, it is actually a notion that was introduced during the lifetime of Saint Clare (certainly influencing later depictions of the saint as the icon of contemplation). The word's root lies in the medieval notion of *contemplationem* as the "act of looking attentively." But contemplation in the medieval sense had nothing to do with gazing out into the world as if from an opened window—as is suggested by a linear perspective. Rather, to contemplate was to engage in the practice of augury or divination. That is to say, it was less about seeing than about seeing through, less about perspective than prospective. Similarly, the word *temple*—which also derives from the word *contemplation*—stood for a demarcated space for auguring. Quite often medieval religious spaces were constructed not in order to allow people to see the transcendent as much as to invite them to transcend their immediate time and space and see into an elsewhere (a function achieved, in what might seem a contradiction, by means of a well-cultivated faculty to immerse in that very space one wanted to transcend).

Conceived in this way, to contemplate was essentially to engage in an extramural activity, and it was an action that, though premised on an idea of seeing, in fact shared more with hearing than with vision. As Gaston Bachelard (1988: 129) writes in *Air and Dreams*, "Profound contemplation is necessarily a hymn." (Recall that Canção Nova means "New Song," which is a hymn title.)[16] From whatever point one enters the song, adjacently, this is its missive: if, as Catholic Charismatics maintain, Saint Clare did not simply see images on the walls of her cell but, by means of inspirited motion, was able to see through into another place and another time, and if seven hundred years later another Sister Clare would receive the vision, while looking at the TV screen in her secluded headquarters, that a monastery of Poor Clares ought to come to Canção Nova, in both cases, the two Clares did not see. Rather, seeing occurred through them—clairvoyantly. Walls and screens led to one another, propelled by a spiritual binding force. Each moment, to-and-fro, prefigured the other, as though in a cosmic game with mirrors. These moments did not occur in linear time, as in a cause-and-effect sequence, but as a kind of convoluted loop, which seems to place time and space always in the middle.

1. Rádio Canção Nova

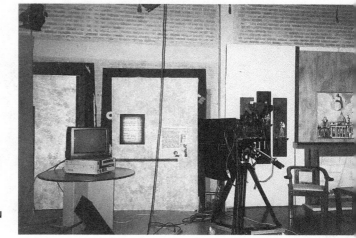

2. Canção Nova studios

3. Canção Nova, Rincão do Meu Senhor, PHN meeting

4. Byzantine panel
Igreja Nossa Senhora do Perpétuo Socorro, Santo Amaro Diocese, São Paulo

5. Santuário Mãe de Deus, São Paulo

6–7. Santuário Mãe de Deus, São Paulo

8–9. Santuário Mãe de Deus,
São Paulo

10. Celebration at Santuário Mãe de Deus, São Paulo

PART II

....

Everything examined deeply enough will turn out to be musical.

—ORSON WELLES (mis)quoting Carlyle in *Filming Othello*

4. THE AEROBICS OF JESUS

························

"Padre Marcelo gives me goose bumps all over," said the woman who, assisted by two helpers, walked toward the sanctuary exit. "This time I dived really deep," she added, sitting down in exhaustion on the pavement and leaning against the main gate. It was a hot day in mid-November in São Paulo. The temperature inside the Santuário Rosário Bizantino must have been around 25 degrees Celsius, even with the new cooling system that sprayed water on the devout during Padre Marcelo Rossi's dynamic worship service, which he has branded "the aerobics of Jesus." Also known as "masses of deliverance," the aerobics of Jesus consists of sing-alongs combined with choreographed physical exercises based on Byzantine techniques of prayer, such as the Prayer of the Heart. First used by the early desert fathers in fourth-century Egypt, the Prayer of the Heart, part of the tradition of *hesychasm*, flourished among Greek monks for ten centuries. Valued for its psychosomatic results, the prayer draws on both vocal and physical activities. The idea is to have voice both punctuate and be punctuated by the bodily rhythmic repetitions of breath and heartbeat, so that one's voice becomes an extension of breath in the form of traveling sound. Once synchronization of voice, breath, and heartbeat is accomplished, the subject is gradually transported through different stages of mystical ascension.

Relying on these ancient ritual techniques, Padre Marcelo has built up a style of prayer that emphasizes physical commitment, bodily transformation, and a living experience of the power of God. Disseminated electronically in different media formats, Padre Marcelo's aerobics have made him famous throughout Brazil. At stake here is how vocalized prayer, aerobics, and technology all share the sign of repetition. Because simple acts of singing, speaking, and even listening aurally affect the body, voice plays a fundamental role in Marcelo's aerobics scheme. In emphasizing his regimen, my aim in this chapter is to highlight the operations of breath in weaving multiple relations and associations, which air-condition the entire field of religious experience. Analyzing the aesthetic physical practice of this form of mediatized prayer allows me to recast the ways scholars have understood the relationship between religion and media and to focus on how contemporary media technologies produce the forms of bodily experience and tactility that have long served to define and account for religious experiences.

In the previous three chapters, dedicated to the Canção Nova religious community, I explored how Catholic Charismatics have, for the past three decades or so, been engaging with mass-media technologies. In a country like Brazil, where progressive public opinion, including within Catholicism, associated mass media and Pentecostalism with forms of alienation, Charismatics had to alter the terms involved in using mass media as a method of evangelization. As described, one of the ways that Canção Nova succeeded in overcoming ingrained negative predispositions to mass media was by curbing the conception of media as being merely instrumental. Charismatics proceeded to rearticulate a form of mediality without eschatology, a providential economy that, as I showed, strives toward the middle.[1]

By "middle," it should be clear by now, I do not mean a mere interval between points. What is particular about the concept of the middle in Charismatic Catholicism is precisely the active annihilation of the idea of something "in-between." Why? Because to say that something is "in-between" would mean adhering to a logic of position. It would be to say that one acts toward an end purpose. But what draws the devotee to the masses of Padre Marcelo is the measure of intensity of motion, bodily and spiritual. It is the extent to which song, prayer, and gesture combine to potentialize subjectivity such that to be present is in effect to be crossing to an elsewhere. This sense of transience, as though the subject is in flight from herself, is powerfully enacted through the rapturing of skin. Skin is not simply an organ that separates the inside and the outside of the body. As we will see, above all skin is an environment that can be regulated.

Let me emphasize, then, that what distinguishes part I of this book from part II is my focus on a single individual rather than on a community. While the Canção Nova Community relies on the idiom of community in order to reenact the Acts of the Apostles in the group setting of a global mass-media enterprise, Padre Marcelo is a solo rider with an inexhaustible amount of stamina, a charismatic and media-savvy young priest, admittedly on steroids, who succeeded in expanding Charismatic revivalism to the masses.[2] Through Padre Marcelo, the pneumatic concerns of the Charismatic movement experience their most concentrated and popularized expression. In response to what he interpreted as a call to become a "trainer of souls," an extension of John Paul II's athletic prowess during his visit to Brazil in 1997, Padre Marcelo has become the Catholic Charismatic Renewal's most prominent gymnasiarch by far. Through his choreographed spiritual aerobics, he waged war on the metaphysical obese; his praying techniques are commandments to muscles and joints; his website is a kind of virtual spa of different practical exercises of prayer and healing with links to medical websites and self-help tips.

Being a soloist rather than negotiating as part of a community has endowed Padre Marcelo with higher powers of flexibility. Soloist though he is, he is not alone, nor could he be, given how the institutional norms are not all predisposed to such flexing as this priest is predisposed to unleash. He was only a novice in 1995, but the Brazilian Catholic Church had already spotted him and his immense energy, which it used to certain ends; the times could not be more welcoming to such agility and lightness, but for that very reason the church was keen to actively monitor and rein in the young priest, assigning a bishop to supervise his every step.[3] Canção Nova Community (of which he was once a part) may strive for a bodily reenactment of the twelve apostles, a fine interweaving between the archaic and the present, but Padre Marcelo would be that and more: he would be Saint Paul on steroids. He would be more than the total sum of all the apostolic parts. He would be the closest incarnation of the circulating third in Brazil's Charismatic revivalism.

What follows in this and the next two chapters is an account of the universe—a network of lateral roots—created and divulged by Padre Marcelo since his rise in popularity in the second half of the 1990s. A singer, film actor, radio broadcaster, writer, composer, spiritual counselor, bodybuilder, soccer player, hang glider, chef and dietitian, hygienist of souls, and priest, Padre Marcelo is a network of personas. He communicates an extraordinary energy, orbiting worlds that seem to defy gravity. He explores ways by which his interventions can be assessed through their effects, and skin is the surface where such effects can become synthesized as felt experience. If properly stimulated, skin can reveal the core and essence of his religious practice.

This is no truer than in the puncturing sensation of goose bumps, an affect Padre Marcelo famously explores in the architecture of his massively attended choreographies. It is as though the operational turning back of breath to itself, central to his "aerobics of Jesus," could be exponentially replicated and spread into the entire body, and that of the entire assembly. Not only did he induce the opening of the body for the circulation of spirit (pneuma) through the power of voice; effectively, he turned bodies into a kind of vocalized skin, a medial space where the natural, the mystical, and the mechanical recursively folded into each other such that none could be said to be anterior to the other.

While there is a great deal of research on conceptualizations of the body in religion, much less attention has been given to the actual participation of the body in creating its own modes of awareness. In the event of a skin tremor, residual forces or theological archives may erupt from their state of latency. What can a bodily reaction such as goose bumps—tiny hairs reaching out like cactus spines in the desert—reveal about the relations among spirituality, technology, and the senses? How can such a rapture of the skin help one to think about a model that brings together mystical experience, media technologies, and the body? The analysis of tremor as a mystical experience has its locus classicus in the work of philosopher of religion Rudolf Otto (1923). Writing in the 1920s, Otto argued that goose bumps express the ecstasy of the body when in the presence of the divine. Implied in Otto's theory is that the religious subject is involuntarily and unexpectedly caught by the unknown. This encounter produces a powerful bodily experience, which dawns on the believer like a revelation. By so arguing, Otto both reflected and enforced the view—very much in vogue during the Romantic period—that the unruly forces of nature were supreme displays of the uncontrollable, which only further confirmed the existence of a higher source of control. Interestingly, the philosophical tradition that influenced Otto's formulations on goose bumps as a human response to the numinous—the *mysterium tremendum* and *fascinosum*—has a strong link to a famous tectonic event: the great Lisbon earthquake of 1755, described by European philosophers of the Enlightenment, including Voltaire, Rousseau, and Kant. As in the interpretations that those philosophers offered about the earth's quaking, Otto's interpretations of corporeal quaking express, albeit in a more phenomenological register, how the natural and the supernatural intertwine and fuse.

With this in mind, an interesting parallel between mysticism and trembling emerges. Both suggest the idea of having been caught by something unknown, being a victim of the unexpected, the uncalled-for, and, perhaps, the indiscernible. One of the concepts that seems to aptly illustrate this complicity between mystical experience and the unexpected is enrapturing. Used to describe mystical ecstatic experiences in Christianity, the word *enrapture* shares the same root as *rapt*, which refers to being kidnapped by an alien force, being a victim of the unknown. And yet precisely due to their strong associations with naturalness and with unconscious affectual bodily response, goose bumps have become an aim of new technologies of media and special effects.[4] In this chapter I explore the ways in which the natural, the technological, and the mystical interconnect during bodily performance. I argue that not only are the natural and the supernatural compatible with technology, but they are actually unthinkable without the technological. I investigate how to situate bodily tremor within the debate about dichotomies between nature, immediacy, and authenticity, on the one hand, and technology, mediation, and reproduction, on the other.

The aim of this chapter, then, is twofold. First, I question the idea of fixed borders that purportedly separate religion from technology, and both religion and technology from the body. By *technology* I am referring here to recording media, such as CDs and tapes, and the internet. However, as I show, the effectiveness of recorded sound rests on a structural homology between the existential properties of technologies of reproduction and the repetitive quality of breathing rhythms, which through Byzantine techniques of prayer enter the composition of a song. In other words, my view is that there is a structural correspondence between modern media technologies, ancient prayer techniques, and what sociologist Marcel Mauss (1934) referred to as *techniques du corps*. Second, I argue that as a result there is no discontinuity between ritual action and everyday life. Catholic Charismatics record music and songs not just for their sound but in order to encode breathing patterns; these patterns have been composed precisely to stimulate listeners to copy and repeat them and so blur the distinction between "recorded" and "spontaneous" breath. In other words, the ritual of breathing recapitulates the media, just as the body becomes a recording technology. Electronic reproduction combines with ritual reproduction. Music becomes breathing and vice versa, both registering and honing the presence of the metaphysical.

Padre Marcelo Rossi

Padre Marcelo's lively choreography and the media attention he attracted raised him high on the religious ladder, requiring him to walk a tightrope from early on. His past experience as a bodybuilder led him to explore a form of muscular ascesis in Christianity, which could not accommodate the bounded logics of conventional religious images and prayer. After an internship in a monastery in Ukraine early in his training for ministry, where he was immersed in Orthodox patristic doctrine, Padre Marcelo returned to

Brazil to highlight a new religious discipline. He liked to refer to himself with the Greek term *kerygma*, the announcer or pathbreaking figure. It was precisely the feasibility of that idea—the kerygmatic power that emanated from Padre Marcelo's novel techniques, his energy, and even his good-looking physique—that caught the attention of the rest of the Charismatic community, of the Catholic Church, and of evangelicals alike (de Abreu 2002).

Catholic Charismatics, who were trying to infiltrate their ideas on grace and pneumatic spirituality into strategic nodes of power, followed his actions with great ambivalence. On the one hand, it was undeniable that Padre Marcelo's trajectory coincided with a new, if not uncontroversial, emphasis on the body and athleticism spearheaded by Pope John Paul II himself, who, after being diagnosed with Parkinson's in the early 1990s, called for followers to become an extension of his own body-otherwise. Yet now that Padre Marcelo had arisen as the great "flock shaker"—combining natural talents with artifice; yoking contemporary tendencies, techniques, and technologies with ancient devotional methods; skillfully orchestrating grace (*kharis*) through the medium of the crowd—Charismatics (or at least some) were wary. They were concerned that the celebrity priest might take things too far and turn the Charismatic doctrine into a parody of itself, producing imposturous breath-controllers and encouraging a narcissistic and virile Catholicism that might lead to rupture and discredit. Was not Padre Marcelo Rossi a confessed consumer of anabolic steroids? Was he not interested in cosmetics (rather than in a cosmology)? Would the Brazilian church really be willing to exchange Leonardo Boff for Padre Marcelo Rossi?[5] How would a concept of celebration such as "the aerobics of Jesus" be made compatible with the mystery of the Eucharist?—a question that elicited both humor and anxiety (with terms like *muscle, mass-builder, bread, ferment* [as fake growth], *elasticity*, and others orbiting around each other) in church headquarters in Brazil, just as it did in the diocese of Santo Amaro (southeast of São Paulo), with which Padre Marcelo to this day remains affiliated.

Marcelo Mendonça Rossi was born on May 20, 1967, in northern São Paulo to a middle-class family of Italian descent. Before becoming a priest at the age of twenty-seven, he spent fourteen hours per day at the gym—his body was everything to him. His father's hope that Marcelo would become a medical doctor was at odds with the boy's uneasiness at the sight of blood. Instead he worked in a beauty parlor for a while and later became a physical education teacher. In the narrative widely documented by Brazilian media about his life, a TV documentary series about the life of John Paul II, which stressed that the pope had been an actor and a proficient athlete in his youth, played a pivotal role in Marcelo's budding ambition. When the pope came to Brazil in 1997, Padre Marcelo made a solemn vow. As the crowd waved at John Paul II, the padre silently promised to do all in his power to keep that waving gesture from withering. Seeing how the same sovereign body could tremble in both strength and decay—the pope's two bodies—Padre Marcelo decided to turn every church arena into regenerative grounds. As he told his audiences, it was a sign of the spirit that the pope, who incarnates the institution, was frail and tremulous. It was the distinctive clue that the church needed seismic renewal and that, precisely through the features of that shakiness in and of the sovereign's defective body, lessons could be drawn as to how to proceed. And so the body of the pope became not the referent to avoid but the very dispositive through which to think tremor and awe. In the very moment that spas and gyms were sprouting on every corner of São Paulo, the church set out to explore new extensions within its tradition that would turn extension into its proper function. Padre Marcelo and his bishop likened this to a "thunder in the heart," "a rumbling in the veins."[6] According to a popular local magazine, when seeing Pope John Paul II in Brazil in 1997, Padre Marcelo exclaimed, "From now on I will only do trainings for God."[7]

From the beginning, media was central to the young priest's training platform. He started with radio, television, CDs, books, a magazine, and a personal internet site, which he still maintains. He then became an actor in two blockbuster films, one dedicated to Theotókos and the other to the Apostle Paul, two important organizing references in his line of reasoning. As his media presence became ubiquitous, his bodily metabolism became an instrument of regulation that influenced people's own bodies and daily rhythms, as followers strove to follow his five daily rules: physical exercise, a midday siesta, five liters of water, two to three egg yolks per day, and frequent prayer of the Byzantine rosary.

Restricted prior to its popularization by Padre Marcelo to a small subset of Charismatics, the Byzantine rosary under his influence would grow to rival the Roman Catholic rosary conventionally used by Brazilians. Its association with the east could in effect articulate, on the one hand, aspects from pre-Romanized (popular) Catholicism where prayer and spirituality conjoined and, on the other, spearhead a doctrine of spirit (pneuma) that could emulate and possibly restrain the growth of Protestant Pentecostalism in Brazil, the Portuguese-speaking world, and all of Latin America. Unlike the Roman rosary—which, with its fifty-nine beads, explores narrative by bonding the collective to a story line—the Byzantine rosary would subject language to the mimetic and quotable powers of the body. It would transfer enunciation into bodily speech such that each word, each phrase, articulates air and not meaning, technique rather than a system of statements. The Byzantine rosary thus becomes a technique of bodybuilding, a mode through which utterance functions to modulate the rhythms of the body to speech and all expression to form.

The Byzantine Rosary

Padre Marcelo structures breath along two main registers of prayer, one of which is the Byzantine rosary, which he presents daily on the radio, the television, and his personal website. In use since the seventh century by Eastern Orthodox Christians, the Byzantine rosary uses a string of ten beads or stones. The particularity of this rosary is that it adjusts prayer to the rhythms of one's breath. While inhaling, the believer thinks, for example, of the words "Lord Jesus Christ, Son of God"; exhaling refers to the phrase "Have mercy on me, a sinner." These sentences, called arrows or ejaculatory prayers and repeated ten times, are contemplated for ten minutes. This practice implies that through the repetition of the same verse, voice and body work together to increase immateriality and the purification of one's self. Unlike with the traditional Western rosary, the practitioner is free to improvise a verse. However, this freedom lies in the fact that the efficacy of the prayer owes less to the referential content of a particular verse than to the word-bearing air or breath invested in it. This means that the verse choice is based on the person's physical or emotional condition, which determines his or her wish to engage with a particular breathing economy.

I would not infrequently see travelers on public transportation or customers lining up at the bank, both young and old, in a tie or wearing flip-flops, holding the shorter rosary in their hand or wearing it around their wrist. Every time I interviewed a rosary carrier about the functions it fulfilled or sentiments it elicited, I was assured of the soothing or prophylactic powers of this way of structuring prayer. For many of the residents of São Paulo, to pray the rosary has become a mode of balancing breath, of restoring rest and relaxation in the gigantic, hot, polluted city. But it can also be a way of centering oneself amid the crowd or rescuing order from the chaotic traffic; it can be a substitute for smoking or a distraction to make distances seem shorter;

it can stretch time or even pace the fluctuations of the stock market, while at the same time engaging the believer in prayer.

Padre Marcelo's website is titled the Online Byzantine Rosary: The Simple Prayer to Heaven. While the Byzantine rosary is based on the ceaseless repetition of the same verse, Padre Marcelo changes the video that accompanies the prayer on a daily basis. Thus he not only keeps his website renewed, but he also associates the material properties of the digital with the mechanisms of respiration (through refreshment and repetition). Most practitioners listen to Padre Marcelo's own daily prayer by accessing his website, tuning in to a Catholic TV station called Rede Vida, or, most commonly, listening to his hugely popular radio program on Radio America. Thanks to mass media, Padre Marcelo has entered the private sphere of many Brazilians. And by "private sphere," I mean at the most intimate level of breath. For many, his voice has become the sonic foundation on which the landscape of São Paulo is built. The unchanging intonations and repetitiveness of the rosary are like the drone of a plane in the distance. Like the sustained note used in Byzantine music, this spiritual exercise rests only on the rhythms of breathing (pneuma), which, as Marie-José Mondzain (2005: 107) has pointed out, is the privileged instrument of the Holy Spirit.

Through online prayer and many downloadable songs, Padre Marcelo helps people structure their breathing rhythms according to their lifestyles and their physical or emotional circumstances. His website appears to be a kind of living organ, which people may access in order to breathe properly, in a balanced manner. Again, the liveliness of the medium is not reducible to its inserted contents. This vitality also follows from how certain operational qualities of the internet—such as movement, lightness, flatness, and repetitiveness—aptly interface with the aerobic world of Padre Marcelo. Content emerges from and into the medium it is made of. This consubstantiality between medium and message is precisely what energizes the Byzantine rosary: words are valued as substantial expressions of the medium of air (pneuma), whose dynamic nature shapes and propels the words toward particular affective results, creating the sense that continuity exists between life on the screen and what is beyond.

The pneumatic techniques of the rosary are also a part of Padre Marcelo's stylized Byzantine ceremonies. He celebrates Mass four times a week at his sanctuary and, on special religious days, in large sports arenas. Many of the songs composed or performed by Padre Marcelo follow the same kind of symmetrical structure as the rosary in that they rely on the rhythms of breathing. His biggest hit, "Erguei as Mãos" (Raise your hands), went through three different sound remixes. The sustained beat of techno music helps to pace both heartbeat and breath. Because in techno the body is supposed to move in sync with breath and heartbeat, it is as though the entire body becomes an extension of lungs and heart.

Ordinarily, Padre Marcelo asks his followers, "Who came here to build up the house of the Lord? Shall we build up God's temple?" The metaphorical tone of these questions morphs into the material sense of bodybuilding through aerobic exercise. Bodybuilding is at once a verb and a noun. On the one hand, bodybuilding is building the body. On the other, bodybuilding is a condition attained through the exchanges and reciprocations that occur during respiration—that is, the outside becomes increasingly implicated in the inside and vice versa. What is significant is that this conception of bodybuilding entails a major reformulation of modern conventional notions of ritual as it pertains to space. Ritual space is no longer a fixed, preexisting dimension that the body simply enters; through the aerated process of building up, ritual space becomes consubstantially identified with the body. Another way of saying this is that bodies do not simply exist in a space, a sanctuary, but are themselves territorial in the sense that to territorialize is to partake in song. Space, thus conceived, is a rhythm. Space is time stretched to the edge.

Stretching the Voice: "Luz Divina"

"Luz Divina" (Divine Light) is one of Padre Marcelo's musical hits from the CD *Páz ao Vivo* (Peace Live). Released in 2001, the album features some old hits by Roberto Carlos, known as the king of Brazilian popular music, adapted by Marcelo to fit the aerobic demands of his prayer techniques and religious practice.[8] As with many other songs arranged by Padre Marcelo, "Luz Divina" matches the symmetrical structure of the Prayer of the Heart, which uses the verses of a song as breathing exercises. One of the particularities of "Luz Divina" is the extreme length of each of the verses, which establishes the air supply and vocal stretching necessary for it to be sung; the song requires rather deep inhalations, putting intense pressure on the vocal cords. It is, he warns, "a song for the experienced." His exhortations therefore need to be all the stronger. As he shouts "Now," "Sing it," "Up! Up!," "Beautiful," "Don't stop," "Ah!," and "Shake it up," he directs the entire choreography of breath.

To the extent that Catholic Charismatics describe the Holy Spirit according to the notion of pneuma—lungs, air, breath—Padre Marcelo operates as a kind of angel who both embodies and organizes among his followers the cosmic exhalations of the Spirit.[9] He does not really sing. He either reads or simply initiates the sentences so as to help his followers recall the lyrics. Like a coach, he often blows a whistle in order to mark the rhythms of both sound and movement. There are moments when the gentle swaying, waving, and up-and-down movements of the multitude visually resonate with the breathing dynamics of their vocalizations. When this occurs, the people's movements resemble the wind blowing through the thick canopy of a forest. Extolled by Padre Marcelo as the biggest pneumatic cathedral on earth, the Amazon rainforest is the magnified expression of pneuma; it has an ecological role in producing oxygen and a spiritual one in producing breath. This resemblance is no accident. Padre Marcelo's attempt to achieve this visual-sonic-pneumatic communion is also an effort to use the harmony of voice and movement to generate a similar accord inside the body. His aim is to create a balance between inner and outer, individual and group, sound and image, religion and nature, technology and the body—a balance that he explicitly models on environmental themes.

As adherents improve their ability to use their voice and control their breath in prayer, they experience feelings of intense love and joy. Because the last of the four stages of the Prayer of the Heart is practically unattainable, the third stage (eponymous with the song's title, *luz divina*) stands for a kind of climax of the prayer. Also called *theosis*, the last stage of the prayer poses the divine as unknowable and the possibility of uniting with God through that unknowability as "glorious nothingness" or "luminous darkness" (Kungurtsev and Louchakova 1997: 24). Conceived as a matter of degree rather than kind, this lack of definition is what permits Padre Marcelo to integrate the necessary flexibility and indeterminacy that will ultimately hold the crowd together in its collective flight. By no means designed as a linear structure moving toward a climax, the ladder structuring the song goes on to coil around itself, recursively, through repetition of the main verse in order to catch up with its beginning. That is, the song not only structures breathing; it performs the breathing cycle in its own composition.

Just as breathing disavows any distinction between inside and outside in favor of the movement between the two, it also undermines any clear separation between form and content, between beginnings and ends. As one breathes, one is inexorably in the middle. Even when a song like "Luz Divina" requires great vocal strain, one is still and already in relation. (Which is, in fact, the very condition of being alive!) The role of the song is precisely to put a focus on this condition. It is at this moment of focused awareness that goose bumps begin to course over one's body. This is an awareness not of something new and unforeseen (as classical theories of the sublime and the ineffable would assert) but rather of something that was already there, potential. Thus, what provides Padre Marcelo's devotees with a sense of both inhabiting and being inhabited by the sacred is not experiencing the novel, anchored in a transcendental elsewhere, but the experience of having the most ordinary, humdrum act of life rescued from oblivion, having each breath express the manifold possibilities lodged in the lungs of a person in the here and now. The rippling sensation of goose bumps on the skin is the spatial counterpart to the temporality of breath. It is, moreover, a physical indication of the breathing self-referential body when it is in touch with itself. Padre Marcelo's voice evokes tremors when he cries, "The Spirit is now passing. You will tremble." Then he adds, "Which is why it is so important to be flexible . . . [so that] you do not break . . . [and] you maintain your balance."

The Structure of Breath

With goose bumps, the body seems to figure and disfigure, as language does in the raveling and unraveling involved in praying in tongues. Padre Marcelo often talks of the luminous beauty of the "language of the angels" as a kind of celestial Esperanto. Glossolalia, however, hardly ever takes place inside the Santuário Rosário Bizantino. Despite Padre Marcelo's obvious Charismatic style, he and his bishop have moved beyond the strict niche of the Charismatic Renewal movement to a form of urban mainstream (popular) Catholicism. When in 1994 Padre Marcelo's power to attract the masses became apparent, the bishop of his parish in the southeastern part of São Paulo revealed his intention to keep Padre Marcelo as his personal disciple. Besides being formed by the old patristic theology, Bishop Fernando Figueiredo is also a confessed adherent of the Catholic Charismatic Renewal and one of the key influential national clerical figures who has moved this form of Catholic revivalism to become ever more subservient to the Roman Curia. While the bishop and Padre Marcelo have co-opted Charismatics' special focus on the Holy Spirit, they strive to avoid religious practices (such as glossolalia and slaying in the spirit) that are highly controversial in Brazil's Catholic

Church.[10] Yet again, this is when the prayer of the Byzantine rosary shows its constitutive significance.

Even though the prayer of the rosary is made in vernacular speech, its formulaic repetitiveness and harmonization with breath allow the practitioner to become engaged in the same kind of deconstruction of meaning that characterizes glossolalia. Thus a person does not need to abandon understandable language in order to experience the kind of ecstatic trance that usually accompanies speaking in tongues. In his study of Catholic Charismatics in the United States, Csordas (1990: 25) recognizes that all language is a "bodily act." He refers to Merleau-Ponty's theory of language as embodiment, in which, Csordas writes, speech is but a "verbal gesture with immanent meaning, as against a notion of speech as a representation of thought" (25). Csordas, however, seems to apply Merleau-Ponty's notion of language as a bodily act in order to justify, and further enhance, the special place glossolalia holds in this notion. He emphasizes the instability of normal language and its phonetic structures so that he can speak of glossolalic utterance as an extension of all vernacular speech in the attainment of freedom—that is to say, beyond all linguistic constraints. In the same paragraph, Csordas quotes Merleau-Ponty as saying that all language manifests the "desire of the human body to sing the world's praises and in the last resort to live it" (27).

As much as I agree with an approach to language as a bodily act, I depart from Csordas's analysis when it comes to accounting for the relation between language structure and the erosion of semantic meaning as they intersect with religious ecstasy. Indeed, my experience among people praying the Byzantine rosary shows that in this case, structured repetition not only is integral to the rosary but is a key catalyst toward the disintegration of referential meaning. The living, bodily quality of sound is fleshed out not because language is being freed from a structure but because language is incarnated and "supernaturalized" as it is made to coincide with the breathing structure that sustains it. As I noted earlier, the dissolution of meaning in the prayer of the rosary happens through the repetitive articulations of sound. The arrows or prayer sentences are aural extensions of breath, which acquire their effectiveness precisely because it is in their nature to elude the rule that determines them. That is, the role of reproduction in breath (as in technology) is to create the conditions for its own denial in the form of spontaneity. I argue that spontaneity thus conceived arises not above or beyond but *through* a structure.

Padre Marcelo and the bishop he works under explore the highly structured compositions of the Byzantine rosary in order to elicit the same sort of mystical experience that speaking in tongues enables. Goose bumps are the silent epidermal counterpart to speaking in tongues. Indeed goose bumps are the most palpable expression of what Csordas refers to as "language . . . incarnate" when writing about glossolalia. But again, I diverge from Csordas in that he suggests glossolalia lacks the temporal contours and resolution of (improvised) musical forms. The song "Luz Divina" shows how musical form can lead to "sung speech"; it also shows how the latter results from a highly structured, nonimprovised audio composition. As Michel de Certeau (1996: 29) asserts, "Glossolalia is a *trompe l'oreille*, just like a *trompe l'oeil*, a semblance of language that can be fabricated when one knows its phonetic rules."

Rather than considering goose bumps—or, for that matter, glossolalia—a "pure act of expression that allows language to exist outside time," as Csordas (2002: 78; see also Csordas 1993) suggests, I prefer to think of time not as an empty dimension but as a substance that bends and folds along with human movement. I understand that when he says that language comes to "exist outside time," Csordas's intention is to refer to something beyond linear time. But to be outside linear time does not mean to be beyond time altogether; it is to inhabit a different conception of time. This is all the more relevant among Catholic Charismatics in Brazil, who actively experiment with the distinction between the Greek word *kairos*—"a time in between" or "qualitative time"—and the kind of quantitative, linear time personified by *kronos*. In classical studies, kairos is sometimes perceived as the mere interruption of linear time when something extraordinary happens. The Charismatic movement, however, emphasizes the qualitative intensity that transforms temporality as such, notably through the figures of recursion and relation.

The Milieu of Relation

When the adherents' exertions cause temperatures to rise in the sanctuary, Padre Marcelo turns on the sprinklers. As the thin threads of water rain down, a cooling mist rises, mimicking the ecology of the rainforest itself. When the temperature gets even hotter, he takes buckets of water and splashes them over his followers, while they continue to hold out their arms in praise. Quakes and tremors ensue. The divine's overwhelming work disperses across the skin, which is at once a surface and a screen, a network and an environment.

Padre Marcelo's services and "Luz Divina" are powerful because, as many people have expressed it, "You dive [mergulho] deep!" Charismatics use the expression "to dive" to describe the experience of baptism in the Holy Spirit. This moment corresponds to the downpour of charismata according to the parable of Pentecost. But, as Padre Marcelo proclaims, for the downpour to happen, people have to practice their aerobics. They have to do their "homework." "You must do so," he points out, "even if you do not have a home," because "the home is literally where the heart is." This refers to breath as the real home: the place where the body and the Spirit dwell and get in touch. Breathing is, of course, a vital activity. Yet by focusing on breath as the main embodied disciplinary religious practice, the ritual itself denies the status of an autonomous, separate stage of prescribed behavior, collapsing any distinction between daily life and ritualized religious practices.

Padre Marcelo records his CDs to have a "live" feel, erasing the border between recorded and live performances, so that when people perform at his sanctuary, they are, in effect, reenacting the "living" experience they had while listening to the CD at home. Conversely, when listening to the recorded version, they recall the experience of singing live at the sanctuary. Live performance and recording devices intermingle; private and public, inner and outer, build on each other. So even though goose bumps can express a suspension of the everyday routine, Padre Marcelo's aerobics are less about taking the body somewhere else than about engaging it in religious (and technological) experiences of the unknown. The rhythm and circularity of songs like "Luz Divina" suggest that even as one is performing, one is also rehearsing; each word, each verse, and each breath are better than the previous, improving one's capacity to surf on the right flow. Like good aerobics, repetition enables higher levels of endurance and staying power. Indeed, the power that is exerted on the bow propels the arrow, which, as already mentioned, is one of the designations for each verse of the prayer.

The exercises of the Prayer of the Heart emphasize the chest area. The pectoralis major, the thick, fan-shaped muscle at the upper front of the chest wall, is what gives the bulky muscular look often associated with male prowess. In women, the pectoralis major lies under the breasts. If breath is the "real home" of the body, then the chest is the source of its energy. Widespread legends about the baptizing of the Amazon River and forest refer to a tribe of warrior women who cut off their right breast so as to better work with a bow and arrow. Myths of the Amazon such as this have been integrated into the larger cosmology of breath inside the sanctuary: the art of shooting with a bow and arrow, for example, is sometimes identified with the strain put on the vocal cords to expel the words of a song through the aperture of the throat.

While drawing on legends of the Amazon, the focus on the chest also relates to the mystical Christian experience of Eucharistic elasticity: the idea that the body of Jesus is less a presence than a flexible apparatus or network—a gymnastic *corpus ecclesia*—that extends to all times and places. This image of a boundless stretch reconnects to the kairotic conception of circular time in its connecting to a sense of the opportune. Conceived in classical imagery as a winged god, kairos is the aperture (the spatial counterpart to the temporal opportunity) in the fabric of life through which the archer's arrow has to pass or, to use a different image, the gap that momentarily opens in the warp of a cloth through which the weaver must draw the yarn. The expelling of the verse out of one's chest into the air is therefore a potentially kairotic moment inside the sanctuary and beyond it. At the sanctuary, mystery and entrepreneurship sail together in pursuit of a spiritual commonwealth under the guidance of the Paraclete.

Finally, the link to the Amazon manifests as a total sensory immersion in the sanctuary's atmosphere. As a person, the third, the Spirit has a temperature and a temperament. Charismatics claim that "the wind says things" and that its tone, cadence, and timbre temper the message. The voice of the Holy Spirit is often described as warm or humid. Warmth and moistness are, of course, universal attributes of the human voice. They are also the two main climatological characteristics of Brazil's tropical weather, which splits between the rainy (summer) and nonrainy (winter) seasons. Nowhere is this combination of hot and humid better illustrated than in the climate of the rainforest—or inside Padre Marcelo's sanctuary in São Paulo. Voice unites the city and the jungle, exposing their resemblances. Both spaces are warm and humid, the humidity in the sanctuary brought into being by the voices and movement of the practitioners. The sprinkler system at the sanctuary heightens these connections. On the one hand, the atmosphere created by the downpouring water has a cooling impact on the body, while, on the other, it underscores the heat and humidity associated with a tropicalized Spirit. The misty atmosphere of the sanctuary works as a spectral visualization of the breath of the Holy Spirit, the valves that run along the ceiling of the 20,000-square-meter sanctuary opening and closing as a way to air-condition the space. That Padre Marcelo also bathes the crowds with buckets of cold water attests to his desire to bring into being a rainforest environment and to render, sometimes in blatant ways, how technique is indelibly implicated in enrapture.

Summary

Followed by the media (which followed the paparazzi following him), Padre Marcelo has repeatedly stated that he is a victim of "artifice." Perplexed to hear this, a journalist once asked the padre how he could make such a comment, given the fact that he himself uses, and not just a little, several means of mass media to celebrate his aerobics of Jesus. In response to the interviewer's puzzlement, Padre Marcelo claimed that the difference between him and "the world of media" is that his use of artifice is "natural," by which he meant that the physiological already bears the print of the spiritual. What on earth could be more natural than air, he seemed to imply, deaf to the oxymoron, as a way of expressing how intrinsic spirituality is to life's basic functions? To be spiritual is a natural thing. "Nothing more natural," in his words. Given Charismatics' emphasis on the preternatural powers of the Holy Spirit, the use of the term "nothing more natural" was soon paraphrased by his followers as "a super-natural." Thus the circle between the natural and the miraculous was established. Miraculous was but a natural superlative (a natural more natural could not be): a super-natural. If technology is an artifice by which to effect such articulation between the miraculous and the (super-)natural, it is only because these notions themselves could never have been conceived outside a certain artificial frame, what in the patristic field Padre Marcelo is trained in is known as "operations" (opus). The miraculous and the natural are not transcendental referents alone toward which one tends, and neither is technology just another means to make that happen. Rather, the very ability to name or recognize the miraculous qua natural is profoundly indebted to techne and craftsmanship.

Padre Marcelo's interest in technique and media technology, as a particular modality of technique, is exclusively concerned with what it can reveal about divinity within the body, how it moves, how the limbs connect, how it hurts if you raise your arms or sit too long. Far from hindering, the subjection of artifice to the functions and skills of the body thus exposes the administrative aspects of naturalness. Given how divine presence unfolds through a body that aptly reveals the principle of its operations and that stresses the formulas through which it functions, nothing is more natural than to use artifice in making that happen—and, moreover, to turn that artifice into the focus of the religious. Since in the aerobic universe of Padre Marcelo the relation between the natural and the artificial is ruled by verbs rather than nouns, the distinction between these aspects collapses.

The relation between the two apparently incommensurate concepts—the natural and the artificial—is governed by a particular conception of action in time. This highlighted perception of action in time pertains to what Jason Throop (2001) calls being "in the midst of action." This is why, as alluded to before in this book, the term *mediation*, often associated with the coming of Christ (Christ as a mediation of God), is inadequate in the context of Padre Marcelo and the Charismatic Renewal more generally. In his actions Padre Marcelo consistently aims to reinstate the logic of Christ's passing through the world in terms not of presence nor of mediation but of Christ as the great articulator, the exemplary athlete whose dynamic image of himself as messiah can be rendered only as a kind of being in action—in short, as always already spirit, pneuma, the third in circulation.

The key phrase in this chapter has been "building up" in the most aerobic sense. Whether through prayer or through songs, Padre Marcelo Rossi's main goal is to inculcate in and physically elicit from his followers the sentiment that each single breath is a bifurcating arrow between the polar extremes of natural and artificial. I have shown that, for Padre Marcelo, to build up is to enter the province of an elongated middle of relation, according to the material reference of breathing as movement that vitally occurs in and through the reciprocations, circulations, and exchanges of "information" between inside and outside. Insofar as breath hinges on repetition, to train oneself in the art of building up is chiefly a question of tuning and modulating the body—the ears, the heart, the lungs, the entire network of skin receptors—toward self-reference. The main purpose of the Byzantine rosary and the musical compositions it structures (and the media technologies, such as CDs and tapes, that record them) is to catalyze the body's breathing cycles. Production and reproduction, inside and outside, means and ends, form and content—all collapse in this logic of bodybuilding. To build up is to experience the sacred that arises from repetition. Religious feelings, however, do not ascend like an arrow in a linear trajectory, arching from a fixed origin toward a specific point. Rather, experience assumes the shape of a spiraling arrow or cursor that moves along the routes of the everyday.

In chapter 5 I examine how a sanctuary becomes a building up. If this chapter has been about building the body (as though it were a temple), the next chapter is about a building that follows the formula of a body in formation, yet another space where the principles of life, reproducibility, recursivity, of body and image, all meet in rhythmic intimacy. This meeting of features relates—indeed is built on—what in patristic Byzantine iconography goes under the name of Theotókos, the Mother of God (Mãe de Deus).

5. SANCTUARY THEOTÓKOS: A CONCEPTION
....

You are extraordinary within your limits, but your limits are extraordinary.
—GERTRUDE STEIN, *Everybody's Autobiography*

In May 2013 I traveled to São Paulo with the aim of visiting the newly in-augurated (if still unfinished) Catholic Santuário Theotókos Mãe de Deus. Located in the southeastern part of the city, a district primarily dominated by industrial buildings, the sanctuary is a massive structure of concrete, the unfinished form of which revealed the layers of material operations: the metal scaffolding, the bricks, the raw cement. Despite a thin rain falling, the builders moved back and forth, bringing with their gestures new additions to the building's gradual—very gradual—building up. A group of three men worked on welding a geodesic dome above the altar. Outside a few portable concrete mixers ingested sand and gravel to produce the material for the con-struction of the office headquarters. A long crane was loading and transport-ing goods from one part of the site to another. It was Saturday morning, and at 3:00 P.M. a televised Mass would be taking place at this largely unfinished space named after the Byzantine icon Theotókos, the Mother of God.

Four times a week thousands of Catholic devotees come from all parts of Brazil to Santuário Mãe de Deus to attend the Masses of Padre Marcelo Rossi.[1] With a total area of 30,000 square meters, the sanctuary can accom-modate up to 100,000 people, which makes it the biggest Catholic building in Brazil after the national basilica. On Thursday evenings, Saturdays, and Sundays the avenues that lead to the sanctuary are jammed with vehicular traffic and crowds of churchgoers, street vendors, beggars, and police provid-ing security.

The purpose of my journey was to conduct a deeper ethnographic analy-sis of the tension in a space that is not finished and yet is immensely popu-lar among Catholics. This tension revolves around the question, "When is a space usable?," allowing me to examine a problem of space through the di-mension of time. This problem is hardly exclusive to the sanctuary but applies to the city's own expression: the overarching sense of spaces in the making recognized in the regularity of the rumbling of machines, the gridwork of cranes and scaffolds, the stream of sounds that jolt, stop, and surprise the passersby and expose the city to the edges and extensions from which futures will unfold.

The trip from São Paulo's international airport to the center of the city offered a legible example of the relentless rhythm of a city's anatomy. Driving deeper into the local landscape, one could see countless homes without a finished exterior. Through the bus windows incongruously juxtaposed reddish bricks transmitted the sense of an organism without skin. The agglomerate revealed the economy of materials involved in the process of the buildings' making: the beams, the ceramic blocks, the mortar lines of brickwork. This is because many of these buildings rise not just to enclose human life but themselves define a kind of life of the economic, an *oikonomos*, where to live is to administrate a living. "The story goes like this," a graduate student at Escola da Cidade, São Paulo's school of architecture, had told me the year before: "a young man, say a migrant from the north, buys a piece of land, a supply of bricks, cement, and gravel enough to build four walls and perhaps a roof. He gets to do a patchwork of low-paying jobs like selling coconut water or [being a] car mechanic and driver, and uses some of the land to grow some vegetables. In time, as savings allow, he buys more bricks, more cement, more gravel and sand. Gets a wife, works on the roof, gets children, works on his family's safety, and so on. The house is built in tandem with its management."[2]

One could not think São Paulo city by any other name. The metropolis is a Pauline technocratic opus Dei, a liturgical masonry where structures rhythmically rise and fall, defined less by its monumental heritage than by the operations that breathe it alive. In its affirmative exposure of the infrastructural conduits of space, the city recalls the latent and abstract worlds of information databases in computational theory, an aniconic landscape caught in the fold of the temporal gerund and indeterminate ongoing. This gerundive quality, as the temporal marker of the city, makes it a space existing at the edge of time.

Not unfrequently such an edge speaks not of progress but of a festering impasse. But that is yet another story, one running parallel to that of the migrant worker who builds his house as bricks allow, in turn, under the heading of another game. I am now thinking of the many empty shells and ghost structures, public monuments to corruption, one encounters in the urban dominion. Never completed or already deteriorated, such spaces exude temporal patina. They are the city's negative heritage. Marked by the insignia of scandal with anonymous graffiti and ciphers, colossal structures of exposed, raw, brute ferroconcrete remain suspended before their futures, as though from the crane that had come in support of them. Others still posit an affirmative state of pendency, of being reappropriated into possible futures, transforming limitations into new potentials. Uncertainty is the language proper to the cemented architectures in São Paulo city, perhaps in view of the malleability of materials, no less of ideas, through which edifications themselves are possible.

Santuário Mãe de Deus in the neighborhood of Santo Amaro is one such example. It embraces incompletion unapologetically.[3] In effect, Padre Marcelo Rossi and his followers have turned the circumstances of its incompletion into its very theological proceeding. Although the sanctuary is dedicated to the Byzantine icon of Theotókos, visitors see no physical icon, only a tremendous hollow space made of cement. They see stacks of tiles in a corner, rebar beams poking out of the walls, raw cement, electric cables, sockets, and water pipes, but no icon at all. There is an iron-grid tower in the middle of the sanctuary where the TV cameraman stands, but he himself is an image producer surrounded by thousands of people, the crowd below like pixels to his screen. Talking to workers, churchgoers, and deacons in the course of several visits to the site, I realized that the disclosing of the industrial components of the space was not a defect or a shortcoming but theology articulated through paste, steel, and bricks, its tools, technique, and management. The nudity of elements, in the brutalist cemented rough edges all around, the spikes, tucks, and blocks, seemed to be part of the dramaturgy of celebration.

Churchgoers, in turn, acted as though the exposure of the means of production, the entire physical infrastructure, was endowed with metaphysical force. And, as I gradually came to realize, that meant this: *If the icon is not in the building, it is because the building—or, better, its building up—is the icon.* But how did it happen that an icon became assimilated to a space rather than contained by it, which is the convention in Catholic spaces? In being internal to—perhaps one could even say, consubstantial with—the sanctuary, the icon seems to challenge all circumscription; the borders of the sanctuary necessarily coincide with that of the icon. What is at stake in this territorializing of the icon that renders visible and puts into play a particular economic model via its plastic operations? Such is the enigma of Theotókos, Our Lady of the Oxymoron, in her ability to claim all space by occupying none in particular.[4]

In this chapter I describe and analyze how the Byzantine icon of Theo-tókos came to work as the matrix-like model for the administration of an architectural project, a Catholic sanctuary, in the city of São Paulo. Were the sanctuary to be simply dedicated to Theotókos—as, indeed, it was initially intended—the building would work as a container of the icon but would not partake at all in its content. As it was until recently, sanctuary and icon did not have the relation that a wall has to its decoration or a container to its content. Instead the icon extended to everything that circulated in the space; indeed circulation is what gave existence to it. My aim in this chapter is to show how this territorialization of the icon-cum-space happened—and, to a degree, goes on happening—at the intersection between a critique of circum-scription and a renewed valorization of transparency. I further emphasize that both these latter aspects link in particular ways to the motif of circula-tion, as the formal structure of an economic narrative. What is distinctive about this economic narrative is a particular semiotic configuration, one that relies on the disavowal of a master referent according to the Byzantine iconol-ogy. By having the referent incarnated in the material, the semiotics of the sanctuary implode all circumscription. In its stead a circular, self-referential indexicality emerges between signifier and signified, notably, a sanctuary relating to its world like a mother's uterus to a child. Though localized in space, the sanctuary is meant to be no mere vessel or channel (for according to the enigma of incarnation what *it* contains is uncontainable) but bound-lessly middle.

Derogatory criticisms of the sanctuary by local architects and art histo-rians who compare that "middleness" to the midgrade quality of a gasoline station, as I often heard it described, ignore how much, in effect, such a de-scription coheres with the form of Theotókos.[5] It is the very manifestation of renewal at the core of Charismatic Catholicism. What is this form? It is the form of a recursive operation, of a circling or movement of turning back and of readapting. It is at once the figure of wholeness and its subsiding. Techni-cally speaking, a Theotókian cycle undermines its own physical limitations; it is a process of implosion of the very worlds it encloses. Theologically speak-ing this is because in Orthodox Christianity, Mary must be contiguous to the infinity of the Son and not a finite vessel. Geometrically speaking, the circle is deployed as a figure of universality, but it does the opposite too: it encloses a world. Or even, it implodes the very world it encloses.

As we will see, the context at Santuário Mãe de Deus in São Paulo is a good example of where theology and geometries meet in the celestial space of Theotókos. Here the transparency of materials—the transparency of the economy—works only in order to distract churchgoers from the whole, from the imaginary totalizations produced by the eye, by drawing their attention instead to the sanctuary's constitutive parts, to the spatial operations that add up incrementally and gerund-like to the *making* of the building. In bringing attention to the extremities and edges of a building, Theotókos will stand the test of its elasticity, an endurance of sorts. It is at this key intersection between whole and part that the mutual entanglements between the problem of transparency and that of representation and circulation are explored. The question, to repeat, is about space as much as about time. In what follows I explore the circumstances under which Padre Marcelo appropriated into the present the ancient Greek notion of *oikonomia*, meaning the administration of the *oikos*, the home. To do this, I must first lay out the nonperspectival economy of the icon of Theotókos and how such a Byzantine icon could become the very matrix or plan for the making of a space: a colossal sanctuary.

Theotókos, Mother of God

Entering the city of São Paulo is somewhat like entering the old Greek gym of Corinth, where the Apostle Paul often went to build up his own theology of Spirit. The Greek gym offered Paul the pragmatic rules from which to grasp a form of spiritual engineering, an athleticism of form and style that drew attention to the peripheral belt of things. It was there on the edge, where means and ends coincide as one, that the space-time of the sacred was to be found. Saint Paul's dictum, which Charismatics often quote, "The body is the temple of the Holy Spirit," concentrates his vision of the bearer of spirit as a bodybuilder at the core, a model for architecture that implicates and renders visible the ensemble of practices and artifices from which it rises up. His approach was to grasp the setups and outfits of language, the building blocks, the underpinnings, through which, in the words of Michel de Certeau (1984: 12), "the prose of the world is at work."

Such emphasis on operations makes São Paulo a fitting city of Paul. And nowhere is this Pauline principle of spiritual edification as powerfully portrayed as in the iconic figure of Theotókos, or so at least according to Padre Marcelo Rossi and his bishop, Fernando Figueiredo, as key representatives of Charismatic Catholicism in Brazil. Whatever passion for bodybuilding Padre Marcelo once nurtured and fleshed out in his being now finds striking translations in the Byzantine Theotókos icon and in the building that bodies it. This again might sound like a stretch, but a stretch it is precisely. It is the story of how the Virgin's celestial body became a hagiographic matrix for the building up of a Catholic sanctuary, a space where modern aerobics and Byzantine metaphysics build on each other but also, it turns out, a redemptive counter to the blasting corruption scandals that, from the second decade of the 2000s onward, have seemed to tear apart Brazil as a nation, no doubt testing its capacity to withstand.

In her study on Byzantine iconography Marie-José Mondzain (2005) suggests a particular regime of seeing as innate to the Byzantine artistic tradition.[6] Following the doctrine of the icon itself, she contends that we pursue a linking of images to power by looking not at the system of signs but at the formal and graphic properties of images themselves. For example, we should examine how, technically speaking, the lines in the Byzantine painting connect the body of a child to that of the mother, the trajectories and intensities of brushstrokes. Are they striated? Are they smashed? Are they muscular? Are they darted? But also, color, light, rhythm, and so on. Accordingly, the icon does not only exist in space but itself has territorial qualities. The icon, she argues, is above all a space-occupying physical being. This intimacy with the "flesh of the icon," that is, with the material and technical tracing of its being, connects to the theological kernel of *schesis*, which describes the icon as a relational entity according to a particular semiosis.

The icon of Theotókos, from whom Padre Marcelo extracts his vision for a sanctuary, is one such example where *schesis* plays the role of a matrix. Meaning "bearer of God," Theotókos is the general appellation given to the icon of the Virgin in Eastern Orthodox Christianity. The title became officially recognized during the Third Council of Ephesus in 431 CE and was given local nuances as it spread to different parts of Eastern Europe, Constantinople, and the Roman Empire. Building on Platonic metaphysics and its central concern with the relation between ideal and earthly forms, Theotókos proposed to capture a relational enigma through which three entities—Father, Son, and Holy Spirit—were synthesized into one. Such a synthesis was extremely pragmatic in its effects. The idea of three divinities, as posed by the Trinity, risked an association with polytheism, thus problematizing the monotheistic status of Christianity. In order to prevent that, the fathers of the church had to find an operational term, a network of personas—an apparatus or *dispositif*—that would organize the relational nature of the Trinity around a single divine principle (Agamben 2009). This operational term—from where the term *apparatus* itself evolved—was the Greek *oikonomia*, which signified the art of household management (*oikonomike techne*) and would become the law (*nomos*) with which the church managed the plasticity of the icon. But then Theotókos entails a theory not only of space but also of time. She is the mother of God, which means she is the mother of the one who gives her being; she is the creator of her own creator. Through such kinship arrangement, that is, the icon comprises a tautological recursivity; not unlike a self-adaptive system, it directs attention to the reality behind its own emergence. While temporally Theotókos relates to the gerund, spatially it connects to *gest*, which means to bear or carry but also to construct or synthesize. It is this complex intersection of different semantic possibilities by which the temporal becomes materialized in space that occupies me in this chapter.

As Concrete as Celestial

When, in 2005, Padre Marcelo announced to his followers that a new sanctuary was to be built in São Paulo, he evoked a structure "as celestial as the heavens." In 2008, while still celebrating Mass in an old clothes factory, he exhibited a model made by the Japanese Brazilian architect and urban planner Ruy Ohtake so that devotees could indulge in the minutiae of spatial details. The design of the sanctuary incorporated the tendencies of contemporary religious architecture, which is characterized by contemplative simplicity, organic forms crafted into curved lines, and juxtaposition. Known for works such as Hotel Unique, Renaissance São Paulo Hotel, and the Tomie Ohtake Institute, dedicated to his mother's work, Ohtake set off to design a major temple commissioned by Padre Marcelo in coordination with the Roman Catholic diocese of Santo Amaro and the nonprofit Associação Rosário Bizantino, which Padre Marcelo runs with his mother. According to Ohtake, the Santuário Mãe de Deus would foreground three features: circulation, ventilation, and serenity.

The new building would be located on the site of a former beer factory in southeastern São Paulo, just on the other side of a large gasoline station. Interlagos, as the region is called, is an area of the city that was long dominated by industrial buildings. Since 2001 it has grown into a desirable residential area for the middle class. Located at the intersection of one of the major arteries of Interlagos, the new Catholic sanctuary would have a capacity of 100,000 people: 25,000 indoor (10,000 seated and 15,000 standing) and 75,000 (standing) in the outdoor area. The curved roof covering the space would create ceiling heights varying between 6 and 25 meters. At the highest point of the building there would be a dome with stained glass in shades of blue, purple, and orange. With a total area of 430 square meters, the altar would be made of reinforced concrete 5 meters high and 20 meters long, the ceiling above it 10 meters high. The altar area would include a space for special guests (100 seats). Under it a large crypt would eventually house the mortal remains of Padre Marcelo and other priests and bishops of his diocese. According to the plan, the sanctuary complex would also include an administration building, an events hall, classrooms for catechesis, a rehearsal hall for musicians, 500 bathrooms, 2,000 parking spaces, a chapel for 25,000 pilgrims, a general shopping area, a bookstore, a gift store, and a cafeteria. The roof of the building would be supported by fourteen pillars. Around the sanctuary in a curved shape would be signage with a 13-meter width and a 40-meter span. On top of it would be placed a 42-meter-high steel cross, which would be illuminated at night so that it could be seen from afar.

The height of the structure would vary from wall to wall. The first wall would range between 7 and 13 meters, the second from 13 to 17 meters, and the third from 17 to 24 meters. The three walls would be curved, and the nonexistent fourth wall would be a row of concrete pillars. In the rear of the building would be seven huge TV screens so that celebrants would be able to see digital images of what was happening on the altar and of themselves, produced and transmitted in locus and in real time. The TV crew would stand on a 3-meter-high tower located at the center of the sanctuary.

As it turns out, almost no correspondence exists today between the model and reality. When I met with Ruy Ohtake in his studio in 2013, he told me (with deep melancholy) that only 35 percent ("if that") of the model had been actualized. Basically all that had been built was the main shell of the sanctuary: roof, walls, and altar. "*A obra em andamento*" (an ongoing construction) is how Padre Marcelo's bishop put it to me, and this is also how the construction workers and the donors of time and money referred to the sanctuary. Visitors spoke of it as a place they had seen evolving from its inception: they were aware of the form of the building, the height of the pillars, the relation between the dome and the altar, what was missing, what had changed, what went wrong. They knew how many months it took to set the roof, how large the altar-cum-stage was, the size of the cross and what it was made of, what was happening next, and how many were presently working on the project. A great deal of information about and around the construction was collected from Padre Marcelo's website, where he continues to update and archive photos and videos of the building's biography. Another source was his immensely popular daily radio program, *Momento de Fé*, on Radio Globo. But it was at the site itself, during celebrations, that individuals experienced most aspects of such information through the vantage point of the participant.

As he had while celebrating in his previous sanctuary, Santuário Rosário Bizantino, Padre Marcelo displayed Ohtake's model within the new sanctuary under construction. In coming to the new, if unfinished, Santuário Mãe de Deus, visitors could have a sense of where things were (not) going but also of where things had come from. Now that he had left the old hangar, he could better claim to be delivering on his promise of offering his many followers a much better place: bigger and more open, a proper temple and not some recovered factory. The fact that they had moved to new premises endowed the present with a distinct sense that things were moving, and moving they should be.

And so viewers not only can report back to the futures modeled and set off in the previous sanctuary but equally imagine the future from which point such a past will be rendered as an altogether different location. They will say, as they do, "It was supposed to be like A, but the Spirit went ahead with B." Gradually the future itself will be transformed, no longer what it used to be according to its model. The model will become a future of the past as the space goes on developing in contractual proximity with what the present brings up, indeterminately. Such is the pliable logic of the gym. The more Santuário Mãe de Deus distances itself from its original model, the more spiritually fulfilled it becomes as the material narrative of anointed adaptability. To make the present an ongoing affair rather than something that is simply there, indicatively, is to live up to the interiority of an icon that strives to have none so that it might shine from all sides.

Iconic Praxis

The year 2010 was a stellar one for Brazil's economy, when the level of inflation decreased to 4.5 percent (in August), an unparalleled vigorous year in domestic consumption and urban rejuvenation. While the rest of the world was undergoing serious economic recession, Brazil was on a roll with both consumption and investment rates reaching extremely positive records. The 2010 presidential elections were on the horizon, and so the country was plastered with optimism and bold promise. The president in power, Luiz Inácio Lula da Silva, gave frequent communications to fellow citizens. He assured them and gave credence to Brazil's lecherous success, including that candidate Dilma Roussef (who would become the first female president of Brazil) would protect the house-nation under construction. For the president this should involve two well-balanced steps: the first is investment, the other is consumption, both public and private, through active participation in the economy. President Dilma, as it turned out, would become president, but, much like the icon of Theotókos, she gestated the one who gave her being: Lula Inácio da Silva.

At Santuário Mãe de Deus things should have been running well in such a time of economic optimism, and yet the latter part of 2010 made it a year of crisis for Padre Marcelo. Revenues from the sales of his media productions had severely declined in the previous two years. The main roof of the sanctuary was nearly ready, and Andrade Gutierrez S.A., the sanctuary's contractor (which specializes in energy-related structures, like electric dams and off-shore oil platforms), wanted its money and guarantees of future payment. It had run out of patience with the increasing interruptions and the missing payments from the Associação Rosário Bizantino. But for Santuário Mãe de Deus (to which it provided basic foundations and the skeleton of the building) what this would mean was about to undergo a twist of fate. In a matter of months since it communicated to Associação Rosário Bizantino that it wanted to bring their contract to a halt, Andrade Gutierrez S.A. was among the names on a long list of operators whose heads, starting in the summer of 2014, would roll under the rhythmic guillotining of Operation Car Wash, Brazil's biggest ever—and still ongoing—corruption scandal.[7]

A turning point in Brazilian politics and economics, 2010 was also the year that the state oil company Petrobras peaked its expansion curve, since its founding in 1953, by attracting the largest share offering in history to be used in developing the newly discovered oil fields (named after Lula) in Campos Basin, Rio de Janeiro. The P-51 platform was built, a semi-submerged structure of portentous metal gridwork, a source of extractive energy and wealth. The new Petrobras platform, its marriage with building corporations and engineering, impacted the imaginary of Brazil as a BRIC nation under construction. Yet it also lent expressive vocabularies to the well-anointed aesthetics of submersed corruption and murky opacity on which calls for transparency regarding oil's business would be appropriated, for no less obscure ends. Brazil's 2010 path to election whirled around three key elements: oil imaginaries, expanding civil construction, and feminine leadership, all of which were handled with strict economic orthodoxy under the direction of a Chicago-trained bank executive in order to reassure markets.

For Padre Marcelo, Theotókos could synthetize all this and more. For one, she, a system of articulable relations, would connect immediate needs and distant contingencies, turning the temper tantrums of Andrade Gutierrez S.A.'s market plan, for example, into the mute sound of the future condemned. She would clear out a heavenly space in the whirlwind of corruption scandals that would sway Brazil starting in 2014 and continuing ad infinitum. Oil and unction would stem but from Spirit alone. Theotókos would be more femme than President Rousseff, the very one who encouraged transparency in investigating the Lava-Jato corruption, and in whose rigid style, televangelical governors found opportunity to repeat the *kick, kick, kick* and *thwack, thwack, thwack* operation brought twenty years earlier on the statue of Our Lady of Aparecida.

But unlike Our Lady of Aparecida, Theotókos would rise above it all through the persuasive powers of an exposed vulnerability; her openness to the uncertainty and rawness of materials would foster a redemptive demeanor among those who saw in such disinhibited incompletion a mark of translucence in such obscure times and in the disowning of calculative ends, signs of a divine design rather than human disorder. Linearity has never been part of her design, however, nor, as we known by now, is it intrinsic to pneumatic inspiration. In fact, according to the latter, the sacred must host within a margin of indeterminancy.

That same year, 2010, rumors were rife that Padre Marcelo and his association had been for quite some time secretly under investigation by the Congregatio Pro Doctrine Fidei, under the leadership of Cardinal Ratzinger. Those rumors included accusations of the usurpation of funds and criticisms of the padre's theological doctrine and shameless self-promotion, which had brought him close to being barred from celebrating Mass. These accusations had lingered since the death of Pope John Paul II in 2005 and were aggravated by Pope Benedict's refusal to receive Padre Marcelo, the biggest public figure in Catholicism in Latin America, during his visit to Brazil in 2007. There had been an enormous amount of media coverage given to that rebuff.

But it was not easy to silence Padre Marcelo. Whether or not the new pope liked him and whether or not his sanctuary was completed, the Catholic Church in Brazil—and in Rome—had to acknowledge that Padre Marcelo did bring back the flock.[8] As people put it, "Padre Marcelo rocked it." He transformed the local scene of devotion as well as the theological imaginary; one cannot say it enough. Called a heretic by some, a holy man by others, he nonetheless brought the element that defined the parameters of modern

Brazilian Catholic architecture: the crowds. Second only to the national basilica of Our Lady of Aparecida in size, the Santuário Mãe de Deus is a project whose scale could be justified only by the staggering number of its weekly visitors, who line up for hours to get a place in the front. This is a feature that has always characterized his celebrations, which is why already back in 2003, when the first ideas about building a sanctuary as a "temple from another world" were circulating, there was talk of a space whose walls would expand and contract in response to the number of visitors it had (de Abreu 2005). No one could tell exactly how this idea of responsive walls would materialize, in form or in budgetary terms; in truth, oftentimes the imaginative stakes of those rumors were impressive enough, as when people started to make anatomical comparisons between the sanctuary's future walls and lungs or between lungs and tents, or between those and the Amazon rainforest, all important items in Charismatic pneumatology in Brazil.

All this and the fact that Padre Marcelo had hired an architect whose renowned ultramodern ideas definitely polarized opinion at church headquarters. Later on, the concept of having mobile and adaptable walls underwent a transformation through time: first it focused on the doors as revolving transparent walls, then as gates that would never shut so people could follow the Mass from the outside, and finally the idea was to have no doors at all, just a cement arch on the three sides of the building from which the stage and fourth wall could be seen. The building was meant to communicate adaptability, the trained ability to let oneself go under the compulsion of spirit. And oil, as we have seen, was the currency that percolated throughout.

Yet such unrestrained borders, physical and imaginary, also created embarrassment in certain Catholic circles, which saw in such popularity a victory of the US-influenced style of megachurches and "electronic agoras" of Pentecostalism, such as Brazil's Universal Church of the Kingdom of God.[9] The idea that Catholics were losing territory to Pentecostals was often materialized in such templar megalomanias. For those who were (still) holding key positions in many dioceses in São Paulo as spokesmen of liberation theology ideals and of the workings of the ecclesiastic base communities, it was dispiriting to see Brazil's Catholic Church succumbing to those same parameters. Indeed the Pentecostal-like scale and aesthetics of the Santuário Mãe de Deus hindered support among non-Charismatic Catholics. Many in the clergy, despite the influential support of Bishop Figueiredo in the Santo Amaro diocese, saw in the architectural ambition of the project a mirror of Padre Marcelo's personal vanity, its incompletion a fitting end.

Over time, though, the church had to resign itself to the evidence. Impossible for the church to ignore were the thousands of churchgoers and pilgrims who came, and keep on coming, to celebrate in a church space that is not even finished. Rather than making an outward condemnation, the church had to find a compromise, a shift in emphasis from the possible resemblances between Padre Marcelo and Pentecostal logics to how to keep the crowds attuned to a Catholic perspective—if for no other reason than to include them in the statistics in the war against evangelical expansion. The Catholic Church would therefore have to make sure that the project of building the sanctuary did not stop completely. The institution was at an impasse.

But then in October 2010, just when the sanctuary seemed to be entering a more serious crisis in sustaining construction following the series of blows detailed earlier, Pope Benedict XVI, who had previously mobilized an investigation of the priest's conduct, awarded Padre Marcelo the Cardinal Van Thuan Prize for the distinctive category of "modern evangelist." It was a sudden shift and inconsistent with prior moments. Publicized and celebrated across the entire media spectrum in Brazil, Padre Marcelo once again ascended to reconstitute his image and the grace he has always claimed to have been endowed with. Having decisively beaten back any maleficence coming from the national headquarters of the church, which had accused him of being a self-centered soloist who cared little for communion, that same year he published *Ágape*, which has become the best-selling book in Brazilian history, with more than 7 million copies sold in just the first year.

In March 2010, Fabio Said Bittar, a devotee of Lebanese descent who often attended Padre Marcelo's celebrations, experienced a crisis. His wife was kidnapped and held hostage in exchange for a large ransom. Negotiations with the kidnappers went on for weeks. Bittar asked Padre Marcelo to address the kidnappers during the televised celebrations on TV Globo. After weeks of agony, the wife managed to escape on her own. This outcome, in the course of intense prayer, prompted Bittar—who was also the engineer and director of the São Paulo–based SOLIDI-Engenharia e Construções Ltd.—to take over the project of construction of Santuário Maria Mãe. Enter the engineer and devotee, the missing piece in a whirlpool of events and variables. Through the grace of the Holy Spirit he would align engineering to the metaphysics of a conception. He would link a place (*khôra*) to uterine bearing. "We move in sync with the possibilities of the sanctuary," Bittar would tell me when I visited him in his studios in the Bela Vista neighborhood of São Paulo in 2013. "Padre Marcelo contacts me and says, 'Fabio, we can proceed with that part of the sanctuary or that unfinished section, et cetera,' and we restart work. We continue or stop as Providence allows: a wall, a room, a step ahead, a step ahead, and so on." Such is the space-time I encountered during my visit in 2013. The denuded concrete, gigantic pipes, and fresh mortar felt musical, and with surprise I found in it a waft of tenderness.

Cut from the Same Cloth

The relations among territorial expansion, crowds, and mass media were integral to the development of the sanctuary. Padre Marcelo would be the operator placed at the exact intersection where Catholicism and Pentecostalism meet, the former in its love for Mary, the latter in its praise for the Holy Spirit. The result was to be centered in the Eastern Orthodox tradition of Theotókos, the tradition where Mary and Spirit were never at odds, as Protestants claimed, but were of the same cloth. As one anointed in Spirit, Padre Marcelo would bring together territory, crowds, and mass media into a fine arrangement, and in that he very much resembles an evangelical. But all that would be tendered to the powers of the mantle of Mary (o manto de Maria), she who is both "territory" and "event," both the space where the evangelical message was sown and its incarnated partaking; may the crowds of the sanctuary relate to an abode like a child to its mother's uterus. Padre Marcelo wanted to build a house as large and as celestial as the heavens. If limits imposed themselves, that was not necessarily bad. He, the inventor of "the aerobics of Jesus," could always bend limits into new extensions, the kind of challenge that was good for his adaptable elasticity and at which he is adept. If, indeed, the conditions of development could move no further, he could always choose to perform these. To perform conditions meant to come closer to the recursive qualities of Theotókos. It would mean that form (the sanctuary) would no longer follow life (matrix) but be life's own manifestation. And that was good.

A thought struck him (and then his bishop), like a connection that had always been there, though perhaps too close to be properly grasped. Father and novice would gather a theological corpus that made all impediments seem in mystical harmony with a divine plan. In agreement with the Spirit that had brought Padre Marcelo to this point, the sanctuary was never meant to be a pointing to a referent, never a representational entity or well-integrated whole, never something that, indexically speaking, would come to exist as simply *there*. Rather, to truly live up the temporality of the spirit of Mary, a house of prayer would have to do justice to the gerundive qualities of an ongoing gestation. It would admit to no circumscription but only to the infinite quality of articulations among entities. What was initially conceived as finite and linear would become inscribed in a structure of infinite middle, the circular ongoingness of a project of building up.

Such considerations would shape all Padre Marcelo's subsequent decisions in carrying out his plans to build a sanctuary, even with all the criticism from within and outside his own Catholic headquarters. Going forward and despite this upswing in fortune, Padre Marcelo would continue to adhere to the semantic edifice through which economic management can be thought not in referential but in performative terms. The sanctuary would not be built in the name of Theotókos; it would not be *dedicated to* the icon, for that would imply an exterior referent. Rather, the icon would be internal to its own operational logic, that is, both nonperspectival and self-reflexively Byzantine. This is to say, the icon would perform its own principle, its Theotókian soundness. To be Theotókos, as we have seen, means to be the manifestation of the cause that gives it (the icon as building) meaning. From 2010 onward the economy would be internal to the sanctuary's being, where each donation, each material contribution, each strike of the hammer, each turning on of the machines, each prayer, each testimony, each breath would partake in the space's gradual, very gradual, construction, its building up. In overlapping with itself, Theotókos regains a new dimension. It enacts the principle of an adaptable self-regulating recursivity as proper to its doctrinal concept (as mother of the one who gives her being).

Oikos: The Anatomy of a Building

Visitors to Santuário Mãe de Deus do not behave with the same kind of reverential attitude they might exhibit in traditional Catholic spaces. There is no saint by the door (or anywhere) toward whom they bow, make a promise, or pay in petition; no urn containing blessed water for ablution; and no center aisle leading to an altar. Roman principles of space organization have given way to emptiness. What people see instead are the raw materials used in the making of the building: the cranes, the scaffolds, the bricks, the cement, the sand and gravel. Materials and tools, however, are not there to be revered. They are not substitutes for religious images. Piled up in a corner of the sanctuary, they expose the relationship between a space and its procedures, its plasticity. Lay testimonies by those who, in one way or another, have contributed to the construction exemplify a reverence for this ongoing staging of disclosure. During celebrations, Padre Marcelo invites the builders, volunteers, engineers, donors, philanthropists, and politician facilitators to join him at the altar. He asks them to talk about their experience as collaborators in the "building of this house," to describe their contribution to the construction, what it has meant to them, and so on. Attendees thus learn about the trajectory of the sanctuary through its "operators" (*obreiros*) but also how their stories juxtapose, like a mosaic, to form a picture of Padre Marcelo's extraordinary journey since his appearance in the mid-1990s.

Padre Marcelo Rossi first started to celebrate in a small chapel adjacent to the diocese of Santo Amaro in southeastern São Paulo in the mid-1990s. Padre Marcelo and his bishop invested in rebuilding and redecorating the building, first named Nossa Senhora do Perpétuo Socorro (Our Lady of Perpetual Aid), proposing to rename it Chapel of Our Lady of Theotókos. The redecorating of the chapel was largely funded by the aforementioned Associação Rosário Bizantino. It was in this diocesan constituency that Padre Marcelo, under the guidance of his personal bishop, was initiated in the doctrinal teachings of patristic thought and of the Eastern Orthodox Church. Assimilating into itself the syntagmatic arrangement of Theotókos, an intensive tutorial ensued in light of the doctrinal and constitutive being of Mary.

Theologically speaking, Theotókos is a relational triumvirate where no one entity encloses the other. Its power relies precisely on abolishing from view any attempt by one element to enclose the other, so as to bring into sharp focus the principle of circulation that binds them. As an entanglement of entities, Theotókos proposes the logic of a functional whole whose parts articulate an *energia* that always exceeds the *ergon*, that is, of a being-at-work over any sense of a final product. The bishop–Padre Marcelo pair would not only become the reforming channels of the Byzantine in terms of a particular aesthetic of the image or style of prayer among the wider Catholic populations of Brazil, but would manage things according to a Theotókian treatise, the defining attribute of which is never put in terms of what it is but of how operations and life connect.

I spoke with Bishop Figueiredo in late May 2013, when protests were happening all around the city of São Paulo and other parts of Brazil. Meeting in the diocese, we discussed how opting for Theotókos as the model that guided much of the "community life" he entertained with Padre Marcelo was primarily a rejection of the authority of circumscription. In his view, Brazil's modern Catholicism had bequeathed to the secular the powers to define and separate in circumscribing the sacred from the nonsacred; it was imperative today, therefore, to summon up a more encompassing, universal "way of doing Church" (*um modo global de fazer igreja*). One of the tenets of Charismatic Catholicism he and Padre Marcelo endorse, he told me, is to show that such an ideology of separation "was never successful in Latin America, certainly not in Brazil," a place so drawn to spirituality. We then talked about Brazil's patron saint, Our Lady of Aparecida, as a holy referent to millions of Brazilians, an icon of the mother and nation that connected popular Catholicism to the secular sphere through the building of a vast sanctuary and basilica where she could be included. That brought us to the polemical moment back in 1995, when the image of Our Lady of Aparecida suffered a major blow.

Bishop Figueiredo disapproved of Pastor Von Helder's actions, calling them an "unreasonable act," distasteful and theatrical.

> BISHOP: What's in the mind of someone who sets out to break up a religious image on live TV, on a religious day. . . . It is to hurt. . . .
>
> MARIA JOSÉ: Hence the upheaval for days and weeks. . . .
>
> BISHOP: The gestures, the kicking, the crushing of the saint to fragments on the day thousands across Brazil adore, pray, make petitions. . . . It was senseless . . . foreign.

Having made clear his condemnation of the pastor's iconoclastic gesture, he proceeded to express how his theology of the image aligns him with the principle that three-dimensional statues, such as the one vilified, do in fact present a problem. For this reason, he and Padre Marcelo invested in redecorating the small chapel in the image of Theótokos, replacing three-dimensional images with flat glass. The bishop referred to statues (the kind that the chapel used to have prior to redecoration) as "too static" (meaning nonpneumatic), thus echoing Pastor Von Helder, who accused the image of Our Lady of Aparecida of being "unable to move." At stake in the bishop's understanding was the problem of circumscription posited by religious imagery in the Western tradition. Religious sculptures occupy a place in time and space that cannot do justice to the idea of an image animated by spirit, which ought to be rendered as nonstatic.

In Brazil, traditionally, Mary is beloved as the mother of Jesus, the loving and sacred channel out of which Christ appeared in the world. But the fathers of the church, Bishop Figueiredo explained, have also told us that there are other ways of thinking "the way of Mary" (*o caminho de Maria*).[10] In old patristic thought Mary is not a channel (*veículo*) through which Christ passes but "a shroud that extends to all" (*um manto que a tudo se estende*).

"She is a celestial body," he continued saying, guiding me to the adjacent chapel and showing the stained glass of Theotókos, through which it is possible
to "see through" and into its entire being. The bishop went on to describe
how in the stained-glass example of "the virgin of contact," a famous depic-
tion of Theotókos, this retreating of borders is operationalized in the graphic
architecture of the icon itself. He pointed out the qualities of the image by
which two bodies, mother and child, form one single entity. With no spatial discontinuity—or what we call "perspective"—existing between one and
the other, a circularity between mother as infrastructure and what she bears
is inscribed in the territorial surface of the glass. The image owes nothing to
representation. Rather, the icon is formed by the material of its being, the formal lines, the colors that graphically constitute her as a body through which
light passes in and out.[11] Each pictorial element in the composition of the
stained glass matters in its capacity to dictate the rules of a territory.[12]

The problem of physical limits posed by religious images is intrinsic to
the birth of Charismatic Catholicism in Brazil (de Abreu 2013a). In the early
years, Catholic Charismatics were willing to dispose of their religious images, arguing that these were in conflict with pneumatic flow. Charismatics questioned the nature of religious icons, particularly in their relations to
space and time. Padre Marcelo and Bishop Figueiredo expanded on this idea
by popularizing Byzantine iconography and Byzantine techniques of prayer,
as seen in chapter 4. Together, they introduced a reforming iconology that
was based on the logos of the icon itself. In doing so, these two major ex-
ponents of contemporary Charismatic Catholicism were able to consolidate
an alternative theory of the icon, one grounded in orthodox Christianity as
a way of reconciling Catholic Marianism and Pentecostalism. This master
synthesis of elements likewise mirrored the logics of a form of sovereign governance that would find maturation in the theatrical politics of the current
Bolsonaro era.[13]

Perceived as *oikos*, the building up of the sanctuary is no longer a mere
means or vehicle for the image. Rather, the icon is its own iconopraxis. The
entire field of incarnated operations constitutes it. Being is never fully there
other than in the form of an abstraction, that is, through the gestures and
materializations involved in the making of the space. The visitor to the Santuário Mãe de Deus must bring constant attention to the point where things
are *standing*, to the wavering edge where time clings. The temporality of the
sanctuary-cum-Theotókos, one could say, is the same as the logics of breaking
news: a room of real-time indefinite expectancy. This is also why Theotókos,

and not just Clare introduced in chapter 3, is so apt to think television, its rhythms of emergence, its structured indeterminacy. The icon of Theotókos becomes what it was always supposed to be in its immanent distending of a work in process, invisible as such but ubiquitously present through its manifold operations. If one does not see an icon in the sanctuary, it is because the icon is all around, and at labor—a Marian supra-masonic body. The icon admits to no exception, no shadow; it involves no perspective. It is flat, brutal, live, and pervasive in its process. It is the entire network of gestures, materials, narratives, events, and the boundless crowd, what allows one to see through and push further the edges of its ongoing making.[14]

Moved by pragmatism more than argumentation, Theotókos is a theology of doings. It is a bundle of operations, the prime function of which is not to represent nor to render present what is otherwise absent but rather *to give flesh to the desire to see*.[15] In Theotókian terms it is tantamount to a surrendering to the rawness of an operation: Operation Icon. This is why Padre Marcelo and Bishop Figueiredo can get away with having an icon within the sanctuary. In not being present, framed, the icon is closer to its theological function of making visible the divine principle *at work*. In existing only between the form of bricks and machines, cement and gravel, hammer and nail, the icon becomes a comment on the nature of the visible itself, the operations of incarnation involved in bodying forth a dwelling space.

The Chamber Burial

But then what rises also digs out a space. The future anterior that became intrinsic to the building-up quality of the sanctuary is perhaps nowhere better dramatized than in the idea of a chambered burial that is to be constructed underneath the sanctuary. It is in this space where Padre Marcelo, his bishop, and other members of the clergy of the Santo Amaro diocese will be buried. What is striking is that plans for constructing a crypt gained ample attention in the talk and prayers of churchgoers in 2013, a year after the official inauguration and opening of the (unfinished) Santuário Mãe de Deus in 2012, a period when it was clear that things would never be according to the initial plan proposed by Ohtake. By then the master modernist architect had little command over his own model, the Holy Spirit having taken the wheel. Acting "according to Theotókos," as Bishop Figueiredo put it to me, required just that. Letting the Holy Spirit take over.

But why did talk of the building of a large crypt, indeed of death and ends, become such an issue precisely at the moment that the future was being robbed of all perspective of an end? Could it be that the moment of its official inauguration as a *corpus ecclesia*, however unfinished (and obstinately called "the Sanctuary of Padre Marcelo" by churchgoers), also invigorated the presence of the institution of death, of sacrifice, and thus of the law of the Father? Or was it precisely because now that the Holy Spirit had taken control of things that the new plan as per Theotókos excluded all planning about the future, that death and ends could be freely evoked as realities that were always already part of an ongoing present? What is at stake here is a double abolishment, one that institutes a new logic of sovereignty: on the one side, the erasure of an origin personified in the architect and creator Ruy Ohtake and, on the other, the ending of ends. That is, it is the end of ends both in the sense of an original plan and in the sense of the end of death. There is no beginning and no eschatos, *only middle*, only circulation between entities.

That the catacombs will be built under the great stage where Padre Marcelo and his large crew of acolytes, musicians, and guest enthusiasts perform four times a week is worthy of comment. Padre Marcelo, much like the Cossack dancer in one of Franz Kafka's writings whose movement of the legs draws him deeper into the ground, eventually burying him, has been existing in a bipolar system (see the afterword). On the one hand, we have his belief that he can extract anything from spirit, from pneuma, from divine afflatus. He had done the unthinkable out of that conception, bringing millions back to the church in the time of its decline. But on the other hand, he had to exist under the shadow of the institutional, of the paternal organism that nominates pneuma yet must regulate, and at points stem, its direction. I am referring to Bishop Figueiredo, the Conferência Nacional dos Bispos do Brasil (CNBB; National Conference of Brazilian Bishops), and, at last, Rome. Where institutional control granted Padre Marcelo a sense of litigation, it also required a continual emptying of his authorial fate. After all, the Holy Spirit is *of* the church and of no one in particular. Yet this double bind only made his movements fluctuate more. He had to learn how to walk on and through that middle zone, to transform it into something of its own valence. He had to live up to it.

Except that to live up to it also meant living down to it. His movements — starting with the mechanical rhythms of expiration and inspiration — would reflect the necessity of balance: between up and down, charisma and institution, life and death, air and earth. Would all that swaying motion and energy in the name of spirit that sets Padre Marcelo from one project to the next, ever stretching, ever readjusting, become the motor or engine digging the catacomb beneath his feet, beneath the stage, beneath the coming to pass? As long as that oscillating movement persisted, the stage too could be articulated as an ongoing, shifting reality in which death or the end is no longer positioned at the end of time but is intrinsic to the cycle of breath, life, and prayer, and, finally, to indefinite labors of the uterine sanctuary. But what to make of this woman-like body that never stops gestating an all-encompassing indefinite? What is left of the feminine when its being has taken the whole of space? What of this *femme fetal* of the oxymoron who takes all space, even a crypt, so as to claim none of it for itself?

Infrastructure: Mater and Matter

Returning to the sanctuary in 2013 and then again in 2014, and then again in 2015, I lingered around the site, waiting to attend afternoon Mass. Individuals walked into the space and scattered across the area, like at a pop music concert. Padre Marcelo had put on a substantial amount of weight. Everybody was talking about it, remembering the times he had accused church members of being obese. He was older now and no longer the gymnasiarch of the earlier days. He had turned to calmer musical compositions and to meditation, counseling, and writing. Leaning against one of the columns, I noticed how the steel alloy scaffolding that supported the roof was horribly eaten by rust and recalled Ruy Ohtake's words; had he known it would take this long to install the plaster lining below the ceiling's metal structure, he would have opted for a stronger weatherproof metal.

The service was nearing the liturgy of the Eucharist. Acolytes entered the altar from backstage. One was holding the monstrance, another swinging a ball of incense. Padre Marcelo interacted with the community, making announcements about the administration of the sanctuary, a book he was writing, a forthcoming event, a particular person he would like to intercede for. He spoke:

> It may look like it stopped in time, but that is not the case. Look well with seeing eyes [*com olhos de ver*], hear well with hearing ears [*com ouvidos de ouvir*]. This temple grows like a plant [*planta*]. And if it is so with trees and things that spring out of the ground that you don't see growing, how much more is it so with the kingdom of God? This place, your house, is built in

the time of God . . . of kairos. What is kairos? The time of God, the time of grace. Our time. . . . I explain it all in my new book, *Kairos: Tempo de Deus*.

Padre Marcelo asked people to come to the sanctuary often so its growth would be less perceptible to them. "Only those who have *not* come here for a while," he added, "will detect how this house grew." To be familiar with the place, as though one lived there, was to become one with its growth. If one did not see improvement, it was neither a sign that the "house is not growing" nor was it because one did not "believe" enough but rather because one came often; by going there often, individuals would become one with the building's own anatomy. Thus, when the basket for the collection of alms circulated or when people made online contributions from home or work, offering money was an act that had to withdraw from the logic of exchange, as the counterpart for what one would see as a final product. Somehow the gaze had to withdraw from the perspective of the whole and enter the flesh of the icon of which the very gesture of giving, or any other gesture, was a part—and as a part it had to remain.

At the same time, such investment of the gaze only comes all the closer to what presumably demarcates itself: the market. Recall Padre Marcelo's pecuniary interpellation: "I explain it all in my new book, *Kairos: The Time of God*." According to the book, kairos is ruled by grace, not by rules of economy. Grace is anti-economics, which shows how *oikonomia*, the operational laws of the icon, and modern economics have moved far apart. Grace, Padre Marcelo and his mother, and Bishop Figueiredo (father) are the mantle of Mary touching all that exists. She supports all. This is demonstrated by the image of women walking around the sanctuary using their bodies as supports for billboards. These marketers publicize Padre Marcelo's new book on kairos, named after the god of qualitative time (as opposed to Kronos's quantitative time). It is a bizarre scene and yet not entirely incongruent with the idea of a gendered infrastructure that both shows and is a dispenser of things.

Walter Benjamin once wrote of the human billboard or "sandwichman" as among the last reincarnations of the flâneur. As Benjamin saw it capitalism entails two ways of dealing with leisure: the figures of the poor and the unemployed and that of the person who explores his loitering. The flâneur, as Benjamin notes, falls in the latter category (see Benjamin 1997, 1998a). By comparing the flâneur, whose idle walk through the arcades embodied the bourgeois consumer culture of Europe, to that which it least resembled, the clochard and the unemployed who worked as human advertisements, Benjamin aimed at prodding a revolutionary moment through the kind of jolting that produces shock. These worlds in tension expose the infrastructure, the jolt in the movement of the machine behind the surface of appearance. The dialectical image constitutes the scene of a certain temporal rupture. It is not a scene organized as progression but as cut and break: fissure.

Yet the women at Santuário Mãe de Deus whose bodies became the infrastructural support for advertisement share little with the revolutionary horizon evoked by such an idea. The kairological apertures in place have become internal to the logic of capital that unfolds through—rather than being disrupted by—jolt and rupture. With that same thought in mind, I looked at the floor and contemplated the cracks in the cement reminding me of Benjamin's gap through which the messiah could enter. The athletic character of late capitalism, in its capacity to foster redemptive opportunities out of critical scenarios, blasted through the cracks. But there was a perverse twist to Benjamin's redemptive gap out of the rubble of history, one that calls on the suspension of the power of shock, dissonance, and the unexpected in its capacity to generate visceral responses that halt the progress of linear history.

In the late 1990s the sociologist Susan Leigh Star (1999: 375) defined infrastructure as "matter that enables other matter." A feminist and a scholar of infrastructural systems, Star made the important claim for researchers to pay attention to the "system of substrates": the often-invisible underworld of infrastructure. As she writes: "Study a city and neglect its sewers and power supplies and you miss essential aspects of distributional justice and planning power" (379). Star's equation of the feminine and infrastructure—an invisible background—inspired a generation of feminist scholars to think about gender through visibility. It is the idea that our (feminist) critical function is to expose what lies beneath and underneath, as infrastructure. And yet this expectation fails to understand how the protocols of critique themselves have changed. Emancipation through exposure made sense in its modernist guise when the figure of opacity was the horizon of critique. But precisely to understand how power works today is to understand that critique's horizon is no longer opacity but conspicuous transparency. This is the cynicism embedded in an aesthetics of *béton brut* today. Not cynicism in the sense of an incongruence of the subject between inside and outside. That is precisely what it is not. Rather it is cynicism in the sense of a caustic reagent that makes things apparent by bringing all to the surface, thereby inhibiting our political ability to mobilize critique according to older protocols. The "cynical reason" for transparency, to use Peter Sloterdijk's (1987) expression, is then in how an economy of exposed materials itself produces opacity. Moreover, it does so not just by simply replacing opacity for transparency but, more problematically, by reconfiguring that relation into an undecidable tone of a chiaroscuro. The problem of transparency—and thus the question of infrastructure—is then what needs to be urgently recognized in the task of redefining the protocols of feminist critique in particular and of modern critique in general.[16]

Accordingly, far from repressed the realities that underlie the built phenomena at Santuário Mãe de Deus are laid bare as part of *both* its economy of display *and* the displaying of its economy. As far as the administration of the sanctuary goes, a continuum exists and must persist between the conditions of possibility and the phenomena to which such conditions give rise. Material form is inseparable from what is at stake in imaginary terms; the plastic elements must share in the same formula that constitutes the philosophy of the icon. What is experienced is the material economy of the *oikos*, whose applied principle is the fluid doctrine of the icon. Theotókos is enabling matter. She is at once *mater* and *matter*. The image of feminine space is explored in Theotókos to the maximum but only to reinforce the substrate of a power that women hardly share.

End of Exception: Summary

Over the past two decades, Catholic thought in Brazil has adapted to vast changes in media and socioeconomic conditions. Against the background of structural changes in the iconic fundamentals of an increasingly technological and mediatized nation, this chapter addressed the economic strategy behind the (still) ongoing (if vastly transformed in new and unexpected directions) construction of a megasanctuary in São Paulo. I have shown how a suspension in claims to economic totality found resources within the theological domain. Forced to interrupt the construction of the sanctuary due to a lack of capital and trust, Padre Marcelo turned his attention to the mechanisms through which to think circulation itself. In doing so, he turned the traditional claims of interruption inside out. This chapter framed the stakes of such operational logics involved in the making of a religious building. For Charismatics it is intrinsic to the form of labor that Santuário Mãe de Deus erases the very entity it promotes. This implies that neither space nor time be framed as finite and containable. There is only the being of an ongoing labor.

We learn from classic politico-theology that the space of exception presumes a transcendental outside, the point from which sovereign decision can be formulated. But if that classic formulation of the politico-theological is our point of departure in studying the particular case of Santuário Mãe de Deus—or that of Brazil's current political moment—we would have to say (at the least) that the rules of exception are going through a displacement.[17] What is involved in this chapter is how the feminine body becomes the infrastructure that gives the paradoxical status of ubiquity to the exception. Doctrinally speaking, if there is one imperative about the Byzantine, it is precisely its nonadmittance of exception. This is because exception would imply perspective, and perspective would imply shadow, which would imply an existing parallel world to a representation.

In the Byzantine aesthetic, no exception is allowed. However to say that it is not allowed does not mean it is not relevant. It can also mean that exception coincides entirely with (and, indeed, has become) the rule; that exception and rule are in sync; that exception is one with the rhythm of its operations. As matrix for the architectonic project, Theotókos makes exception coincident with its entire being. As rumors of what would become a massive corruption scandal involving major local and global corporate construction companies and Petrobras were coursing through the corporate windpipes, it became important for the supervisors of this project that she, the icon, expose her absolute malleability. May the throng walk into this massive sacred space and find the countenance of the Mother of God in the abstract expressions of concrete and formwork. Let the crowds not see the bare state of her being as vexing but rather as what highlights her elastic potential. Still *em andamento* in 2020, Santuário Mãe de Deus calls attention to that long-forsaken yet vital space of the feminine—to the dense foliage of tubes and pipes, mortar, brick and shovel—only to reduce it again to the mere abstraction of a dynamic and reproductive force at work. Theotókos is a phantom-like recurrence made to be everywhere, *extremely in the middle*, so as to disallow her any visibility. That is why, however packed with crowds, however filled the space of the sanctuary is on a normal day of Mass service, it will always still look hollow and vacant.[18]

Addendum

White against white was how the architect Ohtake first envisioned the altar. The white cross at the center, a few inches away from a second curved wall in a slightly oblique position, would transmit a sense of movement and infinity. The reference to Kazimir Malevich's (1918) Suprematist composition

White on White is evident in Ohtake's model: it dispenses with features of representational art like depth, boundaries, and color, and opts instead for a monochromatic slanted geometrical shape. These features, however, never materialized in the building. By the time of its official opening to the public in November 2012, the building was a gray, granular concrete shell of gargantuan proportions. The inauguration took place within crudely cemented walls. On the unpainted cement floor there were a number of white monobloc chairs reserved for the clergy and guests. Electric light replaced the absence of color. "To have the altar illuminated," the technician informed me, "we had to bring a diesel-running 300 KVA [kilovolt-ampere] generator that could be pushed up to 500 voltage." Plenty of plants and flowers. A crimson carpet on the altar marked the center of solemnity. This was aligned with another red carpet, stretching from the ground all the way to a tower located in the middle of the sanctuary, on top of which a cameraperson would oversee the live televising of the event to all Brazil. There were no religious images in the sanctuary, only the clergy, the politicians, and the artists with whom Padre Marcelo and his bishop, the shadow (or he who brings perspective), collaborated in the past, and finally the people, a large standing throng arriving from all over Brazil.

This unconventional order of things had its limits. Padre Marcelo could not continue to appear on national TV as the country's representative leader of Sunday Mass against a gray wall. Nor would the original plan quite work, for a white cross against a white wall would make it look too much like a Protestant Pentecostal church. That was not good for the Catholic Church, nor for mainstream TV Globo, which broadcast Padre Marcelo's Masses. In 2015 an Italian painter named Paolo Maiani arrived on the scene. He had traveled from Rome to give an icon to the Santuário Mãe de Deus. On Rome's recommendation, it was agreed that Maiani would paint a fresco altarpiece, thus interrupting the warehouse aesthetic.

Maiani was asked to paint the figures of the virgin and child at the horizon of the TV cameras, at the center of the sanctuary and slightly above it. Painted on the concave polished stone located in the rear of the nave, Mary holds the child in her left arm while rising up out of a tower of angels. The figure is a variation of Theotókos, a motif painted in the style of neo-Italian realism. Pastel tones of amber, yellow, rose, brown, and aqueous blue are predominant. A dense atmosphere surrounds mother and child within a layered blending of hue. Unlike the still life of the Byzantine icon, where the event of perception is created through the encounter between viewer and painting (for, as we saw in chapter 3, it is a feature of the Byzantine sensibility to turn the viewer into the image producer), Maiani's fresco offers a perspectival representation. Mary and child are depicted with the blasting force of a sudden appearance around which angels, clouds, and light revolve jubilantly at the miracle of an ascension. Likewise departing from the convention of the half-lengthened body of Mary in Byzantine icons, the icon is a whole-bodied figure. She is dressed in a shroud of azurite and gold over a white and crimson tunic. Her left arm holds the child against her chest, while the child's right arm is open, intersecting her upper body. Yet Maiani also references the intimate contact and slightly diagonal dispositions of Theotókos, notably, between the right shoulder and neck of Mary and the neck and cheek of Jesus. These points of contact through the interposition of bodies and draperies are theologically substantive, asserting the noncircumscriptive if incisive contiguity between two bodies, whereby one cannot tell who contains whom, where one body commences and the other ends. There ought to be absolutely no separation between the two anatomical references, for one constantly recreates the other, infinitely.

Maiani's fresco is of a piece with the typical mannerist scenario of contexts of transition and compromise, where instability, tension, and undecidability are thematized through recourse to exaggerated and elongated forms. This happens to the degree that the style spans into a composite baroque dramaturgy, all embraced by the TV cameras. Byzantine art, too, was a style accommodating compromise and tension, but it was one in which it was paramount that the visible not be confused with the divine prototype (Mondzain 2005; Elsner 2012). To do so would be an act of idolatry. But this idea was superseded by demands for a new naturalism of the image in Renaissance Europe. The desire to make art as a vivid evocation of reality, where the relation between seeing and believing can be optimally staged and where lines and materials partake in the making of presence through symbolization and circumscription, was among the factors that led to a schism between Eastern and Western representations of the icon.

But now the long corridor marking the space of tension between those two currents meets a third draft, that of electronic (and later digital) media, to form a new synthesis. How will this synthesis take place in light of all the doctrinal demands, economic constraints, and corruption scandals firing from all sides, at the very moment that orange pigments stain the walls of Padre Marcelo's sanctuary? And so here is how Padre Marcelo and his constituency will act: wherever there is wall, there will be paint. From one side to the other, including the recessed areas that frame and enclose the world of the virgin and child within the borders of its being, there will be a scene, simply painted, as an extension of that sacred bond. In this way icon and space, sovereign and territory, will again coincide—no longer through gray exposed cement but, as in the profusion of an internal bleeding, as a true explosion of color.

6. GHOST CHAIR

....

By the two main entrances to the Santuário Mãe de Deus, stacks of white monobloc chairs are clustered. Once all the chairs inside the sanctuary—a gigantic shell of 30,000 square meters—have been occupied, visitors remove a chair from the pile, take it inside, and align it with other chairs facing the altar. The chairs are arranged as a series of rows in a crisscross pattern that divides the sanctuary's massive floor surface into twelve to fifteen main blocks, each holding about two hundred chairs. The sight of thousands of empty bleached chairs, prior to the arrival of the crowds, brings to mind the pattern of replicative textures, as in the swarming of microorganisms, the stuff of rumor, the airborne. With a seat area measuring 16 by 18 inches and at 35 inches high, the white plastic chair gets easily overtaken by the life that sits on it. Like an adaptable structure, the chair draws expression from the sitter and thus underlines the event of seating as such.

Monobloc chairs have a prominent presence in evangelical church spaces in Brazil and across the world. The banal quality of the chair, its ubiquity, and its plasticity all seem to underline the aesthetics of global adaptability associated with Pentecostal evangelicalism.[1] The command to facilitate the flow of spirit has entered the logics of the design of sermons, spaces, and objects among Catholic Charismatics. This preference stands in contrast to traditional Catholic design conventions, wherein gravity and solemnity are valued as means of anchoring the divine on earth and as modes of expressing authority and tradition.

However, Catholic Charismatics are both Pentecostal and Catholic. As mentioned, before it came to be called the Catholic Charismatic Renewal, the movement went by the ecumenical name of Catholic Pentecostalism. This structural ambivalence has, among other things, pressed this revivalist movement to constantly negotiate the doctrinal, aesthetic, and political demands associated with both of these traditions and, especially, with the conflicts between them. Within the Charismatic movement, what complicates this delicate negotiation is how a conflict between the traditional hierarchy and lay power has absorbed existing discourses between mainstream Catholicism and Protestantism or Pentecostalism. In their critique of the hierarchy, lay Catholics, especially those who are strongly involved in the Charismatic movement, take refuge in the Holy Spirit. In so doing they also explore vocabularies that were made available by the Protestant tradition in its long resistance to Catholicism. In addition to this substratum, nonconformed Catholics also allude to the folk structures that during the premodern era organized lay power as less mediated by the hierarchy. Historically speaking, then, the Holy Spirit emerges as a complex network that operates at once with and against the church, pulled and pushed from all sides to expose, above all, its capacity to stretch in opposite directions, like some amorphous substance. What unites all the parts in the conflict is the sharing of the common refrain according to which the Holy Spirit is on the side of the "members," a term that, as we have seen previously, connotes laypeople as corpus.

Padre Marcelo Rossi, who is sometimes accused of measuring the elasticity of his congregation by his own body, has expressed the opinion that when one sits one obstructs the *unção* (a mix of motion and unction) of the Holy Spirit. He has long criticized, more through his acts than through his words, the inertia and even obesity that he thinks hinders Roman Catholicism. He sees the act of sitting as a form of subjugating the members and not just those at the bottom of the hierarchy. The hierarchy, which necessarily lends legitimacy to his activities, wants to sit down. Indeed, it needs to sit down in order to stage its higher status. But how did such a counterintuitive propriety influence the decision to propose the monobloc chair as a solution to circumvent the subjection of the members? How is the chair able to accommodate such tensions between orders of gravity? In this chapter I analyze the material politics of the monobloc chair in the sanctuary of Padre Marcelo. I concentrate on the articulation of two material qualifiers: containment and gravity. One central line of argumentation in chapter 5—and throughout this book—is how to think the relation between formations, like body and space, outside a more logocentric logic of containment. In this chapter I expand on this with an analysis of the presence and uses of the monobloc chair in the political economy of the sanctuary. If it is true, as I argue in chapter 5, that Santuário Theotókos Mãe de Deus defies containment, how should one proceed in conceptualizing the people and the objects that occupy it for purposes of ritual (Tambiah 1981)?

More than thirty years ago anthropologist Marilyn Strathern (1987) showed how the problem of containment is essentially a problem of context. To put things in context, she argued, is to define the boundaries of a particular setting or situation in order to further inquire about its analytical worth. As some scholars see it, context is what endows a social reality with particularity and, therefore, makes it amenable to comparison. The counter to this view proposes that the worldwide movement of things encompasses processes of decontextualization, which implies that globalization takes things out of their context even as it elicits new ideological and empirical formations about the local. But what happens if the semiotic makeup of the object in question itself defies containment? What if, to twist Burt Bacharach and Hal David's song message, "A chair is not a chair even though there is someone sitting there"?

The monobloc chair is, uncontestably, an icon of globalization. Artists and amateur designers have turned the adaptable plasticity of this object into one of its defining features. But my purpose is not to debate the local and global conceptual implications through the spatiotemporal trajectories of a particular object. Rather, I draw on an object that incorporates in the empirical material itself the status of being context-free. Most chairs tend to be context-specific and authorized, and they often are named for their designers. The monobloc chair, on the contrary, exists in anonymity. As in the orphan cinema movement, this chair contradicts the long tradition of authorship of this kind of object in design history. Instead the monobloc chair is named after its own technical procedure: a molded single piece of polypropylene plastic. What interests me about this aspect of the chair's orphanhood is how it opens up this object to be the sign of circulation of the crowds that come to the sanctuary of Padre Marcelo. The material qualities of the chair—its lightness, portability, and stackability—allow for the constant rearrangement and reassembling of the crowds and the logistic potentials of space.

Those very attributes, however, also create contradictions. If, on the one hand, Padre Marcelo can regulate the crowds by setting up and having available a specific number of chairs, on the other hand, the very portability of the chair poses the possibility of deregulation. Further, if the presence of the chairs pleases those who long condemned Padre Marcelo for forcing people to stand (and move), the association of the monobloc chair with Pentecostal spaces also introduces new pressures for him to convey that the Santuário Mãe de Deus is in fact Catholic and not Protestant or Pentecostal. The chair signifier thus moves in the sanctuary according to these different forces, and ultimately it is because of the chair's inbuilt portability that such tensions are allowed to play out. What follows is an attempt to articulate how that unfolds among Catholic Charismatics in São Paulo.

All Saints' Day

On the afternoon of All Saints' Day in 2013, Padre Marcelo and his bishop celebrated a special Mass at Santuário Mãe de Deus, and several high dignitaries of the church of Brazil and other parts of Latin America were invited to attend. With rumors flying that Padre Marcelo was bankrupt, that he would never be able to pay for the massive construction he had initiated five years before, and that, following the death of John Paul II, he was being ostracized by the hierarchy, the Mass celebration on that date was crafted to have as much impact as possible among the wider population. Helping this effort was the fact that TV Globo, Brazil's chief international network, was providing weekly coverage of his Masses, which, continued to be among the most popular in all Brazil. In 2013 the sanctuary still received an average of fifty thousand people per week, which was three times more than any other Catholic space in Brazil could claim on a regular basis. But the fact that people insisted on referring to the sanctuary not by its official name but as "Santuário do Padre Marcelo" was a point of contention among the church hierarchy, which evoked the axiom that Catholicism has never been a one-man show but a community endeavor. This concern was also associated with the fact that Padre Marcelo often invited to his Masses guests who were celebrities rather than church representatives.

This All Saints' celebration would therefore be a way to soothe the impatient cry by the church that he be a proper Catholic and convey the proper message to the cameras, to his community, and to the world. To deliver on this, Padre Marcelo and his spiritual counselor, Bishop Fernando Figueiredo, worked on preparing the celebrations. Their goal was to observe the traditional conventions of the Catholic ritual while acknowledging the exceptionality of All Saints' Day, when people remember the dead through prayer and with candles and reflect on the future. If everything went according to plan, there would be thirty-eight bishops and cardinals from all around Brazil, Argentina, and Chile in attendance.

The large crowd had already mostly taken seats according to the geometrical arrangement of the chairs. The white seats had been placed and aligned by volunteers, many of whom came to the sanctuary on a weekly basis to help with logistics. Five of the bishops would be seated on the raised altar, but most of them would occupy the first two central rows facing the altar. These two main rows would form a belt of bishops, who would then be backed by other renowned clergy, nuns, and novices. In the middle of the sanctuary, though, were a large number of empty chairs, oddly positioned, and a group of volunteers closely guarding them so that no unauthorized person would sit there. It was clear that those chairs would have a more auspicious function that day.

In an effort to acknowledge the presence of the dignitaries, Padre Marcelo had the bishops enter during the initial procession, by which time the sanctuary was already crowded with congregants, many of them pilgrims. As the bishops went to sit according to their order in the line, attention was drawn to the fact that there was one bishop too many and that an extra chair was needed. A young nun hastened to offer her own chair, and she in turn was offered a chair by a layperson behind her. Seeing the agitation, a volunteer approached with two more chairs and placed them next to the bishop who had been last in line. Apparently two bishops were yet to arrive. But no one took those seats, and throughout the ceremony, the two chairs remained empty. These chairs, however, remained under the attentive eye of volunteers, lest any layperson attempt to occupy one of them.

None of this would be worth much attention except that Padre Marcelo had long resisted having chairs in the sanctuary at all. In fact one of the reasons he had left his former chapel was the impact of its design on the stillness of the churchgoers. As he saw it, the long, parallel cedar benches were particularly constricting of the body's movement. Sitting contradicted his valuing of the vertical body, the body that rehearses its kinetic capabilities. Moreover it affirmed the existence of an exterior object to which bodies accommodate rather than embracing the body's capacity to generate space. Another problem with the benches was that they helped predetermine the crowd's number. They aligned the people according to the benches' size. The benches determined the finite, restricted nature of bodies and of the space itself. In that, they reintroduced the kind of corporeal individuation Padre Marcelo wished to overcome. Through the songs he composed, he imagined a rhythm where people could loftily take the weight off their feet not by taking a seat but by lifting each foot from the ground. For more key than lifting one's foot is to expose *how* gravity is challenged.

As more people kept coming over the years, attracted by his celebrations, the more accustomed he grew to the idea that, in the measure of the possible, he must not predetermine the limits of his crowd. If he embraced the media with all his might back in the 1990s, it was in view of this repudiation of all framing. The emptier the space, the clearer the role of the practice in building up. By not having a specific number of seats in the new sanctuary, Padre Marcelo could potentialize his crowd, his followers rendered always already in terms of those who might yet arrive. The potential crowd, or as Padre Marcelo put it, the "buoyant crowd [*galera animada*]," is the best definition of the crowd at Santuário Mãe de Deus. His audience is a crowd in which there can be concordance between the prospective and the actual number, much like in the womb of Theotókos, described in chapter 5, the child in there is not one singular being but a network of relations, an apparatus.

Padre Marcelo's relation to the crowd recalls Elias Canetti's (1960: 22) notion of "the open crowd," which, as he writes, "wants to feel the sensation of its own growth again." Canetti's reference to St. Paul as the exemplary leader of the open crowd—in opposition to St. Peter as leader of the "closed crowd"—attests to this description; Padre Marcelo often invokes Paul's Areopagus Sermon as the ideal logistical scheme since it is directed against the limiting ceremoniousness of the official temple.[2] The crowd he aspires to construct and coach resembles Canetti's "rhythmic crowd," which, insofar as it is constituted primarily through rhythm, communicates a certain blurring of contours, a trembling of the edges. As I described in chapter 4, some of Padre Marcelo's composition or reinterpretation of songs draws on the mantra-like structure of the Byzantine rosary. The repetitive and heartbeat-like rhythm of the rosary enables songs to be adapted to electronic sound remixes. The Prayer of the Heart, as Padre Marcelo refers to his musical adaptation of the Byzantine rosary, allows him to abstract a rhythm that tunes in to, while honing, the body's mechanical elasticity. His ideal crowd is constituted both as and through rhythm. Using techniques of prayer and song, he draws a pulsation. The beat aligns bodies to a common pounding or motion, a punctuation, that aspires to blur the edges of otherwise discrete presences.

However, as I have argued, this reduction of the crowd to a rhythm is hard to maintain. This is especially so because his recruiting from repertoires of popular culture, in the very moment it introduces alternative techniques such as the Byzantine rosary, also reactivates elements from popular Catholicism. If, on the one hand, his rhythmic compositions favor a kind of abstracted anonymity, on the other, the very success with which he accomplishes this also makes him quite popular. Paradoxically, the rhythms that ought to disavow singularity for a common beat also turn him into a leader—even a saint or patron—and reconnect him to old logics of popular sanctity. Thus, while churchgoers bring their rosary beads to the sanctuary so as to attune the beat of their heart to prayer, they also bring personal belongings, like photos of their kin, driver's licenses, and employment cards. His role is therefore one of constantly working on the balance between abstraction and concrete existence. He pulls things one way in the hope that in so doing their opposites will also appear.

Now that thousands of monobloc chairs have convened in the sanctuary, Padre Marcelo has had to erect a bridge between his personal stylistic wants and those of the hierarchy. He has resigned himself to the idea of having chairs in the sanctuary. Yet as became clear on that particular All Saints' Day, his mode of resignation also inspires in him a certain theatricality or staging of sorts, as though to declare that he, again, is in control of things at the sanctuary, even those things he would rather not include. The guarded, empty, and oddly arranged white monobloc chairs in the middle of the sanctuary were an example of such an acting through opposites. Shortly after the opening of the ritual, a group of young novices and deacons dressed in immaculate white vests came from behind the altar, descended the long cement zigzagging ramp, and crossed the sanctuary to the strategically positioned empty chairs. Following the herd of neophytes, who moved in line across the space accompanied by electrified solemn hymns, the congregants indulged in a kind of medieval popular dramaturgy of the Last Judgment of deceased souls.

The motif of the parade of souls in popular Catholicism, which is characteristic of All Saints' Day (when the torments of hell are compared to and overcome by the joy of eternal paradise), was integrated into a performance that chose violence as its referent, notably the memory of the brutality that many in Brazil suffer every year. This became evident as the coiled movement of the procession's celestial corpus, like angels bearing the deceased's souls up to heaven, occupied their assigned seats. Sitting down in a particular order, the novices' distinctive white clothing illuminated a literary scheme according to a relation of signification in space and time. They formed a pattern that made legible the three capital letters of the word *paz* (peace). Sitting in relation to each other, their bodies became calligraphic. Their figures bestowed semantic order on an otherwise abstract, disordered agglomerate of chairs. Through a sitting that wrote, the novices' bodies exceeded their own individuality. Who ever doubted that writing is a bodily craft?

Seated bodies became signs for a provisional inscription. As markers, the novices related to the chairs the way a pen relates to paper. Their literary marking in space absorbed the conditions facilitated by the chairs' support: white on white. Still, the chairs went beyond the function often attributed to paper as a simple support or inert surface. It was precisely because Padre Marcelo did not consider the chairs to be neutral matter in the building that he set out to involve them in a theatrical scene of legibility. In other words, the chairs were not mere physical supports; they did not simply exist under their occupants like some inert surface. By partaking in the operation of writing PAZ, the chairs subverted the conventional power of such an object to circumscribe, becoming instead a technology of inscription. Only those looking from the stage or those watching at home on television could decipher the words, and Padre Marcelo added his voice to the choreography so the congregation would know: "Angels of peace"—that is what the novices were. And like a wave that erases in view of future inscriptions, a massive applause ran through the place.[3]

What mattered most, this time around, was to curb critical talk amid the skeptical clergy. While, partly, the sanctuary had started to include seating to accommodate the clergy, the chairs also proffered new possibilities to address the body as a candidate for sitting. One option was to form a continuum between chair and sitter, support and body, so that the chair—in becoming an extension of the action of the sitter—entered the materiality of that action and function. The novices were not just sitting on chairs, thus allowing the sign to impose its will on the thing. Rather their sitting itself deliberately brought up a new system of signs, at least to those who were able to read through the white inscription of its being.

For some, including me, there was a tinge of comedy at the sight of cardinals, bishops, archbishops, and other Latin rite patriarchs—those Canetti (1960: 183) describes as "the temporal lament mummified"—adorned in their heavy cassocks, scarlet silk rabats, crosses, miters, and other official regalia, sitting on plastic chairs. The deceptive, even ghostly appearance of the chairs under such patrician occupants was a topic of some wayward talk in the cantina after the celebration and also in the car of the female congregants who offered me a ride to the city center. The humorous reactions of the women followed on the heels of a disproportionate amount of debate, as they recalled it, about which chair Pope John Paul II would sit in during his last visit to Brazil in 1997, the third during his mandate. Speculations in the public domain as to which designer, which carpenter, which materials would accommodate the Holy Seat back then offered the terms of the problem of how and where to seat the hierarchy in the space organized by Padre Marcelo. "Tradition is a springboard to the future, not a footstool for resting," said the driver of the van proverbially, prompting all the more laughter among those present.

The classic linguistic question, as in Bacharach and David's famous song "A House Is Not a Home," about whether a chair is still a chair even though no one is sitting there, may give a hint as to whether a chair is still a chair despite someone sitting there (see Van den Hoven 2013). However inadvertently, Padre Marcelo had highlighted the flexible qualities of the chair, not only its actual materiality but its transformability: its plasticity. Canetti's (1960) thoughts on sitting, for example, evolve from an image of the chair as an object that is rigid, an object that intrinsically exerts pressure on the world. His model is the king's throne or the soft but heavy upholstered chair, which are sites of the exertion and maintenance of power. ("The dignity of sitting is a dignity of duration" [452].) Canetti writes:

> When a man sits it is physical weight, which he displays, and if this is to make its full effect, he needs to sit on something raised above the ground. In relation to the legs of a chair he actually is heavy. If he sat on the ground (or stood for that matter) he would make an entirely different impression, for the earth is so much heavier and more solid than any of its creatures that the pressure they exert is insignificant in comparison. The simplest form of power is either in terms of height—in which case he must stand—or in terms of weight—in which case he must exert visible pressure. (453)

If it were up to Padre Marcelo, power would stand, not sit. As it is, however, he must make way for a certain gravity, a certain weight, that will function as the hierarchy's positive endorsement of his style and space of celebration.

On All Saints' Day anxieties ran high among churchgoers and volunteers, an apprehension that the presence of the hierarchy, sitting there in all solemnity, would affect the agile elasticities of spirit that Padre Marcelo had made himself famous for, not least through his uniquely popular aerobics of Jesus. There was an incongruence between the rigid squad of clergy in the front and the calisthenics members in the back, between the well-defined figures at the altar and the irregular, open-ended, and sometimes closely crushed adherents at the rear of the building. But at least to some degree Padre Marcelo was able to expose the manageability of the chairs beyond their proper function. He could move them in space and rearrange them. He could show them to be chair and antichair at the same time, to be a ghost chair.

As Chairs Kept on Arriving . . .

It was around 2005 when the monobloc chairs "began to arrive out of no-where" at the sanctuary, said a volunteer, who stood with three other women. "The first chairs were just there, like if the wind dragged them . . . and those stayed and more kept arriving [*foram ficando, mais chegando*]." This was Padre Marcelo's second sanctuary since he had left his small parish in Santo Amaro. "A wanting for chairs," the volunteer noted, "came from the people too." She continued, "First, people began to bring camping chairs with them and sit in the outer ring of the crowd, next to the wall. But because [most people] would be standing up while praising, they were not able to see anything. So the administration of the sanctuary, with the permission of Padre Marcelo, ordered a [large] amount of chairs and established that only those who needed them [elders, children, disabled people] would sit in the front rows with other special guests." That year in early April, Pope John Paul II passed away, and for a while this tamed the normal vivacity and stamina of the masses. As previously discussed, the pope had been an enthusiastic supporter of Padre Marcelo, and rumors had it that the next pope would be less favorable to the verve and dynamism he offered. That fear found a correlate in the worry that the introduction of chairs would substantially change the comportment the padre had long fought to instill among his congregants. People were concerned that the chairs would interfere in the rhythm he sought in prayer, song, and dance and therefore affect everyone's motivation to engage corporeally in the mass. In sum, the fear was that the center of gravity would no longer be in the echoes of sound and song but in the axis that connects the sacred to the ground, where power is traditionally deployed.

Ironically, the first chairs started to arrive at the sanctuary not as a result of pressure from the hierarchy but due to the fame of Padre Marcelo. To this day some churchgoers line up outside the sanctuary starting as early as four in the morning. Dozens of others spend the night there, wrapped in sleeping bags, waiting for the big outer gates to open at around 5:15 A.M. But people also brought chairs. Mostly these were light and foldable, which, given that the celebration lasted between two and three hours, sometimes on scorching hot days, were helpful. Workers at the sanctuary, however, discouraged them, asking congregants who wished to sit to retreat into the cafeteria or go outside. In time a discourse on fatigue and endurance began to take form. The effort to come early and wait entitled some to see sitting as more than just a privilege. Gradually the front rows were strictly occupied not only by those "specially in need" but by the hierarchy of the church. Behind these first rows were a few other rows for special guests, such as nuns and friars from various orders but also celebrities and politicians. And behind these sitting dignitaries and personalities was the standing congregation, which regularly could add up to thirty thousand people. Padre Marcelo feared that once a few chairs were allowed for those people, it would be difficult to reverse the process. The chairs would attract more chairs, and still more would come, virus-like. Chairs would introduce a ranking within the realm of the assembly that could be balanced only by more seats. To curtail this, Padre Marcelo bought wooden benches and placed them on the large altar so the hierarchy, inclined to querulous comment, could look over the crowd as he did.

One time, back in 1996, while celebrating in the small chapel of his diocese in southeastern São Paulo, Padre Marcelo had improvised a sound system on the patio of his church. Turning the street into an extension of the church, he began to celebrate Mass in the open air. As news of his astounding celebrations spread, attracting more people and the media's attention, the street became impassable. Eventually the surrounding arteries leading to his chapel were filled with standing celebrants on service days. The police and volunteers had to guide the crowds and reroute traffic; public authorities, including the mayor, apologized to the neighborhood's residents. The gesture of bringing the Mass outside the walls of the church or, better, joining those inside the chapel with those outside, thus worked as a commentary on the nature of the crowd Padre Marcelo wanted to produce and mobilize. His audience was not a crowd formed of discrete bodies positioned in time and space but a crowd formed through rhythm. The difference concerns the subtle perception of a crowd emerging through resonance, through the idea that rhythm overcomes the separateness of presence, where the specificity of number abstracts into the possibility of enumeration, the possibility of a counting on the way to becoming more. It is as though the rhythmic choreographies he introduced, drawing thousands to his chapel, his street, and his neighborhood, had the power to make the total bigger than the sum of its parts. Embracing the repetition of lyrics, melodies, and accompanying movements, the crowd became its tempos and syncopations. He would be the chief leader of a parade creation he branded "the Carnival of Jesus," the "yeah, yeah, yeah of Christ," and like all good parades in São Paulo it caused a lot of tumult and disorder in the normal traffic of the neighborhood, making the journey taken by churchgoers and curious visitors quite arduous.

At the turn of the twenty-first century, Brazil's main TV stations competed for Padre Marcelo's presence. He was known as the "priest of all medias," the "priest of all marathons," the "priest who never sits, nor does he let sit." The renowned liberation theologian Frei Betto, who was Lula's spiritual adviser, accused Padre Marcelo of being a "celebrity priest" and suggested that he ought to stop and think about what theology is. "Instead of running an average of ten kilometers on his treadmill and another ten kilometers from one radio station to the TV studios," Monsignor Beltrami from the archdiocese of São Paulo (introduced in chapter 3) had said to me on a visit in May 2001, "he should take time to stop and ponder if this is what Catholicism in Brazil is supposed to become."[4] What all these voices signaled was discomfort but also an indelible admiration for Padre Marcelo's energy, his ability to embody the powers of media in its capacity to be in different places at the same time.

For the sake of the monobloc chairs, it must be stressed again what a force he represented. On any given Sunday he could be celebrating Mass somewhere in the city; be a guest on *Domingo Legal*, Brazil's most popular talk show; appear on the cover of a magazine; be heard on his daily program on Radio America; be seen in the cinema, acting in two major films he also directed; be heard in a disco through his immensely popular techno mix "Raise Your Hands"; and more. His ambition was to embody the extramural qualities of sound, or to personify—as he did in one of his movies where he played the archangel Gabriel—the electric qualities of angels (de Abreu 2005). He wanted to be in one place, vanish, and then appear somewhere else; to be like a lightning flash that both strikes and illuminates; to be effective, like Saint Expedito, the saint of urgent causes, and a much-favored figure among those who follow Padre Marcelo (de Abreu 2013b).

It soon became clear that Padre Marcelo had to leave his chapel in southeastern São Paulo and celebrate elsewhere in the city. By 1998 he was offering Mass in gyms, football stadiums, parks, and at racetracks. Pressed by his peers in the clergy to settle down and be associated with a single location, Padre Marcelo rented a large hangar in an industrial area of his diocese. He alternated celebrating at his sanctuary with an intense presence in the media until these coincided: the media started to come to the sanctuary and film his celebrations. And despite the constraints imposed by the hierarchy to have a spiritual home, he went on finding ways to return to his idea of a congregation formed by the phenomenon of its motion. He endured things. His insistence on celebrating with the doors open, his aspiration to build a sanctuary with "expandable walls" (see chapter 5), and, as it turns out, the lack of doors in his Santuário Mãe de Deus—all are reiterations of how to challenge containment. His followers, his publicity agents, and the media kept rounding up the number of visitors per celebration: twenty thousand or forty thousand, seventy thousand, two million. . . . This counting was launched into the public realm, only to be inflated, contested, and amended, and it worked to reinforce the impossibility—or nondesire—on the part of Padre Marcelo to turn presence into enumeration. And what chairs could do justice to such an ambition?

The chairs kept arriving. People brought them to the sanctuary first for the practical reasons already mentioned, then in imitation of what others were doing, and finally in response to the concession of the sanctuary leadership. "If you think you will be too tired," Padre Marcelo started to tell the congregation, "you can bring your own pew [*banquinho*]." But the variety of seats interfered with his sense of the collective and the need for free limbs to go up and down, to make the blood flow and people's faces scarlet and sweaty. (He liked that exertion.) Finally he permitted the monobloc chairs, thousands of them, in the sanctuary. The chairs have altered the space in significant ways. And yet they differ substantially from the church's conventional bench design, with its dignified aura of durability and weightiness. The ease with which the chairs can be assembled and disassembled, stacked and unstacked, or even discarded altogether highlights the plasticity of the space.

Those practical qualities synthesize in their material being a model for thinking about subjectivity in urban São Paulo. At the same time, however, these very light features also constitute a threat to the anchoring structure upon which the lightness of Padre Marcelo also depends; in addition, the lightness of the chair poses a risk to the proper governing of crowds qua individuals, and so measures must be taken to safeguard the space from falling into utter disarray. What ultimately has turned the monobloc chair into such a performative object is that it allows for the coexistence of opposites, a chair that incorporates the ambivalence of a movement that is both Catholic and Pentecostal. As an object, it both determines and comments on the power structures that govern the relation between Padre Marcelo's desire for an open crowd and the Catholic Church's fear that too much freedom of the members will send ripples across the measured steps, heavy canons, and rigid sermons of the hierarchy.

Prior to celebration—or in its aftermath—the sight of the chairs in the sanctuary triggers the kind of encounter Mario Perniola (2004) calls "the sex appeal of the inorganic." In the sensuous apprehension of its material being—

its chairness—one feels momentarily how the monobloc chair could be rendered a kind of material contrivance of spirit. This is quite evident when due to the wind currents running through the building (which to the detached observer looks more like one of those roadside, open-ended, and beautifully roofed gas stations), the lightness of the monobloc chair eerily manifests: the chairs start to drift in the wind, forming crowds of their own, in ways that expose the incontrovertible necessity for regimentation of some kind in order for lightness and plasticity not to be confounded with disorder and dilution. This is why the hundreds of volunteer workers at the sanctuary, identifiable by their blue vests, make sure that the chairs return to the endless similitude of their existence. Intensifying the twilight zone between materiality and spirit, form and content, container and contained that the chair communicates are the ritual-bound, preternatural manifestations of miracles, prophecies, and revelations that take place in such crowded celebrations. And there again the chair forms an important compromise, made of plastic as it is, between the posture of standing up and the act of lying on the ground as, in the course of the ceremony, anointed individuals, paradoxically, give in to gravity in order to "repose" (*repouso*) or "slay" in the Spirit.

On a visit in 2019 to the (still) unfinished Santuário Mãe de Deus, I saw a metal structure on the ground just for the first five rows of the sanctuary, the belt area where the bishops, cardinals, politicians, personalities of the star system, and other noble guests take a seat. The idea is to yoke these monobloc chairs at the front to the metal frame so the chairs, and perhaps their occupiers, go nowhere. It may ultimately, then, return to the original model proposed by Ruy Ohtake, according to which the first row of chairs—more like carmine chaises longues, designed to take the weight of the dignitaries—would be convened, while in the back the crowds stand in praise.

Gravity

The problem of gravity, its sensorial and normative force, has a traditional role in the designing of religious spaces and the disciplining of the religious self. In modern physics, gravity is defined as the force of attraction that moves bodies toward the center of a celestial body. In the Christian tradition, gravity can be seen in terms of how the religious ritual of the Mass translates into a problem of how actual bodies, a mass, both human and nonhuman, relate to each other in relation to a celestial body. In the modern interior design of churches, the cross has come to occupy the central position and serves as the prime celestial body to which all other bodies are oriented. It is the sign that mediates both the vertical relationship between heaven and earth and the horizontal relationships of worldly life. While the term *Mass* refers to the ritual of celebration as a whole—the Mass liturgy—it entertains a metonymic relation with the properties of the Eucharist. Throughout Christianity the coming together in communion has been the Eucharist's prime operative power. In medieval discussions about the appearance of the Eucharist and the consequent replacement of the early Christian loaf by the wafer, it became important to have the principle of mass communion embodied in the material properties of the host. The corpus of the mass should be encoded, substantiated, in that of the Eucharist.

In the same period that the corpus of the host was becoming lighter and flatter—on the way to translucent—the setting of the liturgy was getting increasingly heavier and object oriented. It was as though the movement of bringing authority from heaven to earth demanded that a certain amount of weight be invested in the visual arguments proper to an ecclesiastical setting as encoded in the seat, scepter, and regalia of the pope. Liturgical iconology, furniture, and insignias should signify aspects of religious and civil sovereignty while commonplace emblems like altars, ambries, oil cabinets, baptismal fonts, chairs, communion rails, hymn boards, lecterns, pulpits, pews, rosaries, kneelers, and the buildings constructed to hold them ought to be material renditions of the aim to persuade through weightiness. The choice of heavier materials—stone, wood, metal—supported that goal and carried forward the challenge of testing faith through the art of bending and working these materials in sculpture and engraving and by drawing spiritual and institutional lessons from it. As a whole, church materials were selected in response to notions that associated earthly authority with weight.

But where weightiness was paramount in bringing celestial power to earth, its negation allowed certain objects, like the monstrance, the chalice, or the Bible, to be lifted into midair. Size, shape, proportion, symmetry, and balance were qualities valued in this weight-lifting activity. The Mass ritual was thus not only a means to draw the gaze of the spectator to the cruciform nature of the gestures performed by the priest: sideways and upward. It was equally about implicating such gestures in the muscular politics of the institution, expressed in the ever-reiterated goal to grow and expand into the universe as *catholos*. Thus the orthopraxy of the elevation of objects did not simply defy the gravity brought into them by design (Stolow 2013); it was paired with the ambition that such weight become encoded in the body of the ecclesia. In that capacity, the ecclesia has always been God's celebrant as much as a weight lifter. In medieval Europe the contrasting dynamics between gravity and weight lifting found iconic equivalence in the enclosure of the host in a heavy monstrance, which in turn was overcome by the priest's gesture of elevation into the air so that the entire community could partake in the edification of the church. This exercise was replayed in the ritual of communion, the replication and distribution of the host among the congregation, in its capacity to both affirm and disown the human body and its fleshly presence.

The relations among the host, the monobloc chair, and the community are thus not simply metaphorical. What these three entities share is not resemblance by likeness but resemblance in dynamism or rhythm. Host, chair, and community apply to their procedural being the principle of opposites, that is, the paradox that enables the affirmation of gravitas in the very moment that denies it. This is the same paradox by which the gaining of human form and mass in Christ has, for Charismatics, the power to express the unbearable lightness and ghostliness of God. As Caroline Walker Bynum (2006, 2007) has documented regarding medieval sacramental practice, the force behind the ritual did not come from its context but from the power to exalt the paradoxical nature of Christ: the double nature of spirit and flesh, incarnated in passing like a flashing light. Accordingly, the fortitude of the sacrament was given by the ability to expose its cardinal vulnerability. The value of the host lay in its capacity to resemble what it took as its prototype: the kenotic and kinetic sense of making present an invisibility. This idea has already been explored in chapter 3, where I argue that the efficiency of the Eucharist draws on a strategic vulnerability, a certain reputation for ruination that works to highlight its contraries, what it is as much as what it is not. For Charismatics, the Eucharist expresses the orthodox principle of contraries that spring life forth as the supra-emanation of the *corpus ecclesia*: from the divine, to the vicar, and finally to the members. The procedural and structural aspects that govern the relationships between host and community, divine and human, lightness and gravity—more than the given and the representative outcomes involved in the celebration—converge in the composite notion of "mass." Mass refers at once to congregation and to matter, to the act of gathering and to flesh, to flock and to stock.

The profusion of baroque aesthetics in Brazil in the seventeenth and eighteenth centuries highlighted that composite sense of mass by integrating it into an aesthetic composition. The artists of the baroque worked on the enhancement of volume through the play of light and shadow, and the sculpting of form tended toward the infinite through the elimination of the boundaries and limits of the image. The excesses of the baroque and the games in perception it offered the viewer are among the reasons that the gravitational pull of the cross became important during the reforms of Catholics in the latter part of the nineteenth century. While the proliferation of saints and statues throughout the colonial period had the power to create a corpus of the teachings of Christianity, this material profusion also contributed to the dispersion of power away from a core authoritative center. What nineteenth-century reformers like the European Catholic order of the Redentoristas attempted to do with the incisive and violent reduction of popular saints was to combine the need for gravitas with strategies of containment. Once a powerful proselytizing method, the culture of saints—and its many hierarchies—was substantially reduced during the modern period to fit the axis model as embodied in the cross. The cross became the promotional sign that would pull sacred power down to earth while enabling relationships on the ground to cohere by anchoring individuals in relation to a center. In a period preoccupied with techniques of modernization, the cross became a means to frame the public domain. Previously deployed as an instrument of colonial subjugation, the cross became for the modern religious individual what the grid has been for the urban planner: a means to measure and rationalize space.

This preoccupation with rationalization included air space. The search for the highest geological points to plant crosses or religious icons—as in the image of Christ the redeemer standing on top of Corcovado Mountain since 1932—was part of a larger effort to reconfigure the status of air space from thick substance to empty dimension, a kind of secularization of the air (de Abreu 2015). Crosses could be high in the air, but they were not of the air. A cross is an object identified by the borders of its materiality, but the air has no boundary between its ends and beginnings, no inside nor outside; the cross differentiates between the object and the surrounding atmosphere, while the air expresses a nondistinction between event and milieu.[5] In an attempt to develop a vital new relation to the earth, particularly in the aftermath and spirit of Brazil's independence from colonial rule in 1888, the country embarked on projecting the values recorded on the flag, "Order and Progress," which it borrowed from French positivism.

In Catholicism this vital relation to the ground found expression in liberation theology, including its earthbound metaphysics and grassroots politics of freedom and exile. The dissociations between the center of Rome and the periphery of local gravities throughout the twentieth century tightened further the connections between liberation theology and the earth as an idiom for liberation and redemption. The ideological and moral uplifting of populations was bound to a rhetoric of the land articulated in both political and folkloric sources. It is this reliance on earthbound vocabularies to articulate religious and political concerns that Catholic Charismatics most vehemently dismiss. For example, I witnessed at a press conference in Curitiba some Charismatics suggesting that liberation theology is heavier than the cross they are trying to carry, implying that the real load of their credo is ideological more than religious.[6]

The arrival of the Catholic Charismatic Renewal in Brazil in the late 1960s precipitated a number of doctrines and practices that posed a challenge to the previous requirements for gravitas and circumscription of the sacred. The importance attributed to the cross as a prime attractor of institutional power by a modernized Catholic Church inspired Brazil's Charismatics to criticize both the dramatics of the crucifixion and the formal features of the cross. In an attempt to detach from the more thespian scenarios of the Passion, Catholic Charismatics invested in finding innovative ways to attach doctrinal thinking to new material and performative repertoires. This enterprise hinged on a correlation according to which the Passion is to death as Spirit is to life. A prayer group leader once said to me, "In biblical terms, we say here that the Charismatic movement is a shift from the gravity of St. Matthew's Passion to the joy of resurrection in St. Luke."[7] The localization of pneuma in the region of lungs and pectorals, as argued in chapter 4, offered Charismatics new criteria for valuing the upward, the vertical, and the kinetic. To be baptized in the Holy Spirit, the preternatural endowment of the Charismatic revival experience, is to turn those bodily coordinates into the core of an exercise of charismata onward and upward.

In this new orientation toward vertical mobility, the act of sitting evokes the demons of habit and inertia, of conformity and portliness, which eventually lead to rigidity and death. The anointed, or good, Charismatics stand up not just because they ought to be ready to leap but because by leaping, they update their capacity to do better in the future. Charismata puts one constantly on call. "Those bishops that insist on staying seated, they will never speak in tongues," the leader of a Charismatic prayer group in São Paulo told me during the twentieth anniversary of the Charismatic movement in the town of Aparecida. The five-day event in Aparecida do Norte had been fraught with tensions between the hierarchy and lay people, and remarks imbued with innuendo kept traveling from one side to the other. "And it is not because they refuse to do it. It is because as long as they remain bent like that, their body is as sealed as the walls of Jericho." By standing, in contrast, the body is poised to move. Insomuch as it moves, the body constantly reassesses its balance, symmetry, and pace, qualities that Charismatics see as the best direct access to the heart and lungs.

Summary

In the first week of May 2010, Padre Marcelo fell off his new antigravity treadmill. In the fall, he twisted his foot and had to be in a wheelchair for three weeks. Talking about his accident, he emphasized the sensation of the air pushing under his feet, through his legs, lifting him slightly up. He prided himself on running with his eyes closed, so ordinary an activity it had become, and he adamantly explained to the media that the fall had been caused by envy, or *olho gordo* (fat eye). His book *Ágape* was selling extremely well, like no other book in Brazil's history, with a record 10 million copies, and dismissing the rumor that he had failed to adapt to the ultramodern new exercise machine, he saw his accomplishment as being the ultimate cause of his fall. In any case, the incident did not deter him from going about his life. Despite the advice from his family and bishop that he ought to rest and recover, he met his commitments and celebrated Mass from a wheelchair.

On May 9, Mother's Day, he entered the altar rolling his wheelchair, creating a major wave of commotion across the largely female audience. "A chair with wheels," he said, "is not so bad." Then, over the microphone, he shouted the usual "Shall we now shake the house? Shall we spring?" The event started with his usual roster of songs, helped by Brazil's popular singer Hebe Camargo. For many of those present, it was extraordinary to see the priest known for defying gravity confined to a chair. But it also offered him an opportunity to stage the overcoming of such restricting limitations. He was able to admit that sometimes one does need to sit down. He was learning that lesson. But the accident also reinforced his point that chairs are lofty sites of indulgence, that chairs can turn people into spectators, not participants; they can be pulpits attesting to the idea that the body can never be built up enough. The convention of sitting churchgoers, Padre Marcelo continues to assert, misses the fact that the light of grace is still best reflected while standing and ready to jog in the directions the Holy Spirit may call forth. To stand is to both act and expose the necessity of practicing religion. It is the minimal requirement for the Spirit to initiate its dramaturgy of unction and devotion.

Notoriously unstable, the monobloc chairs still remain in the sanctuary of Padre Marcelo, as mentioned, as though brought there by the wind. The colloquial expression notwithstanding, among Charismatics "carried by the wind" can easily be rendered as "blown away by the Holy Spirit." The counterpart to this inspirited wind that carries and brings, however, is the cheap throwaway chair associated with the drafts of industrial capitalism. The biography of this molded plastic object reflects the double nature of spirit and globalization. The monobloc chair, as mentioned, not only is anonymous but identifies itself with its mode of production, its manufacturing process, its spirit. The chair is at once a completed object and its infrastructure, at once the sign, the form, and its conditions of possibility. It is simultaneously a chair and its concept, Theotókian. It is no wonder that another chair that, by authorized design, succeeded in tapping into the fame of the anonymous monobloc chair would be called the air chair. Mostly associated with outdoor settings, the monobloc chair is emblematic of the spatial ambivalence of Padre Marcelo's sanctuary in demarcating inside from outside. I wonder what will happen, chair-wise, if the padre ever completes the building of Santuário Mãe de Deus. In its current shape, he can argue that better chairs, perhaps made of stronger plastic, will come in the future to accommodate those who should be granted the option of sitting. But as the completion of the sanctuary slowly progresses, the monobloc chair seems to best synthesize the spirit of the place and the logic of the open crowd.

EPILOGUE: THEOLOGY ON THE RUN

....

The modern project of critique of religion attempted to replace the continuous concept of history in Christian theology. Yet Christian theology too has a tradition of interruption in temporal continuity. The theological dwarf in Benjamin's (1968) thesis alerts us to such presence in history. The historical materialism embodied in this figure lies in the aperture, the gap of the opportune or incision, opening in the medium of time so that "a breath of the air that pervaded earlier days caresses us as well. . . . In the voices [we will] hear an echo of now silent ones" (Thesis II). But while great investment has been made in interrupting linear narratives of time—an effort to which Benjamin was committed—there has been much less focus on scrutinizing the less progressive, when not outright (or even alt-right) conservative, powers of interruption he likewise analyzed.

Brazil's Catholic Charismatics frequently pull out Greek theological phraseology in social exchanges—not armchair theology but more like what Benjamin called "theology on the run," the function of which is to grant asylum to something in jeopardy by attaching to it the semblance of popular culture. Charismatics have long recruited ways to shake language out of its semantic torpidity, as it were, by taking verbal communication to the gym. One of the ways to do so has been through the deploying of Greek terms as though to interrupt more canonical formulations of language. Terms like *kharis, kairos, kronos, khora, kerygma, kenosis, schesis,* and more appear in Charismatic speech and prayer, not everywhere with the same frequency but enough to count it a feature of the movement.

The function of those terms is to join other figures of speech, such as tautology, alliteration, and parataxis, in endowing language with gymnasiarch qualities. Their purpose is to interrupt the forward motion of language so as to better experience its "workout," enabling corporeal and lateral dispensations. Positing a challenge to what they consider the metaphysically obese, Charismatics nevertheless adopt the same logics characteristic of the obesogenic environments that underpin contemporary body cultures in dietary regimes or physical exercise. They proceed through bipolar oscillation and basal paradoxes in ways that, according to the philosopher Peter Sloterdijk (2013), are distinctive of the "heroic-holy-athletes" in their ability to hide the contradictory nature of their message through overexposure and overemphasis. These holy athletes who seek "to embody the privilege of emanating directly from the exception" (276) must place paradox at its very core—one with life and breath and gesture—so as to maintain the dialectic between opposites and make it look at once natural and artificial. That is their charismatic elasticity.

Though smaller communities of the Charismatic movement had employed those terms before the mid-1990s, it was former bodybuilder Padre Marcelo who brought theological notions to sport the masses. There is his best-selling book *Kairós: Tempo de Deus* (Kairos: The Time of God), his best-selling CD *Ágape Musical*, and *Philia*, a book to combat depression "by applying Phili" (*aplicando Philia*). And then there is metanoia, as in *Metanoia Wi-Fé: Descubra a Senha Que Vai Revolucionar a Sua Vida* (Metanoia Wi-Faith: Discover the Password That Will Revolutionize Your Life). There is also *Ágapinho* for children and soon enough *Ágon* for the afflicted and those skilled in the arts of winning graces over impossible situations or dire circumstances. Then in 2014, after undergoing a severe and nearly suicidal diet to lose 35 kilograms in six months, Padre Marcelo published a book titled *Ruah: Quebrando os Paradigmas de que Gordura e Saúde e Magreza e Doença* (*Ruah*: Breaking the Paradigms That Obesity Is Healthy and Slimness Is Illness), which again became a historic best-seller in Brazil in offering Brazilians "tips for a healthy diet." As he clarified to his audiences, the Hebrew *ruah* was chosen as an alternative to Greek *pneuma* because, being a book about diet, it suits better the soft winds from the underbelly (whereas pneuma, as we saw, is located in the chest). Be that as it may, the media wanted to hear Padre Marcelo admit that his change in weight was a direct reflection of his oscillations in mood, his bipolarity that he, in turn, both highlighted and blocked in letting the world know about his daily treadmill exercises.

At the same time, this bipolarism is also inflected by the logics of celebrity that suffuse Brazil's star system. An example is the famous epistolary exchange between the liberation theologian Frei Betto and Padre Marcelo published in 1999 in Brazil's most widely distributed newspaper: "Dear brother ... the bigger the flight, the bigger the fall."[1] Bipolarity would appear again, during a religious show in Canção Nova Community, which always looked on Padre Marcelo's incomparable fame with both anxiety and admiration. In front of a crowd of thousands an intruder brutally pushed the priest from the stage, making him fall, headfirst, onto the asphalt below, by the crowd; given his past investment in depicting himself as archangel Gabriel, perhaps the woman was pushing him to fly up, not fall down. It was all unclear, and little explanation was offered. The fact that she was later diagnosed with bipolar disorder doesn't help either.

When in November 2018, after an official visit to Brazil's prime military aeronautics base in the Paraiba Valley, President Jair Bolsonaro came swiftly to the nearby Canção Nova Community, he was overpowered by tears of joy. On live TV Monsignor Jonas Abib together with other founding members of the media community and Father Eduardo Dougherty, the American Jesuit who introduced the Catholic Charismatic Renewal to Brazil in 1969, prayed for the newly elected president. In collective praise, the president and the audience brought glossolalic speech to the site of the wound due to the alleged stabbing suffered by Bolsonaro during a campaign rally in September 2018. Padre Jonas then told Bolsonaro that he is the "president that Brazil needs" and that he was chosen to be sovereign "of this great nation not by the people but by God." It was a theatrical spectacle where suddenly the dramaturgy of sovereign power in the Bolsonaro era—and somewhat oddly the themes of this book—came into full view, suturing the man's middle name (Messias) to image, to incision, and to powers of bodily speech.[2]

For Charismatics, speaking Greek, as with speaking in tongues, highlights first and foremost the ability to communicate. The incision it introduces to the flow of ordinary speech, by virtue of its estrangement, exposes the operations of speech. The foreignness of speech, its conspicuous archaism, alerts the body to its gestural potentials; it is what shapes the body-evangelist.

By the same token, however, Greek words assume the form of a political compromise in the idiom of theology. Precisely because it is archaic and anachronistic, Greek affords Catholic Charismatics the distinctive sounds of revivalism in view of a certain orthodoxy in doctrine as well as in practice. It helps them to distinguish themselves from non-Charismatic Catholics and evangelicals while not having to decide for *one or the other*. Greek speech testifies to a practice beyond decision into that of incision, cutting through ordinary speech. At times its eruption resembles electrical short-circuits, while at others it is well patterned in a phrase's arc—nonetheless affecting it in the manner of a counterplot, as though speech were in tension with itself.

Benjamin (1968: 261) famously posed theology as an alternative to the modern cult of progress, "to homogeneous empty time." Inspired by Marx, he associated revolutionary force with the powers of interruption and shock in making transparent the powers of fiction. In calling attention to the fact that reality is a fabrication, he demonstrated that individuals could imagine futures otherwise. But when the power of shock becomes inalienable from sovereign governance, the exposure of the operational apparatus is—or can be—the way for hegemonic power to hide in plain sight. This conspicuous co-optation of the rules of medial apparatus, and of fabrication, is what is involved in current forms of mimetic populism that are erupting around the world.

The power of dissimulation lies in the ability of the ruler to make shock a generative expression. This, I think, is the logic to explore in the linkage between new media, mimicry, and governance. If the power to shock once depended on its exceptionality, what happens when exceptionality no longer has the power to shock? And if exception no longer holds as exceptional but has become the structure of ruling, what happens to sovereignty? This typology that enables power to take form from and identify with the mechanics of interruption—in the case of the Charismatic Renewal, as a kind of breath—requires that we fathom how power works in our political present. Where strategies to interrupt the logics of decisiveness that have long underpinned the forward directionality of knowledge are necessary, one must also note how interruption and open-ended systems have come to lodge themselves in contemporary modalities of governance. In that, applied theology might be more fit—worked out—for the task of helping us address the political dramaturgy of our time than we were led to believe.

AFTERWORD: ON BIPOLARITY

It has been nearly two decades since I first started work on this book, and during that time Brazil has entered a new political and cultural moment. Swelling under Bolsonaro's regime of (non)exceptionalism, this moment can be described as—indeed is being propelled by—a rhythmic oscillation between poles. Sovereign decision-making seems to be suffering from a kind of bipolar disorder, bouncing swiftly between one extreme and the other. On the level of subject formation, for example, we notice two opposite and yet simultaneous tendencies: the global neoliberal subject is defined by his or her ability to adhere to a logic of unrelenting circulation and flexibility, but the era is also witness to a return to the adopting of frames that enforce the overriding relevance of identity politics and sectarianism. Where the former evolved in the 1990s as a move to decenter the subject as permutable and open-ended, the latter, perhaps reactively, fosters renewed value in positionality and closure. A strange form of flexible rigidity seems to describe the synthesis between these extremes. My interest is not in defending the vehement claims of one or the other side of this pole. What strikes me is precisely the undecidable sway between the two as a defining feature of action and doctrine in present-day Brazil—and Brazil is not alone in this regard. Just what is at stake in the middle space created in the wake of these oscillating opposites is the question this book has explored through the example of the Catholic Charismatic Renewal in the state of São Paulo.

It is my hope that this work exposes what I see as a pattern of operation in the political era of Bolsonaro. The operational logics of sovereignty that characterize this administration, its specifics notwithstanding, are breaking free of their context and becoming applicable to other emerging forms of populism around the world. Such logics constitute elements of a certain baroque sensibility, the kind of "Baroque-Byzantinism" that Walter Benjamin ([1963] 1998a) also noted in *The Origin of German Tragic Drama*. These are indecisiveness, surrealist shock effects, a taste for conflict and ministerial intrigue, temper tantrums, interruption and discontinuous utterances, gestural extravaganza, buffoonery, apocalyptic thought, martyrdom, and despotism.

I begin this book in 1995, with the kicking of a statue of Our Lady of Aparecida by a pastor of the Universal Church on live TV and the forensic dramaturgy that ensued. What interests me about the incident is the power of iterability to affect perception to the extent that, even though the statue suffered no definite injury, publics across different arenas perceived that it had, describing it over and over again in discordant terms and scales. The more the televised scenes of the attack circulated, the deeper the incision went, soon to become the very amphitheater and stage-form for the rise of Charismatic Catholicism in Brazil in the 1990s. Thus exposed, the incision releases the ghostly scenes that traverse this book. Such ghostly scenes are operations.

In between two technologically mediated injuries—that of Our Lady of Aparecida and that of President Jair Messias Bolsonaro during his campaign in 2018—Brazil went through a period of colossal transformation in every possible sense: economic, social, religious, aesthetic, political, judicial. As with the perceptive qualities of the injury to the statue of Our Lady of Aparecida in the mid-1990s, so the highly media-reproduced stabbing of Bolsonaro during his campaign in 2018 highlights the nature of political theater in contemporary Brazil. Just as it became irrelevant whether Pastor Von Helder actually shattered the statue to pieces, so it is whether Bolsonaro was stabbed. Much like the statue of Our Lady deepened the mediatic perception of a fracture in the very moment of trying to overcome it, so Bolsonaro's multiple post-stabbing surgeries to his abdomen (a total of four within the first year of his mandate) to restore health from an insalubrious hernia also contribute to deepening it.

The reiterative powers of incision speak for a new order of the perceptible. They rhythmically puncture the political. From the physical blows to the statue of Our Lady in the 1990s to the chutes and ladders in Operação Lava-Jato, the rise of the courtier, the ejection of Dilma Rousseff and the striations of the parliamentary field, the jailing of former president Lula, the rise to power of Bolsonaro, and the *Intercept* revelations of "Vaza Jato" inflicting Brazil and beyond, the political tirelessly strides on shock. The image that politics wants us to apprehend is a kind of a Byzantine mosaic where more important than the single fragments of a panel are the dynamic thresholds or intervals between scenes. It matters less what is being shown than what the rhythms of moving from one scene to the next do to perception.

In the process, a distinctive form of Catholic revivalism arose, one embedded in much larger capitalist and entrepreneurial networks.[1] The primary concern of this Catholicism is to revitalize a whole *corpus ecclesia* through its gestures and articulations, one that is capable of bending in opposite directions. Indeed what is distinctive about Charismatic Catholicism is how it uses a language of operations unmoored from a narrative-teleological conception of time. In such a setting, actors are no longer *in* place, standing up on a stage, as it were; rather their gestures partake in the very stage-form in which those same actions unfold. The progression of narrative happens not through decision as hitherto constituted but through incision, interruption, and rhythm.

He a Catholic, she an evangelical, Jair and Michelle Bolsonaro symbolize and highlight at the supreme level of the state the kind of marriage (and tensions) internal to Catholic Pentecostalism that this book analyzes. State and church powers converge by way of a tactic that draws political energy through the inclusion of what best opposes it. The embracing of Mary by Catholicism, and of Spirit by Pentecostalism, positions Catholic Pentecostalism from the start as a religion of compromise—a compromise that builds on and is embodied by the very tension of opposites it highlights. As argued in this book, it is this unresolved tension that makes Charismatic Catholicism a practical doctrine of the gymnasium, just as it is this unresolved compromise that allows it to recuperate Eastern Orthodox Christendom via the Byzantine in contemporary Brazil. It is an astonishing operation that Charismatics do, for it thrives on maintaining tension while conserving the demands of an older orthodoxy. It exercises anew the muscle of a much deeper elasticity, a corpus familiar from earlier periods. Popularized in Brazil by Charismatics through prayer disciplines, pneumatic doctrine, and iconography, the adaptation of Byzantine practices adjoins premodern counter-reforming repertoires to introduce a kind of pneumatic baroque into the contemporary. It is "an epic stretching," in Brecht's words, the defining feature of which is precisely the ability to extend and bend to different traditions and protocols: a propaedeutic of the gymnasium through its "members."

A similar investing in the suppleness of form characterizes the body politic of Bolsonarismo. During the open session of the Câmara dos Deputados in 1993, Bolsonaro famously declared, "I am in favor of a dictatorship, a regime of exception" (quoted in Fishman 2018). In 2018, twenty-five years following that pronouncement, he captured the presidency under the national campaign slogan "Brazil before Anything; God above All." His victory followed a media event—his stabbing and subsequent uttering of the slogan while in recovery—which had radically altered the course of his campaign; Bolsonaro would no longer engage in public debates or even try to persuade voters, instead modulating the affective consequences of his injury to the punctuating dynamics of social media. With each tweet piercing and polarizing the fragile body of democracy, he operated in the space of exception even before formally assuming power. And yet, when he did eventually assume presidential power, he went on behaving as though he were still in the heat of the campaign. Such craft in moonwalking—the ability to backslide in the very movement of going forward—might be unprecedented in a ruler, and yet these, and other dancing steps, are among the regime's signature moves.

Defining the rule of law and sovereign decision-making in the rhetoric of exception seemingly puts Bolsonaro at the center of a Schmittian understanding of political theology. In its classic formulation, in line with Westphalian order, the politico-theological centers on the problem of sovereign decision. As the Schmittian dictum goes, the "sovereign is he who decides on the state of exception." But while slogans such as "Brazil First," "America First," or "Brexit Means Brexit" may suggest a will to restore sovereignty around the logic of positionality—of what stands before and above—they operate in a distinctive power arrangement. Bolsonaro and his American counterpart, Donald Trump, warn that a decision will take place, threaten that they will decide. The capacity on the part of these leaders for making things decisive is, however, precisely what is disabled in the process; if there is any sense of the exception, it is the exception from decision itself. This is not to say that new laws are not instituted or overturned. It is that their enactment occurs in the fearful shadow cast by sovereignty's lack, one that will require continuous confrontation with the exception and the extreme so that in time, exception will be everywhere and nowhere in particular. Sovereignty today assumes the form of a rhythmic echo between opposites, a bouncing of sorts, whereby indefinite transience has the last word.

Extreme indecisiveness is more than simply not being sure of how to act; it is a constitutive dimension of the political act itself. As the late feminist literary critic Barbara Johnson (1986: 35) notes, "There is politics precisely because there is undecidability." Johnson is interested in the relation between the deviousness of language—what she explores as techniques of oratory—and the directing of violence. It is the idea that, paradoxically, the more indirectly aimed, the more slanted the move, the more effective the targeting will be. "What," she asks, "could seem farther away from budgets and guerrilla warfare than a discussion of anaphora, antithesis, prolepsis, and preterition? Yet the notorious CIA manual on psychological operations in guerrilla warfare ends with just such rhetorical treatise: an appendix on techniques which lists definitions and examples for these and other rhetorical figures" (29). It is precisely the abstraction that bestows such rhetorical operations with an apolitical aura that can more easily be smuggled across worlds, not the least, the bodily.

When the pendulum of decision moves back and forth in the reign of Bolsonaro, say, between appointing one person to preside over the Directorate of Evaluation of Basic Education only to dismiss him twenty-four hours later, when legal protection for minorities is revoked so suddenly as to produce whiplash, when workers are fired en masse as part of a *despetização* of the government only to be, hours later, exonerated for fear of paralysis due to lack of know-how, or when, dramatically, he proclaims, "The Amazon is ours," and that the way to prevent destruction by fire is to eliminate the forest itself, for which he needs "new partnerships," the president is not just tossing from one side to another in view of finding the best solution. The rhythmic movement of an undecidable back-and-forth becomes the act itself, the nonarrival that highlights the effort of bringing a muscle back in shape.

It is a floor-gymnastic attitude Bolsonaro adopts. While the use of bodily extremities—of the hand and, even more, of the fingers—has always been a component in the choreography of sovereign decision-making (as in the use of the thumb by the sovereign in the either/or decision to give or take life), with Bolsonaro we are witnessing the use of gesture as performative of a particular kind of power. Rather than signifying, gesture for Bolsonaro exhibits a certain motor function of the extremities, a double-jointed rotation between one thing and the other. To be *at once this as well as that*: authoritarian and flexible, despot and neoliberal, sovereign and beast, the arsonist and the fireman. For example, the same gesture that allows Bolsonaro to choreograph a shooting (by using his thumb and index finger) also allows him to flip and rotate the fingers, and thereby turn that same gesture into the letter *L* (for Lula). In so gesturing, the sovereign not only puts forward his gestural warfare but also stages a mockery of Lula's sovereignty by indexing (literally) the size of his penis. As theatrical as it may sound, Bolsonaro's "acting" owes nothing to the power of figurative representation but to the ability of working on the muscular radius, the articulations themselves—of the wrist, hand, and fingers—that allow him to alternate between poles. With a slight rotation of the wrist, the sovereign can say *this* as well as *that*—and he does it incisively, hurtfully. At stake here, I suspect, is something more than a simple replacement of the "head" for the "extremities" but the reappearing of a whole corpus of governance and stage-form that is having (and will have) tremendous repercussions, not least when it comes to containing the very fascination it unleashes.

Unlike the stiffness of the old sovereign who held a scepter of history in his hand, the Bolsonaro sovereign adopts an oddly flexible form of authoritarianism. His virtuosity as leader is constituted by, and will continue to be, the suppleness and mediality of gesture. His characteristic gesture-turned-meme pro-guns campaign inaugurated a new communicative register in Brazil's political setting. The gesture of the gun sign soon spread among Bolsonaro supporters across the country. It was seen at every pro-Bolsonaro street demonstration, incorporated into choreographed choruses among the youth as a grand finale of their collective dances. During his presidential campaign street merchants sold T-shirts with imprints of the candidate waving his gun gesture. The examples are many, but perhaps the most memorable of all (in how it combines sovereign vulnerability with hardline gesturing) was when Bolsonaro, in the hospital recovering from a stabbing he allegedly received while campaigning, performed the handgun signal to the TV cameras. Virality and virility thus became the twofold impetus in sovereign gesture.

What is perplexing is how gesture in Bolsonarismo combines extreme semiotic violence with attention to minority rights. The fact that First Lady Michelle Bolsonaro broke protocol by gesturing her inaugural speech in sign language or that she translated the entire campaign into Brazilian sign language is but one portent signaling the central role gesture occupies in this new political era. Gesture here should not be reduced to the communicative powers that sign language otherwise entails. During her inaugural speech in sign language, Michelle Bolsonaro was not only communicating with a minority. She was also coordinating efforts with the president's notorious militarized choreographies of gesturing. She was, as mainstream media described it, drafting "compassion" for minorities but only to align its dynamics to the dictates of nonargumentative reasoning that characterized Bolsonaro's campaign. Hannah Arendt's critique of compassion in *On Revolution* (1963) was in how, being not uncapacious of expression, compassion has often been recruited by regimes that prime communication through gesture and countenance. There on stage Michelle Bolsonaro's compassion did not lead her to gesture. Rather, gesture made her compassionate.

Compassion thus becomes coordinated with the possibility of gesture to cut out. Rather than bonding the minority referent it indexes within the space of inclusion, the gesturing during Bolsonaro's presidential inauguration event dramatized the impossibility to contain, like an admission to the forthcoming—and ongoing—governance through chaos, through that which is, indeed, "out of hand." In being, as though severed from the body it belongs to, gesture in Bolsonarismo thematizes the stagecraft within which it unfolds. The cutting powers of gesture mimic and intensify the incisive tweetable moments that set things in circulation. Most striking of all is how the sovereign applies the logic of incision to his own body. The relentless media exposure of Bolsonaro's scarred abdomen in the course of a series of surgeries, the daily tweets and televised communications sent from the hospital to the nation, all display a desire on his part to draw power from incision: to make the wound literally operational, or his name is not Messias. Each time he revisits his anesthetized gut, he gives a stage to the logics of citation that he so wishes to communicate as key to his place in power. Like Donald Trump, or George W. Bush before, Bolsonaro says he will rule the country from his gut in ways that pour scorn on older logics of sovereign decision.

Much like the theatrical dramaturgy of a Byzantine icon, Bolsonaro makes acts and grounds coincide. The ability to act out one's grounds becomes the condition for self-reference; it is what sets effects chasing their own causes. It is the point at which acts and indexes, by virtue of that circuitous recursive topology, are never vertical or horizontal but slightly tilted, slightly slanted. As with a Byzantine icon, sovereignty hypostasizes presence through withdrawal; the sovereign is not there, he is forever *after* himself (in that precise sense of *after* as at once anterior and posterior). His throne is the tweet and the tweet his throne. Baroque, grotesque, insane, he makes a parody out of tragedy. This topology describes the stagecraft of much contemporary evangelical and state theater in Brazil and other sovereign regimes of our time. It is a motion that produces an ever-shifting ground as it discards what preceded it. As put by US trade representative Robert Lighthizer during a recent interview on Trump's indecisiveness, "We don't know whether we're going to get a conclusion. That's the problem. *We are running very quickly somewhere*" (Holden et al. 2017).

I cannot think of a better parable to describe this order of things than that offered by Kafka, the master of impasse. In a reflection on writer's block, he describes the following scene: A man whose house is unsafe starts to build another house out of the material of the first. However, in the middle of the process he is overcome with exhaustion (Kafka 1954: 350). What follows is a scene of oscillation between two houses that ends up producing a third space. What is characteristic of this third space is its fissured both/and for one or the other house. Indeed, the project of building a house entirely succumbs to the rhythm of its exertions. Kafka likens that rhythm to a Cossack dance, whereby the man goes on scraping and throwing aside the earth with the heels of his boot. He then associates that emerging middle space with the graveyard that will eventually bury the agent creating it. (One thinks here of Benjamin's [(1963) 1998a: 70] description of the demise of the ruler "as he loses himself in the ecstasy of power.")

I see the Cossack dancing as the order of the action of an automaton, whose motion reproduces that fissured "both/and" as undecidable. The rigidity of the upper body (authoritarianism) is compensated by sharp thrusting movements of the lower parts (neoliberalism). The waist is the contact point between the two parts. It is at once the anatomical appliance for rotary motion between the upper and the lower and where the center of the executive order is located. The waist is also what supports the act of squatting, comfortably, lower to the ground while on the face a smile is firmly planted, all the while the digging of the graveyard unfolds.

Rhythmic incision rather than transformative decision characterizes contemporary power. The levels of performative paradox and tautological reductionism across Brazil's political spectrum (but also globally, across regimes) require more flexible modes of understanding how today's authoritarianism combines with neoliberalism to produce a centralized extremism. A form of tyrannical flexibility becomes subservient to, and a condition for, the play of contraries. What is bewildering about the form of sovereignty we now confront is the displacement of the "before and above all" in the very moment of promoting it as the defining central slogan of the nation-state. This paradox provides the rhythm new regimes are running according to, a baroque-like drama, which in constantly drawing our attention to oscillating opposites— the bouncing between this and that—increases the likelihood that we will fail to see the totalizing powers of an open-air circle.

NOTES

....

Introduction

1　As the anthropologist Eric W. Kramer (2001: 45) writes, "The reaction to Von Helder's televised attack on the statue was so profuse that the impression of injury and physical violence grew in proportion to its narration in the media." Kramer describes an erroneous notation by David Lehmann that the image was attacked with an ax, implying that even anthropologists are not immune to what technological iteration does to perception. See Birman and Lehmann 1999.

2　Despite many readers of Benjamin insisting that this was his own vision of things, the attentive reader of this important thinker will know that he was always and primarily interested in authoring the spirit of an epoch. Above all, his authorship ought to express the ability to voice that epochal spirit. It is, therefore, wrong to think that Benjamin mourned the loss of the aura associated with art, just as it is to think that he regretted the novel superseding storytelling. It is not that painting or storytelling stood for something gone, which would point to an idea of nostalgia. Nothing about his writings could be further from this idea. Rather his interest in painting and storytelling was in how precisely untimeliness, due to the advent of new technologies, becomes part of its own critical function. Benjamin was fascinated by how "new" media could contribute to expose the anachronism of older media; by way of a kind of retardation of the message, the medium's communicability (the techniques through which perception is shaped and apprehended) becomes all the more apparent. (For more on this important idea see, for example, Weber 2008: 113; see also Hirschkind, Caduff, and de Abreu 2017.) To this capacity of media to partake in their own critique, Benjamin attributed a form of Romanticism, an idea that to my knowledge has been insufficiently explored. Nevertheless, see Weber 2008: 20–30.

3　Judith Butler's (1993, 1997a) important work on "citational practice" informs my own take on the reiterative structure in Charismatic ritualized and daily practice. My qualm is with whether the emphasis on matter and materiality in Butler's incisive writings does justice to the focus on operations Brazil's Charismatics offer and stage. Jacques Derrida (1988), on whom Butler expands, posited that citation is not a secondary example of the performative, but it is that which reveals the structure of the performative. While this idea has highlighted the need to pay attention to materiality, it has also produced the assumption that structure and infrastructure are intrinsically material and, therefore, nonideological. But what if infrastructure is not the exclusive domain of the material, no less than superstructure, as Louis Althusser (2014) also noted, is the province of ideology alone? My reading is this: the common association of infrastructure to materiality draws on modernity's understanding that power operates through opacity. This conception then dictates that the task of critique is to expose (bring consciousness to) "the material infrastructural conditions" as a gesture of overcoming opacity. Yet, my ethnographic engagement with Charismatic Catholicism in Brazil requires that I rethink such determination around the relation between opacity, materiality, and critical function in modern thought. For it is not opacity that underpins the logics of this religious revivalist movement but rather overt exposure. The Holy Spirit anoints, and the function of this anointment is preternaturally rendered by Catholic Charismatics as "seeing through." The question then is what is the political nature of this exposure? What does the power of "seeing through" bodies, buildings, and media screens that this book describes and analyzes do to our inherited paradigms of critique and denunciation? My take is that an emphasis on transparency, the way Charismatics apply it, happens at the cost of a semiotic displacement that disavows the power to index anything in particular. What the showing shows is but the site of an operation that brings the site into full view, totalizing it. The epistemic model that comes to mind is the oil platform anthropologist Hannah Appel (2012) investigates in relation to oil and modularity in Equatorial Guinea. As Appel shows, oil economies function through a radical openness of the "how" that, paradoxically, colonizes the entire space by way of evacuating all specificity and context. This includes the specificity of the how itself. Performative, self-reflective, and modular, the "how" is transferable to elsewhere(s). Charismatic Catholicism aspires to derive its force precisely from a mode of "anointed universalism" that is untethered to any context, even as such effort all the more entails the mobilization of contextual possibilities in which such decontextualization takes form. To go full circle back to Butler in this thinking, see Amy Hollywood's (2012) superb reading of Butler, Derrida, and the problem of meaning and context.

4 What Marie-José Mondzain (2005: 154) in her work on the Byzantine icon calls "the making of the meadow." To talk of mediation would for Mondzain be tantamount to calling the icon art, but as she writes the icon is not art but economy; it is work and it is a network of relations.

5 This exemption of eschatology, then, is an interesting paradox in Charismatic thought in particular, given Charismatics' reliance on Pauline theology that is often associated with a doctrine of ends and messianic return. Yet, this loss of eschatology becomes an end in itself in establishing the dramatic element of

theater that Charismatics draw from the Bible, particularly from the Book of Acts.

6 In Charismatic terms temporality thematizes the operations through which time itself is perceived. This often involves engaging tensile dynamics between opposites whereby, for instance, an experience of fullness is best experienced through emptiness, that is, the point at which one extreme is about to become the other.

1. The Media Acts of the Apostles

Portions of this chapter first appeared in "Breath, Media, and the Making of Canção Nova Community," in *Aesthetic Formations: Media, Religion, and the Senses*, edited by Birgit Meyer, 161–82 (New York: Palgrave Macmillan, 2009).

1 Stories such as these circulate among Canção Nova media publics and in the CCR more generally. They are repeated time and again and gain the status of myth or parable that often ends up being inserted in sermons or proselytizing.

2 All biblical passages are from the New King James Version (1982).

3 Nelsinho, in conversation with the author, Canção Nova, May 12, 2001.

4 Laércio, in conversation with the author, Canção Nova, May 13, 2001.

5 Charismatics repeat this phrase as part of a common archive (familiar forms of reproducible sentences and gestures or sometimes simply gestures). They customarily create sentences, proverbs, and idioms whose purpose is to be cited. This creates a cycle of circulation of citable speech, that is, language poised to be transported elsewhere.

6 Nelsinho (a member of Canção Nova), Canção Nova website, accessed November 9, 2015, www.cancaonova.com/cnova/eventos/coberturas/2004 (no longer available). He repeats the story here: "PHN Diácono Nelsinho Partilha Historia com a Canção Nova," posted by Canção Nova (Oficial), February 4, 2016, accessed May 22, 2020, https://www.youtube.com/watch?v=XUrRQTE1_uo.

7 The Acts of the Apostles (in Greek, *Praxeis Apostolon*) is the fifth book of the New Testament. Acts narrates the story of the early Christian church, with special emphasis on the ministries of the twelve apostles and of Paul of Tarsus.

8 I draw on Charles S. Peirce's linguistic-anthropological distinction between referential terms and indexical terms, the latter being words that refer to the aspect, truth-value, or spatiotemporal coordinates such as *that* or *then* (see Silverstein 1976: 25). See Maurer 2002 for a fascinating account of the relation between the abolishment of anteriority in semiotic terms and the operations of financial derivatives in neoliberal logics through the articulation between mathematical technique and what he calls the "theological unconscious."

9 In Austin's conception of the performative, theater would fall into what he considered "parasitical" and nonfelicitous precisely inasmuch as he considered theater an instance of the extra-ordinary, which he opposed to ordinary performative speech-acts (Austin [1962] 1975; see also Weber 2004: 7).

10   The new canons and sacraments introduced by the modern church in the latter part of the nineteenth century led to what Charismatics regard and condemn as an excessive rationalization of the Catholic Church, which they see as synonymous with opacity. Charismatics then associate opacity with rationalization and the sensory regime of "seeing" in opposition to transparency, bodily experience (anointment), and "seeing through."

11   *Seeing* (indirect, opaque) and *seeing through* (direct, transparent) express an epistemological divergence within the Catholic Church according to which the church "knows," whereas Charismatics experience. Charismatics sometimes employ the figure of Peter, the stable rock, to comment on this rationalization, contrasting him with Paul, the traveler, who made a church wherever he went. Charismatics echo the vision that John Paul II was an evangelist who criticized the petrifying elements of the Roman Catholic Church. On this point, see Hervieu-Léger 1995; and Mitchell 1996. According to Charismatics, the ideal is to convert the possibility of seeing (here associated with Saint Peter and the church) into that of seeing *through*, as modeled by Saint Paul and the CCR, thus challenging the instrumental mediations of the church in light of claims for a more direct access connecting believers and the divine.

12   Again, what is noteworthy about this alternative to modern critique is how Charismatics' endorsing of "transparency" and "directness" capitalizes on discourses of opacity internal to those protocols in order to suggest a new logic of fluidity and flexibility. It is an extraordinary move that must be grasped through a fresh—and no less flexible—critical reading of how right-wing movements and groups today draw on older progressive logics to mobilize their own agenda. So often depicted as whimsical and playful, the caustic Holy Spirit interventions toward "seeing through" can be compared to the cynical reasoning that imbues Brazil's contemporary political system, a system where practices of exposure (of corruption and otherwise) happen not because of a commitment against opacity but because of the disarming power of exposure, its preemptive and its immunizing potentials. The rising of a new critique will have to find a form to account for the opacities of exposure itself.

13   Interview with Nuno Carvalho, follower of PHN *Generation* Canção Nova, November 2001.

14   Canção Nova is not only the most well-known and most sought-out *comunidade de vida* of the Brazilian Charismatic movement but is also the example that launched the model for all of Brazil. In 2000 Brazil had a total of two hundred *comunidades de vida*, rising to three hundred four years later (de Oliveira 2004: 111). This is not to say that all communities work with media. Most, however, not only use media materials from Canção Nova but also transmit Canção Nova's media productions on a local and transnational level. Canção Nova, in turn, has grown through the years institutionally and in personnel. From its first twelve members in 1978, in 2001 the community consisted of three hundred internal members and nearly seven hundred associates spread

worldwide throughout its sixteen mission houses. Here is one of the many online videos about the birth and evolution of the community: "Um Pouco da Historia da Canção Nova," posted by TV Canção Nova, March 18, 2009, https://www.youtube.com/watch?v=NlyY7t8aoHQ.

15 Formed by men and women, intermarriage in the community is not infrequent. Individuals, however, are aware that they might be called in prayer to move to other missions or houses of Canção Nova, within and even outside Brazil for long periods of time. To be able to accept such calls with docility and obedience is a demonstration that one understands that what brought two people together is the same force that might keep them apart for long periods.

16 In this sense the technological is never a replacement that frees the individuals from circulating oil (unction) as a principle of public order, as for example in Angie Heo's (2018: 193–95) account of Samya's oil-exuding hand, for which reason she had to be "secluded from public visibility." Rather, oil, or chrism, in the way Charismatics operationalize it, falls into the category of the sacrificial *hiéron*, as opposed to *hagion*, as adopted by Byzantine theological debates of such icons as Our Lady of Theotókos and Our Lady of Contact. Why sacrificial? Because, unlike the prohibitive *hagion*, it allows itself to be shared and thus contaminated, "violated." As Heo notes in her study on Coptic Christians in Egypt, the difference between *hiéron* and *hagion* as also explored by Marie-José Mondzain in her work on Byzantine iconography, draws on the writings of Émile Benveniste (1971: 168), a linguist who was interested in the idea of a middle voice as a kind of subject in circulation, whose being partakes in and rises from being at once the center and the process of a subject formation, in the "effect of being affected, in the middle."

17 Early in 2001, when I first visited Canção Nova, there was talk of how not to let "errors in the administration of oil" affect the "fluvial" structure of the Charismatic movement, a striking parallel to the sinking of P-36, at the time the world's largest semi-submerged oil platform, where twelve people were killed after a massive explosion. The associations of spirit and oil would go through all sorts of excurses, innuendos, and cross-references, and one can only begin to imagine the slippery slope opened by Operation Car Wash in 2014, by which time oil, state, and corporate businesses were becoming indistinguishable.

18 The Portuguese word *meio* relates to being in the midst, to environment (*meio ambiente*), and to means of communication (*meio de comunicação*).

19 The fact that the CCR evolved as a predominantly upper-middle-class movement among university scholars affiliated with conservative Catholic groups only deepened the rift separating it from the local, progressive, left-wing Catholic Church, whose alleged preference for the poor proved irreconcilable with what Charismatics considered the CCR's spiritually oriented, Americanized televangelical industry.

20 Press interview during the 20th National Encounter of the CCR—Aparecida,

July 25, 2001. The National Congress of the CCR is an annual event spread across five days that gathers all important personalities, sectors, and lay members from all over Brazil, Latin America, and other parts of the world. The congress is an attempt to bring Charismatic Revivalism and the Catholic Church together into one mega-event, through a combination of religious rituals, testimonies, and press interviews. In this national encounter in the National Santuário da Aparecida do Norte, I witnessed people quaking and falling in the Spirit by the mere passing of Padre Jonas in the corridors where the main stalls representative of the CCR movement were selling their products and informing visitors and participants about their missionary activities.

21 See Toca de Assis, http://www.tocadeassis.org.br (accessed May 25, 2020).

22 See, for example, various opinions about the profile of Padre Jonas in section "O Que Dizem Dele" [What people say about Him], in "Monsenhor Jonas Abib," Canção Nova, accessed February 11, 2020, http://www.cancaonova .com/portal/canais/pejonas/textos.php?id=34.

23 Mass of the Audio Club, November 7, 2001.

24 In his letters, Saint Paul enumerates the different charismata in terms of charisms of the word, which include glossolalia and prophecy; charisms of action, including charity and miraculous cures; charisms of cognition, which include the gift of knowledge, discernment, and science. Charity, however, is the charisma he extols as the foundation for all others. Charisma shares with charity and charm the same etymological root in *Kharis*.

25 For example, on July 30, 2001, the difference between ins (3,332,918.24 reais) and outs (2,336,393.27 reais) ended up positive (996,524.97 reais). Only during the previous week did the flow of souls actually accelerate. See Canção Nova 2001.

26 To say that it mediates (or, for that matter, im-mediates) would mean it mediates *between* this and that, say, between sacred things and technical attributes. But what the operational logics of incarnation in Charismatic terms suspend is precisely this idea of the in-between, or even of the interval as space in between. In the recursive operation of the camera that looks back onto itself, making origins and ends spiral, that space field of an in-between that mediation (much like presence) implies also undergoes a transformation. What was in between becomes an indefinite middle in the self-recursive return of the image to itself. It is possible to trace this idea to Paul's engagements with the philosophies of the gymnasium in Greek Corinth (see Dutch 2005; Forbes 1945). Following the discipline of the gymnasium, with its focus on exposing the powers of articulated rhetoric through the example of well-oiled bodies, Paul reworks a theory of spirit as "articulator" that challenges Aristotle's conception of the medium on which conventional theories of mediation depend. As Samuel Weber (2001: 52) writes, "The main tendency of the Aristotelian concept of the medium is that of an interval, a space between constituted and preexisting poles or points: a space in short, whose emptiness is framed by

what it is not, empty, such that a continuum exists." It is this continuum as a defining feature of the interval or in-between space that Paul and Charismatics alter in their practices. Their own sense of interval is more like a figure in the theatrical experiencing of Constantin Constantius (pseudonym of Søren Kierkegaard) inquiring on repetition, about which Kierkegaard writes, "[But] instead of such continuity, he [Constantius] encounters disjunction and doubling in the theatrical 'coming-goings' (of gesture) . . . [that is] 'the clear-cut separation of opposites breaks down' encircling instead a dynamically uncanny third space, [one] 'that is empty in its plenitude, isolated in its separateness'" (Kierkegaard [1843] 1964: 52).

27 Or what my students Ben Bieser and Aaron Su call *pneumatoliberalism*, after a conversation with me in my office at Columbia University. See http://c-j-l-c .org/portfolio/pneumatoliberalism-a-conversation-with-maria-jose-de-abreu/.

2. Confession, Technically Speaking

1 Coffee shops of Jesus is one among many projects Charismatics have created to stimulate and proliferate a variety of juxtapositions between Christianity and public life in the form of fun religious-oriented practical events. Other examples of how Charismatics draw on and absorb from the arenas of popular culture are "the carnival of Jesus," "the aerobics of Jesus," or the heavy-metal Jesus Rock Band. See chapter 1, note 16, for more on the political stakes of this co-option of profane elements by Christianity through the distinction between the *hiéron* and *hagion*.

2 Here it would be interesting to compare and distinguish the status of accountability in terms of either "response" or "answer." Samuel Weber (2017: S160–61) operates with this distinction on the basis that whereas the function of an *answer* is to bring closure, a *response* encourages and propels the cycle by means of "a next." In that sense, to respond is not to bring closure or to enclose but to sustain the circuit as open-ended (see Carlson 2008). Thus, for example, Walter Benjamin used the novel as an example of a medium that embodies the logic of "an answer," notably, through the function of the reader who survives the end of the novel (and thus survives the end by becoming spectator to his or her own death), unlike in storytelling, the purpose of which is to keep up indefinitely with the question "And then? . . . And then?" In other words, the purpose of "response-ability" is to revive the question of "a next" (see Masco 2012; de Abreu 2013a; Caduff 2018). Weber (2017: S161) writes, "If there is a response to this question, it is another story, which like all stories, repeats and modifies earlier ones." My point here, as throughout the entire book, is to restate how Charismatics suspend the idea of eschatology or ends in a guise that redefines the very idea of a *medium* as that which maintains one in the indefinite middle or milieu as a spatial aspect, yet a spatial that is essentially temporal. Space is carved out of a rhythm or ongoing sway. In this affirma-

tion of middleness, Charismatics not only attune themselves to the temporal sensibility of neoliberalism but do so in ways that recall the counter-reforming baroque logics and aesthetics as powerfully articulated in Benjamin's ([1963] 1998a) *The Origin of German Tragic Drama*. What matters is neither origins (pre-) nor ends (post-) but rather to draw these into the "maelstrom" of an interval that rhythmically absorbs the "before" and the "after" into itself and as middle/ing.

3 Wittgenstein ([1922] 2001: 54–55) then compares tautology to contradiction: "A tautology leaves the infinite whole of logical space open to reality. A contradiction fills it, leaving no point of it for reality." While I am interested in the sway of opposites it does not follow that it is about contradiction. What makes the scene I am describing alien to contradiction is a regime of practice. As Michael Lambek (2016: 6) asks, "While propositions can be described as contradictory to one another or even internally self-contradictory can the same be said for practices (like smoking and jogging or advocating for clean air) or for commitments (like to a partner and a profession, or even to one friend and another)? From a certain perspective these might be considered inconsistencies rather than contradictions. They could produce conflict (again different from contradiction) and the sense of being pulled in opposite directions—situations that get resolved through practical judgment and sometimes rupture. They could also lead to various tactics or strategies, including (unconscious) repression, (subconscious) rationalization, ambivalence, self-deception, (conscious) lying, or attempts at compromise," or, as he himself studies in Malagasy spirit possession, to irony and double stance. See also Lambek 2010.

4 Efforts to digitalize Canção Nova started well back in the late 1990s through a Canção Nova website or by participating on Second Life but only on April 2, 2018, did Canção Nova achieve the ambition of installing digital TV (Channel 59.1) within São Paulo, available to 18 million people across eleven cities.

5 As studies on hip-hop have noted and not unlike the experimentation with word and sound explored here, one key feature of the genre is subordination of the written to the oral. In performance, voice actualizes the written text so the latter becomes alienated from its original enunciation. This stylistic procedure encloses the oscillation between singing and speaking. When combined, these two functions attempt to reveal the mechanisms of reinterpretation—not just how a song is sung but what singing itself does to the song. The mechanisms of tension and release, of rise and fall, of return and ellipse, shape a song to become an abstract doubling of the rhythmic scene of the body. For a broad variety of approaches to this idea, browse the *Journal of Hip-Hop Studies*.

6 This is the core idea in Jacques Derrida's engagement with J. L. Austin's ([1962] 1975) notion of the performative in *How to Do Things with Words*, an idea that Judith Butler (1997b) then explored to new heights regarding questions of gender and processes of materialization through ritualized convention and repetition of norms. See also Cavell 1995. Benjamin (1968) also deals with these

points through the theater of Brecht and the centrality of citation in staging the operations of theater themselves (hence the reason one says *citability*, the ability to cite, more than just *citation*). In any case, Butler's work really marks a moment in which meaning and matter are at odds. Yet as religion scholar Amy Hollywood (2012) underscores, there is a lot of work to do regarding the fraught relationship between those two concepts. In my own reading I think this involves stronger conceptualizing of the interval created by the displacement between norms and iterability, that is, what happens to the very notion of interval in the ritualized repetition of norms (see chapter 1, note 26). For an exploration of this idea in another context, see de Abreu 2019, 2020a.

7 This comparison is inspired by Roger Caillois's (1984: 31) text on mimicry, where he compares the "false corpse-like rigidity" of the phasmid insect to the "spectacle of mimicry" in *The Temptation of Saint Anthony* by Gustave Flaubert. I quote him at length: In Flaubert's description "plants are now no longer distinguished from animals. . . . Insects identical with rose petals adorn a bush . . . . And then plants are confused with stones. Rocks look like brains, stalactites like breasts, veins of iron like tapestries adorned with figures." In thus seeing the three realms of nature merging into each other, Anthony in his turn suffers the lure of material space: he wants to split himself thoroughly, to be in everything, "to penetrate each atom." The emphasis is surely placed on the pantheistic and even overwhelming aspect of this descent into hell, but this in no way lessens its appearance here as a form of the process of the generalization of space at the expense of the individual, unless one were to employ a psychoanalytic vocabulary and speak of reintegration with original insensibility and prenatal unconsciousness: a contradiction in terms.

8 It is worth revisiting the whole passage in "Publics and Counterpublics" (2002: 90) where Warner stresses the importance of self-reflexive circulation in the production of a public. Warner, however, is referring to a level of discourse, which may not go subcutaneously enough, as it were, to capture how among PHNers what gets communicated is the very signal of a communicative circulation as it is taking place. As he writes, "No single text can create a public. Nor can a single voice, a single genre, even a single medium. All are insufficient to create the kind of reflexivity that we call a public, since a public is understood to be an ongoing space of encounter for discourse. It is not texts themselves that create publics, but the concatenation of texts through time. Only when a previously existing discourse can be supposed, and when a responding discourse can be postulated can a text address a public."

9 It seems appropriate to refer to Lúcio Pinheiro dos Santos, who, according to Bachelard (on whom Lefebvre draws), coined the term *rhythmanalysis*. Pinheiro dos Santos, a Portuguese philosopher and scientist, went into exile in Brazil during the military dictatorship in Portugal, and the original document on *ritmanálise* remains lost to this day. For Pinheiro dos Santos the universe,

including the moral and the ethical, consisted of rhythm and undulation. In recent years there have been serious attempts at recovering Pinheiro dos Santos's phantasmic work. See, for example, *O Filósofo Fantasma* by Pedro Baptista (2010).

10 With her usual brilliance, Sedgwick (1993: 29) draws attention to the descriptions of the heroine of Denis Diderot's *The Nun* in terms of the "oddly unanchored imperative of ignorance."

11 Thus as a researcher on-site at Canção Nova I was once called on by a female participant whose hand had darkened when interceding for me as she saw "I needed it." As the event unfolded, I (confess that I) was not immersed in "participation" (I hardly ever was) and that (devilish) "darkness" translated my presence into a "short-circuit" or "blackout" in the room. That night my tapes were confiscated and examined by members of the community, and I would learn that a lack of participation is comparable to knowledge, which in turn relates to diabolism. What they have in common, I was told then, is that they divide and separate. It became clear to me how my "dark presence" enabled Charismatics to highlight the very risks they so energetically protected themselves against; this was above all the risk of the boundedness of the sacred, and this fear of boundedness targeted the modern episteme as much as those religious traditions that emphasize separation (*hiéron*). If Canção Nova had to overcome all the prejudgments attributed to any collaboration between mass media and the sacred—as it did in Brazil, partly due to an intellectual demonization of televangelism—it was because Charismatics understand, much like Nikephoros, the patriarch of Constantinople, articulates in his *Antirrhetici*, that all institutions (churches, bodies, words, lungs, icons, things) are abodes of the *hagion pneuma* (Mondzain 2005: 147). Charismatics at Canção Nova endow electronic media with the powers of the aperture that Nikephoros attributed to the icon when he said it was "a graphic opening toward the divine." Accordingly, whatever interrupts the natural (read, artificial) circulation of the icon must not be simply eliminated but itself illuminate what is at stake, notably, the operational mechanisms of an iconicity. This is why writings on the Byzantine iconography will highlight how (after Nikephoros) the value of the icon resided in how its technical properties (its management, its *oikonomia*) instituted "a formal resemblance that was nothing but the very possibility of thinking" (Ghosh 2011: 75).

12 Ideally then Charismatics potentially differ from the Aristotelian distinction between "first actuality" (sometimes translated as "realization") and "second actuality" as espoused in Aristotle's *Generation of Animals*. Aristotle was interested in defining the range of the soul, and for that he considers the borderline notion of sleep (or that of plants). To that end he introduces two senses of actuality: one corresponding to knowledge possessed, and the other to knowledge exercised. Accordingly, Aristotle considered sleep as something one possesses but not something one exercises. However, Charismatics propose that

sleep can—and should—involve exercising or what Aristotle called the second order of "realization" (Aristotle 1942: 41–42). See Agamben 2016 for an engagement with Aristotle's views on sleep and virtue. Agamben quotes Aristotle: "Supposing someone to be asleep all his life, we should hardly consent to call such a person happy. Life indeed he has, but life according to virtue he has not" (7). See Agamben 2016: chapter 1, "The Human Being without Work"; chapter 5, "Use-of-Oneself," in considering the relation between ethics and auto-affection.

13 There is a Christian tradition of connecting respiration to spiritual education of the body as noted by mystic and anatomist Emanuel Swedenborg, for example, in "Influx and Intercourse between the Soul and the Body" (Swedenborg 2009: 561–76). Unlike Charismatics, who draw on *The Philokalia*, one of the first books from which the "prayer of the heart" was taken, Swedenborg reclaimed what he called a discipline of "breathless time" or "internal breathing." As he wrote in his diary, "When we draw breath a host of ideas rush from beneath as through an opened door, into the sphere of thought; whereas when we hold the breath and slowly let it out, we deeply keep the while in the tenor of our thought, and communicate, as it were, with the higher faculty of the soul, as I have observed in mine own person times out of number. Retaining or holding back the breath is equivalent to holding intercourse with the soul; attracting or drawing it is equivalent to intercourse with the body" (quoted in Bigelow 1888: xlviii).

14 Thus, both opposing—and yet mirroring—the psychoanalytical reading of the fetish according to which the denial of a feared absence through its replacement also highlights the absence it means to cover up. See Ivy 1995: 10.

15 I borrow the notion of autoimmunity from Jacques Derrida, particularly his "Faith and Knowledge" in *Acts of Religion* (2002).

16 "Its [the Catholic Church's] elasticity is in fact astonishing in that throughout history, it has managed to form alliances with the most opposed tendencies and groups" (Schmitt 1996: 6). As Schmitt insists this outstanding elasticity is rooted in epistemology; indeed, it is epistemological, a form of knowing in the sense of "grasping" or "comprehending." On the relevance of Schmitt's ideas to think present logics of "militarized thinking," see Weber 2005.

17 This command to stretch things to limits through tension and conflict characterizes the complexity of the Catholic Charismatic movement in Brazil. As mentioned, what is distinctive about this overt effort to take things to the extreme is how the more extreme one goes, the more one is able to assert the center (personified in the figure of Rome) it wants to distance or decenter itself from. This idea of a complexion of opposites, where unalloyed oppositions remain in order to fold into a center, distinguishes Carl Schmitt's ([1923] 1996) *complexio oppositorum* from *coincidentia oppositorum*, or "unity of opposites," recovered from Heraclitus by the fifteenth-century Neoplatonist Nicholas of Cusa. Contrary to the former that expresses a kind of open-ended vitalism

through the maintenance of opposites, *coincidentia oppositorum* explicitly expresses as its luminous and ultimate goal the reconciling harmonizing of opposites. See Certeau 1987 for a fabulous analysis of this idea in theories of the gaze and visual iconography. See Carlson 2008 for an exploration of this idea in both medieval theology and our technomediatic present.

18 Here it is worth making the distinction between *glossolalia* and *xenoglossia*. The latter posits a linguistic alterity within the self that might be more appropriate to Charismatic Christianity according to the image of the outpouring of Pentecost and the cenacle, or upper room. Also given the link between body and building in Brazil's Charismatic Christianity it would be interesting to think of the cenacle in terms of the pectoral muscle as an upper room in the body, as opposed to the lower body, normally associated with the feminine (as in *Ruha*). (See Cooper-Rompato 2010 for a gendered approach to xenoglossia.) For a brilliant analysis of the linguistic and stylistic differences between glossolalia and xenoglossia in relation to the inventory of speech sounds in Canção Nova, see Bonfim 2015.

19 As in Walt Whitman's (1961) famous poem in *Leaves of Grass*.

20 Conversation with Dunga in Canção Nova House Mission (Casa de Missão) in São Paulo, March 2003. It is here that Dunga broadcasts his PHN talk show, hugely popular among young Charismatics, the confessional counterpart to the festival show and PHN camping at Canção Nova this chapter describes.

21 Émile Benveniste's (1971) important study of the "middle voice" touches on a regime of address congenial to that used in the PHN confessional show. What hails in the middle voice, according to Benveniste, is the relational entity of something like a third person. He posits a theory of performative utterance (much like Austin's performative acts) in which grammar is spatialized. His idea of the middle voice shows that in the active tense verbs denote a process that is realized starting from the subject and outside of it: "In the middle . . . the verb denotes a process centering in the subject: the subject is interior to the process" (168). The voice of the third is, therefore, the voice that renders open the operations involved in its "utterance." It does so, however, only as it reproduces a context that is already authorized (see Silverstein 1976, 1992; Lee 1997).

22 As Heller-Roazen (2002: 93) puts it, "Language is sundered from its semantic and intentional ends."

3. Outstanding Elasticity

1 While the TV program is titled *Adoration Thursday*, the ritual of looking at the zoomed host is best known as *Adoration Hour*.

2 The inspiration for the Holy Hour is Matthew 26:40, when in the Garden of Gethsemane the night before crucifixion Jesus asks Peter, "So, could you men not keep watch with me for one hour?"

3 In his thoughts on television, Samuel Weber (1996) draws attention to how in

English we use the verb "to watch" when referring to TV instead of "looking at" or "seeing," as we relate to a photograph or a film, respectively. As Weber explains, the choice of this word has to do with the regime's own fantasies of directness translated into the idea that the image on the TV screen is somewhat alive. Even though the operations of filming are taking place elsewhere, this *elsewhere* is also *present* in the here and now of transmission.

4 Conversation with Roberta, São Paulo, May 5, 2001. Despite not being involved with media elements of the Charismatic movement, Roberta played a key role in introducing me to informants in the field throughout the years. And I am thankful.

5 In *24/7* Jonathan Crary (2014) notes how in different parts of the world the late 1990s worked on developing techniques of wakefulness and hypervigilance and how these happened in coordination with the rise of new global markets and in response to the alternative rotating distributions of daylight and night across the hemispheres. The call for constant vigilance, he explains, has to do with what he describes as "a contemporary imaginary in which a state of permanent illumination is inseparable from the non-stop operation of global exchange and circulation" (5). This call for maximum alertness is connected to a change in our current culture of temporality, one that tends to emphasize the "live" qualities of time defined as an event. Yet it is this emphasis that also produces a distinction between live time and dead time and thus between active and passive, productive and inert. Paradoxically, what it is to be live, what it is to be active and productive also becomes associated with, and indeed defined by, a sovereign form of vulnerability, precisely the kind that requires vigilance and permanent looking after.

6 As we learn in Marx's *Eighteenth Brumaire of Louis Bonaparte* ([1852] 2012), coins (and wafers) did not merely concentrate value in themselves. Above all, coins were valuable in their performative ability to chase and communicate with their own cause. The value was in circulation itself. What coins communicated was a certain spirit of contradiction made possible, above all, by the ability to circle without encircling.

7 The analogy of wafer and coin was important in medieval debates of the late twelfth century. The dangerous possibility that coins could be confounded for wafers tightened all sorts of mirrorings between these two species. A kind of diplomacy existed between both: the wafer lent the coin its aura of sacrality and sacrifice in exchange for "a certain purity of metallic substance" proper to *denarius* (or pennies). Importantly, the virtues of an ethical exercise were not in one or the other but in the space between them.

8 See how Caroline Walker Bynum (1995) deals with this Catholic legacy in "Why All the Fuss about the Body? A Medievalist's Perspective."

9 Bynum (2012) reflects wonderfully on these logics in medieval conceptions of presence to talk about the role of paradox and contradiction as a scholar and a thinker.

10　Kumler (2011: 180–81) continues, "The wafer was an object produced by mechanical means whose exceptional value in medieval Christian culture was paradoxically linked to its infinite repetition, to its presentation of the same details of form and facture week after week. In this way, the host dissembled; it refused any figural or morphological relationship to its paramount referent and end state, Christ's body. It embraced processes of multiplication while maintaining its claims to realize Christ's singular presence."

11　Peter Brown (1981, 1983) has explored the predicaments of this phenomenon. As he and other scholars explain, regimes of sanctity always operate on the fault line between the exceptional and the imitable. See also Castelli 2004.

12　Interview with Monsignor Arnaldo Beltrami, São Paulo, March 18, 2001.

13　"Many leaves, too few grapes." Interview with Monsignor Arnaldo Beltrami, São Paulo, March 18, 2001. Monsignor Beltrami had strong past affinities with the liberationist cartel—famous for its interventionist profile in local and international political arenas—that spearheaded the archdiocese of São Paulo during the military years. Beltrami had been a comrade-in-arms to the Franciscan leader Don Paulo Arns, who was then the president of the archdiocese.

14　Known throughout the Catholic world for his role as a human rights activist and critical opponent of the military state, Don Arns became a hero to many liberal-minded priests and to Franciscans in particular. The simplicity, desire for equity, and care for the underprivileged that Saint Francis personified went well with Marxist ideas. Saint Francis worked as a legitimizing model on which to draw when calling for political activism and critical intervention pursued on Catholic grounds. After his retirement, Don Arns became a writer and an associate of the church and convent of São Francisco in the old quarter of São Paulo city. It is there that on specific days and after written solicitation, journalists and researchers like myself have a chance to talk to the former church activist.

15　Sister Rita continued: "There have been some experiences already with some young girls who stayed here at the sacristy for a week or so, with our orientation and with our madre. It cannot be for too long because it is very small here still, but if after this second year of experience, everything goes well, and with the grace of our Lord Jesus, it will be a real monastery when the cells and the inner cloisters are built. . . . Because it works like this: each monastery of the order has its own autonomy. Each monastery has its madre, its *mestra*, and its vicar. It is not dependent on another monastery. But every time a new monastery is founded, there is a monastery in the region that adopts it and gives it some supervision until the monastery runs by itself. So we became a kind of adopted monastery. The federal madre has also a word to say about it. In 2000 a new madre was appointed to run the monastery of Marília. Of great help was that she had been appointed by the federal madre too, so she played a big role in allowing this provisional monastery. By that time our own madre needed to solve the problems of this monastery here in Canção Nova. That year of experience was over, and the documents in Rome were still not ready. So the madre of Marília, she took responsibility for this monastery here and asked the bishop of Lorena for another year of experience. This new federal madre, she is more experienced. So she is now organizing the documents so that we have a definitive 'yes' to our permanence here."

16 Still thinking of the idea of "real presence" in debates on the Eucharist (and despite my nonphenomenological approach), it is worth mentioning that Bachelard (1988), in *Air and Dreams* as in his *Psychoanalysis of Fire*, likens the power to contemplate to "a function of the unreal," which he describes as the imaginative force that enables a person to create new images instead of adjusting to reality as given (see, e.g., 129–45).

4. The Aerobics of Jesus

Parts of this chapter appeared in "Goose Bumps All Over: Breath, Media, and Tremor," *Social Text* 26, no. 3 (2): 59–78.

1 The logic of the end of time thus is addressed in terms of being forever in the middle. To say that the ends are in the middle as such—that is, as medium—is also to disinvest the notion of medium from any idea of instrumentality in the sense of a means to an end. On the contrary, the end of all mediation is interruption. It is mediality as such. It is useful to compare this idea to logics of the end of time. See Stewart and Harding 1999. I deal with this idea in greater detail in de Abreu 2013a.

2 He often tells the media that he was once an assiduous user of steroids, a resource that still tempts him, especially when faith seemed to wither and stress abounded, thus suggesting a parallel between anabolic steroids and the Holy Spirit (pneuma) in altering, by enhancing, membrane fluidity. He admitted to using steroids again as he recovered from a radical diet on which he lost more than 30 kilograms (data is not conclusive). These oscillations in mass, fat, and metabolism in Padre Marcelo's body are themselves indicative of a powerful narrative and national fantasy projected on the concept of movement rendered in spiritual and physical terms. For a now-classic feminist perspective on "weightless bodies," see Bordo 1993. See also Berlant 2011.

3 Bishop Fernando Figueiredo will be the ever-present shadow everywhere Padre Marcelo goes. But then Bishop Figueiredo has been formed by Orthodox patristic doctrines—he will be the linkage between Byzantium and São Paulo, between pneuma and aerobics.

4 Composers, filmmakers, and phone-sex services are all aimed at tuning the skin, gearing the magical effect of media to the production of bodily affect. The goth singer Marilyn Manson, for instance, draws on dark emotional elements from horror films to generate "horripilation," a musical genre whose goal is the root of the word *horrify*—to stand on end. This deliberately addresses the hairs of the body and visualizes skin as a sort of twilight zone. A

Japanese project of noise reverberation, Merzbow moves beyond the ear into the skin and bone fabric. Among contemporary classical composers, the Pole Krzysztof Penderecki and the Hungarian György Ligeti have similarly tried to use music to generate a sensory experience of horror and fear. In a more cinematic register, the work of Linda Williams shows us the power of pornography to affect the body and to turn the viewer into a "corporealized observer." Likewise worth mentioning are the cinematic compositions of the postwar American film artist Ken Jacobs, as an example of how the medium of cinema can be used as a means to both stimulate and make us aware of our body tropes, physical experiences, and realities.

5 Pope John Paul's call to invite the power of the Holy Spirit to shake the otherwise stiffened contours of the Vatican was interpreted by some as running counter to the spiritualities of consciousness proposed by liberation theology. One of the climaxes of this tension happened in 1985, during John Paul's mandate, by the Congregation for the Doctrine of the Faith (directed at the time by Cardinal Joseph Ratzinger, the future pope Benedict XVI) against Frei Leonardo Boff, Brazil's distinctive theologian and emeritus professor at Rio de Janeiro State University. Ratzinger's censoring of Boff's (1985) book *Church, Charism and Power: Liberation Theology and the Institutional Church* and later the conflict over his presence at the ECO-92 Earth Summit in Rio de Janeiro led Boff to leave the Franciscan religious order and priesthood. During John Paul II's mandate, calls for changes in Latin American orientations were sweeping and decisive in the popularity of the Charismatic movement in Brazil. There were conspiracy theories running throughout the dioceses of Brazil about the interpenetration of a certain anti-Roman affect within the Vatican. The rise to stardom of Padre Marcelo Rossi and of the Charismatic Renewal as a whole against the withdrawal and excommunication of Frei Boff fomented sotto voce recantation and commentary that the Vatican of John Paul II was bathing in well-oiled Greek doctrines of the *gymnasion* of Paul, away from well-seated sophistry and ideology and toward a new orthopraxis whose focus on the spirit and the corporeal—and concomitant removal from view of the blood and sacrifice of the Passion—belied a turn away from sociopolitical matters.

6 Padre Marcelo, *Domingo Legal* (talk show), December 26, 1999.

7 "O Padre e o Rei," *Isto é Gente*, October 28, 2001; see also de Abreu 2005.

8 On November 2, All Saints' Day, Padre Marcelo and Roberto Carlos performed songs from the CD live in a massive sing-along with a crowd of 2.4 million people. The success of the album led in 2001 to a Latin Grammy for Best Christian Album, though Padre Marcelo and Carlos could not pick up their award due to the cancellation of the ceremony following the attacks on the World Trade Center. The events of 9/11, however, made the CD even more powerful, as the title, *Peace Live*, seemed eerily prescient. If the album represented a breakthrough into the sphere of political aesthetics by tying Padre Marcelo's

religious music to political events, then the goose bumps it induced could be seen as an affective monument to the lives lost on 9/11.

9 This self-imagination as angel became particularly explicit in *Maria, Mae de Deus* (Mary, Mother of God; 2004), his first feature film. In this film, which was widely circulated in Brazil, Padre Marcelo plays both the archangel Gabriel, who conveys the message of the advent to Mary, and himself. That Padre Marcelo juxtaposes in the same diegetic space of the film his playing *of* (not as) both archangel and himself captures the ideas expressed in chapter 1 about the nature of dramatic form in Charismatic theatricality and the conception of mediation, the idea that in acting one is not just representing or entering someone else's shoes, as the structure of empathy would frame it. Rather, to act is above all to enter a relation of ex-citation or reiteration between what was before and what comes after. It is, in other words, to work and reflect back on the articulations through which things become rendered as citable: the citability of acts. Acting, in short, is an expression of an operation of recursion, a process that, as we will see in chapter 5, is itself "incarnated" in the icon of Theotókos on which—more than to whom—Padre Marcelo models the structure of his film. For more on the structure of this film, see de Abreu 2005.

10 As made explicit in CNBB's (1994b) published polemic *Orientações Pastorais Sobre a Renovação Carismática*, admonishments were penned by chief leaders of Brazil's Catholic Church against the abuses in using the gifts of the Holy Spirit (*os dons do Espirito Santo*) by Catholic Charismatics.

5. Sanctuary Theotókos

1 Hereafter Santuário Mãe de Deus. Some people refer to it as Santuário Theotókos or simply, as most call it, Santuário do Padre Marcelo.

2 Interview with Gerónimo Silva in Escola da Cidade, São Paulo, August 12, 2012.

3 Given that the construction of the Santuário Mãe de Deus is still ongoing, I shall from here on refer to it in the gerundive term so as to highlight the irreducibility of the building to an indicative "is."

4 As Mondzain (2005: 164) also refers to this icon, which I'll explore below. See also Csordas 1995 on the central role of oxymorons (and short-circuits) in Charismatic thought.

5 The Santuário Mãe de Deus resembles in style and in concept the kind of "drive-in" church spaces described by Erica Robles-Anderson (2012) in her study of the Garden Grove Community Church in the United States, an aesthetic that combines the automobile and the cinema. Unlike the Garden Grove or the Universal Church in Brazil, however, Padre Marcelo's project is far from obtaining the kind of capital, institutional, or corporate support undergirding such megachurches.

6 The brilliance of Mondzain's (2005) analytic descriptions in *Image, Icon,*

Economy has informed my ideas and shaped the structure of this chapter, perhaps even of this book.

7 Andrade Gutierrez S.A. is Brazil's second largest construction company and is one of more than thirty construction companies being investigated in the sprawling probe that has ensnared senior executives and high-ranking politicians in Latin America's largest economy. The franchise operates in many parts of the Lusophone world, including in Mozambique and Angola, but also in other areas of the African continent with substantial activity around oil and gas extraction, such as Nigeria, Ghana, and Equatorial Guinea. The company's Latin American operations are based in Colombia, Peru, and Venezuela. Its projects include hydroelectric power plants, thermoelectric power plants, nuclear power plants, petrochemical plants, mining, the steel industry, refineries, harbors, subways, sanitation and urbanization, airports, railroads, and civil engineering. Globally the company focuses on mining, harbors, logistics terminals, highways, and industrial plant projects (such as steel and petrochemicals). Given this line of operation and projects, it is quite astonishing, not the least conceptually speaking, that Andrade Gutierrez was hired to construct a sanctuary dedicated to a Byzantine icon. The emphasis on oil and anointing that imbues the entire theology of Charismatic revivalism, including (if not mostly) Padre Marcelo's approach, and the company's selective interests in extractive energies, including Petrobras, is an irony worthy of a film script. In 2018 the construction company signed a 1.49 billion reais ($381.49 million) deal to settle corruption allegations against it as part of the so-called Car Wash graft investigation. Andrade Gutierrez is part of a larger unlisted Brazilian conglomerate that owns a stake in companies, including a toll road operator (CCRO3.SA). CCR, the road operator, in November 2018 agreed to pay a fine of 81.5 million reais for irregular financing of political campaigns. See Paraguassu 2018.

8 As many voiced and others published the largest Catholic nation was becoming Protestant. See, for example, Birman and Leite 2000.

9 There are many studies of the Universal Church in Brazil. I highlight the works of Campos 1996; Birman 2001; and Oosterbaan 2017.

10 The expression "way of Mary" seems to have a double meaning. Like the English *way* (*caminho*) it signifies both path and mode or manner. This homonymic aspect of *caminho* enforces the idea of this chapter whereby a path is not simply there but is inseparable from the technical proceedings—the techne—involved in its making.

11 In making this point Mondzain (2005) outlines a key distinction between *perigraphé* and *graphé*. Whereas *perigraphé* means "circumscription," a line that demarcates and contains the limits of space and time, *graphé* implies a "retreat of borders." Thus Mondzain writes, "It therefore becomes important to assert that Christ did not pass through his mother as one traverses a canal; that would suppose two forms; the form of the canal and the form of Christ.

No. The virginal womb and the child are one and the same form. The actual womb of the Virgin, strictly speaking, formed a precinct around that which is infinite, limitless. Inscription is therefore the perfect characteristic for determining the space of something that has none" (161).

12 This is what is meant, as Mondzain (2005: 151–70) articulates, by the idea that the Byzantine icon ideally is above all "a treatment of space." Its role and effect are primarily of a geopolitical nature.

13 A few questions can be raised: How, according to such doctrinal elements, does the statue of Our Lady of Aparecida relate to Theotókos? On a second level we may ask how the iconoclastic assault on the statue of Our Lady of Aparecida on live TV relates to Theotókos. On a third level still we could ask how this in turn relates to the culture of the image in the Bolsonaro era.

14 As Agamben (2009: 7) also notes, it is to the Greek term *oikonomia* that one must turn in order to comprehend the implication of what Michel Foucault meant by *apparatus* as "the network that is established between elements." Theotókos, in other words, is an example of the apparatus, an image that shows nothing but how power relations become territorialized. To repeat, Mary is space that does not contain because the infinite, her son, much like the crowds of Padre Marcelo, cannot be contained. For a historical and anthropological conflation of the body of Mary with the horizontally boundless crowd, see de la Cruz 2015.

15 Here again Mondzain (2010: 308) puts it powerfully when distinguishing between image and vision. She writes: "We do not see the world because we have eyes. Our eyes are opened by our ability to produce images, by our capacity to imagine. These capacities are why we need vision in order to be able to speak; this is why the blind can speak as long as their capacity to imagine is intact. In the capacity to incarnate the powers of seeing, in fact we forget and even find absurd the desire to see something at all." See also Mondzain 2009; and Mitchell 1996, 2005.

16 It is indeed ironic that we arrive at a concept like "post-truth" in the very age that is obsessed with exposure, truth, and visibility from the commodification of "making-of" of film (especially those that have explored special effects), to the interior redesigning of restaurants that allows cook and consumer to glance at one another, fostering a direct totem-like circuit and bonding between the pan, the stomach, and the pocket. The entire episode of Lava-Jato scandals must be studied in this light.

17 This is also suggested in the work of Valentina Napolitano and Carlota McAllister through the concept of theo-politics as alternative to political theology. See McAllister and Napolitano 2019.

18 Which is not to say that a sense of the transcendent is totally abolished. Rather, the transcendent is being displaced toward a new order of the material and the visible. What is powerful about this embedding of transcendence in the material is that it explores the idiom of transparency and "middleness"

in ways that evoke a sense of power vacuum. Yet again the idea of vacuum itself needs to be redefined in light of what conceptions of presence are in place. What happens to the idea of localization and vacuum when the figure of power is not presence, not mediation, but operation? See Reinhardt 2016 for an astute assessment of this reconceptualization of the transcendental, particularly regarding the recent turn to materiality and ontology.

6. Ghost Chair

1   The plastic monobloc chair calls on a conceptual clarity between plasticity and elasticity. For James Gibson (2015: 20) the *affordances of elasticity* are to be differentiated from *plasticity*. If in the former the tendency is to regain the previous shape after deformation, the latter's tendency is to hold the subsequent form. Catherine Malabou describes plasticity as that which is at once capable of receiving and giving form (Malabou and Butler 2010). The materiality of plasticity—and, therefore, the plasticity of the subject—reveals its own explosiveness in ways that are irreversible. Once this explosion has taken place, it is not possible to go back. Elasticity, on the contrary, entails what Butler (1997: chap. 1) calls "a stubborn attachment." The force exerted in detachment tends to run in direct proportion to reattachment. Yet, this movement of reattachment also exceeds it in producing a form of resistance from within (Butler and Malabou 2010). Beyond material affordances, however, I will insist that for Catholic Charismatics "elasticity" or "plasticity" is predictive of neither subjects nor objects but operations that precisely blur the contours of and between the two.

2   In drawing on Paul's Areopagus Sermon as recounted in Acts 17:16–34, Padre Marcelo is following Pope John Paul II in linking Paul's Areopagus to the advent of modern mass media as a means of evangelization of and reform within Catholicism.

3   Every year on All Saints' Day, Padre Marcelo works on staging the word *paz* in unanticipated ways. (*A Paz* is also the title of one of his most popular musical CDs.) One year he involved a jet that towed a banner with the word *paz* written on it, red petals falling over the crowd from the aircraft. Even though it is expected, the refrain of *paz* during the celebration of All Saints' Day also allows for things to go wrong. Thus even those who were not able to read the message through the bodies of the novices were still able to read it through a structure of expectation. And that, for many, was enough. He had done it again.

4   I met Monsignor Beltrami a number of times while consulting the library of the archdiocese of São Paulo during my field research in 2001. He was the coordinator of the Department of Communication of the archdiocese and played a key role in determining the relation of the Catholic Church with the means of mass communication in Brazil. He was also an outspoken critic of the methodologies of communication of the Catholic Charismatic movement.

5 Ironically, technology's very power of denying air of its substance has, in time, led to an almost complete identification between both. It is the state we witness today whereby technological sophistication aspires to become one with air itself. That the world of computation has become suffused by aerial analogies and (hyper)ventilatory rhetoric—equating gravity with old media—and that the default meaning of "cloud" has become "server-based data storage" are symptoms of such conflation between a natural phenomenon and technological advancement.

6 Seminário Teologia da Renovação Carismática Católica–Curitiba 2001.

7 Congress of Renovação Carismática Católica in Marília–São Paulo, 2001.

Epilogue

1 Letter published in *Folha de São Paulo*, November 20, 1998. For a full account see https://www1.folha.uol.com.br/fsp/opiniao/fz20119808.htm.

2 In this way repeating a scene I have described elsewhere, of Padre Jonas inflicting a ritual of humiliation on Padre Marcelo during the 20th National Meeting of the Catholic Charismatic Renewal in Aparecida do Norte, July 23–27, 2001. For more details, see de Abreu 2002.

Afterword

1 Shortly after the stabbing episode, Catholic Charismatics at Canção Nova Community (to which chapters 1, 2, and 3 were dedicated) hosted President Bolsonaro on a special live TV show. Gathering on-site key representatives of Brazil's Charismatic movement, the leader of the community sanctioned Bolsonaro as "God's chosen to be the ruler of Brazil." He then called on the audiences for a collective prayer in tongues. The breath of tongues was meant to bring renewal into Bolsonaro's wound, even as it also validated the look of pain on his face. Yet, prayer in tongues was also an indicator of the redistributive relation between signifier and signified that goes on characterizing much of his presidential mandate. See "Bolsonaro na Canção Nova 30 de novembro 2018," posted by Educar na Fé—Canção Nova, November 30, 2018, https://www.youtube.com/watch?v=Oz-rLf6whEA; "Presidente Eleito Jair Bolsonaro. Visita a Região do Vale do Paraíba em SP," posted by TV Canção Nova, November 30, 2018, https://www.youtube.com/watch?v=SbhBoHpRtRs.

BIBLIOGRAPHY

....

Abib, Jonas. 1999. *Canção Nova: Uma Obra de Deus: Nossa História e Missão*. São Paulo: Edições Loyola.

Agamben, Giorgio. 2005a. *State of Exception*. Translated by Kevin Attell. Chicago: University of Chicago Press.

Agamben, Giorgio. 2005b. *The Time That Remains: A Comment on the Letter to the Romans*. Translated by Patricia Dailey. Stanford, CA: Stanford University Press.

Agamben, Giorgio. 2009. *"What Is an Apparatus?" and Other Essays*. Translated by David Kishik and Stefan Pedatella. Stanford, CA: Stanford University Press.

Agamben, Giorgio. 2016. *The Use of Bodies*. Translated by Adam Kotsko. Stanford, CA: Stanford University Press.

Alter, Joseph. 1993. "The Body of One Color: Indian Wrestling, the Indian State, and Utopian Somatics." *Cultural Anthropology* 8, no. 1: 49–72.

Alter, Joseph. 2006. "Yoga at the *Fin de Siècle*: Muscular Christianity with a 'Hindu' Twist." *International Journal of the History of Sports* 23, no. 5: 759–76.

Althusser, Louis. 2014. *On the Reproduction of Capitalism: Ideology and Ideological State Apparatuses*. Translated by G. M. Goshgarian. London: Verso.

Anderson, Benedict. 1983. *Imagined Communities: Reflections on the Origins and Spread of Nationalism*. London: Verso.

Appel, Hannah. 2012. "Offshore Work: Oil, Modularity, and the How of Capitalism in Equatorial Guinea." *American Ethnologist* 39, no. 4: 692–709.

Arendt, Hannah. 1963. *On Revolution*. New York: Viking.

Aristotle. 1942. *Generation of Animals*. Edited by A. L. Peck. Cambridge, MA: Harvard University Press.

Aristotle. 2012. *Magna Moralia*. Miami: HardPress.

Artaud, Antonin. 1958. *The Theater and Its Double*. Translated Mary Caroline Richards. New York: Grove.

Asad, Talal. 1993. *Genealogies of Religion: Disciplines and Reasons of Power in Christianity*. Stanford, CA: Stanford University Press.

Asad, Talal. 2003. *Formations of the Secular: Christianity, Islam, Modernity*. Stanford, CA: Stanford University Press.

Austin, J. L. (1962) 1975. *How to Do Things with Words*. Oxford: Oxford University Press.

Bachelard, Gaston. 1988. *Air and Dreams: An Essay on the Imagination of Movement*. Translated by Edith Farrell and Frederick Farrell. Dallas, TX: Dallas Institute.

Baptista, Pedro. 2010. *O Filósofo Fantasma*. Sintra, Portugal: Nova Águia, Zéfiro.

Barthes, Roland. 1978. *A Lover's Discourse: Fragments*. Translated by Richard Howard. New York: Hill and Wang.

Barthes, Roland. 2007. *What Is Sport?* Translated by Richard Howard. New Haven, CT: Yale University Press.

Bataille, Georges. (1976) 1993. *The Accursed Share*. Vols. 2 and 3, *The History of Eroticism and Sovereignty*. Translated by Robert Hurley. London: Zone.

Bedos-Rezak, Brigitte. 2000. "Medieval Identity: A Sign and a Concept." *American Historical Review* 105, no. 5: 1489–533.

Bedos-Rezak, Brigitte. 2008. "In Search of a Semiotic Paradigm: The Matter of Sealing in Medieval Thought and Praxis (1050–1400)." In *Good Impressions: Image and Authority in Medieval Seals*, edited by Noël Adams, John Cherry, and James Robinson, 1–7. London: British Museum.

Benjamin, Walter. 1968. "The Work of Art in the Age of Mechanical Reproduction." In *Illuminations: Essays and Reflections*, edited by Hannah Arendt, translated by Harry Zohn, 217–52. New York: Schocken.

Benjamin, Walter. 1997. *Charles Baudelaire: A Lyric Poet in the Era of High Capitalism*. Translated by Harry Zohn. New York: Verso.

Benjamin, Walter. (1963) 1998a. *The Origin of German Tragic Drama*. Translated by John Osborne. London: Verso.

Benjamin, Walter. 1998b. *Understanding Brecht*. Translated by Anna Bostock. London: Verso.

Benjamin, Walter. 1999. *The Arcades Project*. Translated by Howard Eiland and Kevin McLaughlin. Cambridge, MA: Belknap Press of Harvard University Press.

Benveniste, Émile. 1971. *Problems in General Linguistics*. Translated by Mary Elizabeth Meek. Coral Gables, FL: University of Miami Press.

Berlant, Lauren. 1991. *The Anatomy of National Fantasy*. Chicago: University of Chicago Press.

Berlant, Lauren. 2011. *Cruel Optimism*. Durham, NC: Duke University Press.

Berliner, David, Michael Lambek, Richard Shweder, Richard Irvine, and Albert Piette. 2016. "Debate: Anthropology and the Study of Contradictions." *HAU: Journal of Ethnographic Theory* 6, no. 1: 1–27.

Bigelow, John. 1888. *Emanuel Swedenborg: Servus Domini*. New York: G. P. Putnam and Sons.

Birman, Patricia. 2001. "Future in the Mirror: Media, Evangelicals, and Politics in Rio de Janeiro." In *Religion, Media and the Public Sphere*, edited by Birgit Meyer and Annelies Moors, 52–72. Bloomington: Indiana University Press.

Birman, Patricia, and David Lehmann. 1999. "Religion and the Media in a

Battle for Ideological Hegemony: The Universal Church of the Kingdom of God and TV Globo in Brazil." *Bulletin of Latin American Research* 18, no. 2: 145–64.

Birman, Patrícia, and Márcia Pereira Leite. 2000. "Whatever Happened to What Used to Be the Largest Catholic Country in the World?" *Daedalus* 129, no. 2: 271–91.

Boff, Leonardo. 1985. *Church, Charism and Power: Liberation Theology and the Institutional Church*. London: SCM Press.

Bonfim, Evandro. 2015. "Glossolalia and Linguistic Alterity: The Ontology of Ineffable Speech." *Religion and Society* 6, no. 1: 75–89.

Bordo, Susan. 1993. *Unbearable Weight: Feminism, Western Culture, and the Body*. Berkeley: University of California Press.

Brown, Peter. 1981. *The Cult of the Saints: Its Rise and Function in Latin Christianity*. Chicago: University of Chicago Press.

Brown, Peter. 1983. "The Saint as Exemplar in Late Antiquity." *Representations*, no. 2: 1–25.

Buck-Morss, Susan. 1986. "The Flaneur, the Sandwichman and the Whore: The Politics of Loitering." *New German Critique*, no. 39: 99–140.

Buck-Morss, Susan. 2007. "Visual Empire." *Diacritics* 37, nos. 2–3: 171–98.

Butler, Judith. 1993. *Bodies That Matter: On the Discursive Limits of "Sex"*. New York: Routledge.

Butler, Judith. 1997a. *Excitable Speech: A Politics of the Performative*. London: Routledge.

Butler, Judith. 1997b. *The Psychic Life of Power: Theories in Subjection*. Stanford, CA: Stanford University Press.

Bynum, Caroline Walker. 1995. "Why All the Fuss about the Body? A Medievalist's Perspective." *Critical Inquiry* 22, no. 1: 1–33.

Bynum, Caroline Walker. 2006. "Seeing and Seeing Beyond: The Mass of St. Gregory in the Fifteenth Century." In *The Mind's Eye: Art and Theological Argument in the Middle Ages*, edited by Jeffrey F. Hamburger and Anne-Marie Bouché, 208–40. Princeton, NJ: Princeton University Press.

Bynum, Caroline Walker. 2007. *Wonderful Blood: Theology and Practice in Late Medieval Northern Germany and Beyond*. Philadelphia: University of Pennsylvania Press.

Bynum, Caroline Walker. 2012. "Why Paradox? The Contradictions of My Life as a Scholar." *Catholic Historical Review* 98, no. 3: 433–55.

Caduff, Carlo. 2018. "After the Next: Notes on Serial Novelty." *Medicine, Anthropology, Theory* 5, no. 4: 86–105.

Caillois, Roger. 1984. "Mimicry and Legendary Psychasthenia." Translated by John Shepley. *October*, no. 31: 16–32.

Campos, Leonildo. 1996. *Teatro, Templo e Mercado*. Petrópolis: Editora Vozes.

Canção Nova. 2001. *Revista Canção Nova*, September.

Canetti, Elias. 1960. *Crowds and Power*. Harmondsworth, UK: Penguin.

Carlson, Thomas A. 2008. *The Indiscrete Image: Infinitude and the Creation of the Human.* Chicago: University of Chicago Press.

Carranza, Maribel. 2002. *Renovação Carismatica Católica: Origens Mudanças e Tendências.* Aparecida, Brazil: Editora Santuário.

Castelli, Elizabeth A. 2004. *Martyrdom and Memory: Early Christian Culture Making.* New York: Columbia University Press.

Cavell, Stanley. 1995. "What Did Derrida Want of Austin?" In *Philosophical Passages: Wittgenstein, Emerson, Austin, Derrida,* 42–65. Cambridge, MA: Blackwell.

Certeau, Michel de. 1984. *The Practice of Everyday Life.* Berkeley: University of California Press.

Certeau, Michel de. 1987. "The Gaze of Nicholas of Cusa." *Diacritics* 1, no. 3: 2–38.

Certeau, Michel de. 1996. "Vocal Utopias: Glossolalias." *Representations,* no. 56: 29–47.

Chiang, Ted. 2019. *Exhalation.* New York: Knopf.

CNBB (National Conference Bishops of Brazil). 1994a. *Comunicação e Igreja no Brasil.* No. 72. São Paulo: Paulinas.

CNBB (National Conference Bishops of Brazil). 1994b. *Orientações Pastorais Sobre a Renovação Carismática.* No. 53. São Paulo: Paulinas.

CNBB (National Conference Bishops of Brazil). 1995a. *Diretrizes Gerais da Acção Evangelizadora da Igreja no Brasil 1995–1998.* São Paulo: Paulinas.

CNBB (National Conference Bishops of Brazil). 1995b. *Litúrgia da Radio e da Televisão.* No. 33. São Paulo: Paulinas.

CNBB (National Conference Bishops of Brazil). 1997. *Igreja e Comunicação: Rumo ao Novo Milénio. Conclusões e Compromissos.* Doc. 59. 2nd ed. São Paulo: Paulinas.

Cohen, Anthony P. 1985. *The Symbolic Construction of Community.* London: Taylor and Francis.

Coleman, Simon. 1998. *The Globalisation of Charismatic Christianity: Spreading the Gospel of Prosperity.* Cambridge: Cambridge University Press.

Collu, Samuele. 2019. "Refracting Affects: Affect, Psychotherapy, and Spirit Dispossession." *Culture, Medicine and Psychiatry* 43, no. 2: 290–314.

Cooper-Rompato, Christine F. 2010. *The Gift of Tongues: Women's Xenoglossia in the Later Middle Ages.* University Park: Pennsylvania State University Press.

Crary, Jonathan. 2014. *24/7: Late Capitalism and the Ends of Sleep.* London: Verso.

Csordas, Thomas J. 1990. "Embodiment as a Paradigm for Anthropology." *Ethos* 18, no. 1: 5–47.

Csordas, Thomas J. 1992. "Religion and the World System: The Pentecostal Ethic and the Spirit of Monopoly Capital." *Dialectical Anthropology* 17, no. 1: 3–24.

Csordas, Thomas. 1993. "The Somatic Modes of Attention." *Cultural Anthropology* 8, no. 2: 135–56.

Csordas, Thomas J. 1994. *The Sacred Self: A Cultural Phenomenology of Charismatic Healing.* Berkeley: University of California Press.

Csordas, Thomas J. 1995. "Oxymorons and Short-Circuits in the Re-enchantment of the World: The Case of the Catholic Charismatic Renewal." *Etnofoor*, no. 8: 5–26.

Csordas, Thomas J. 2002. *Body, Meaning, Healing*. New York: Palgrave Macmillan.

Csordas, Thomas J. 2004. "Asymptote of the Ineffable: Embodiment, Alterity, and the Theory of Religion." *Current Anthropology* 45, no. 2: 163–85.

Csordas, Thomas J. 2008. "Intersubjectivity and Intercorporeality." *Subjectivity* 22, no. 1: 110–21.

de Abreu, Maria José A. 2002. "On Charisma, Mediation and Broken Screens." *Etnofoor* 15, nos. 1–2: 240–58.

de Abreu, Maria José A. 2005. "Breathing in the Heart of the Matter: Why Padre Marcelo Needs No Wings." *Postscripts* 1, nos. 2–3: 325–49.

de Abreu, Maria José A. 2012. "The FedEx Saints: Patrons of Mobility and Speed in a Neoliberal City." In *Things: Religion and the Question of Materiality*, edited by Dick Houtman and Birgit Meyer, 321–35. New York: Fordham University Press.

de Abreu, Maria José A. 2013a. "Technological Indeterminacy: Medium, Threat, Temporality." *Anthropological Theory* 13, no. 3: 267–84.

de Abreu, Maria José A. 2013b. "TV St. Claire." In *Deus in Machina: Religion, Technology and the Things in Between*, edited by Jeremy Stolow, 261–80. New York: Fordham University Press.

de Abreu, Maria José A. 2015. "Worldings: The Aesthetics of Authority among Catholic Charismatics in Brazil." *Culture and Religion* 16, no. 2: 175–92.

de Abreu, Maria José A. 2019. "Medium Theory; or, 'The War of the Worlds' at Regular Intervals." *Current Anthropology* 60, no. 5: 656–73.

de Abreu, Maria José. 2020a. "States of Extreme: Body Politics, Quick Takes, States of Exception." *Political Theology Network*, February 11. https://political theology.com/states-of-extreme/.

de Abreu, Maria José A. 2020b. "Acts Is Acts: Tautology and Theopolitical Reform in Theopolitics in/of the Americas." *Social Analysis: The International Journal of Anthropology* 64, no. 4.

de la Cruz, Deirdre. 2015. *Mother Figured: Marian Apparitions and the Making of a Filipino Universal*. Chicago: University of Chicago Press.

de Lima, Délcio Monteiro. 1987. *Os Demónios Descem do Norte*. Rio de Janeiro: Editora Francisco Alves.

Derrida, Jacques. 1988. *Limited Inc*. Edited by Gerald Graff. Translated by Jeffrey Mehlman and Samuel Weber. Evanston, IL: Northwestern University Press.

Derrida, Jacques. 2002. *Acts of Religion*. Edited by Gil Anidjar. New York: Routledge.

Derrida, Jacques. 2005. *Paper Machine*. Translated by Rachel Bowlby. Stanford, CA: Stanford University Press.

de Oliveira, E. M. 2004. "O Mergulho no Espírito Santo: Interfaces entre o Catolicismo Carismático e a Nova Era (O Caso de Comunidade de Vida Canço Nova)." *Religiao & Sociedade* 24, no. 1: 85–112.

de Vries, Hent. 2001. "In Media Res: Global Religion, Public Spheres, and the Task of Contemporary Comparative Religious Studies." In *Religion and Media*, edited by Hent de Vries and Samuel Weber, 4–42. Stanford, CA: Stanford University Press.

Didi-Huberman, Georges. 2003. "The Imaginary Breeze: Remarks on the Air of the Quattrocento." *Journal of Visual Culture* 2, no. 3: 275–89.

Dolbear, Sam, Esther Leslie, and Sebastian Truskolaski. 2016. "Walter Benjamin and the Magnetic Play of Words." In Walter Benjamin, *The Storyteller: Short Stories*, ix–xxxii. London: Verso.

Durkheim, Émile. 2001. *The Elementary Forms of Religious Life.* Translated by Carol Cosman. Oxford: Oxford University Press.

Dutch, Robert. 2005. *The Educated Elite in 1 Corinthians: Education and Community Conflict in Graeco-Roman Context.* London: Bloomsbury.

Elsner, Jaś. 2012. "Iconoclasm as Discourse: From Antiquity to Byzantium." *Art Bulletin* 94, no. 3: 368–94.

Engelke, Matthew. 2007. *A Problem of Presence: Beyond Scripture in an African Church.* Berkeley: University of California Press.

Engelke, Matthew. 2010. "Religion and the Media Turn: A Review Essay." *American Ethnologist* 37, no. 2: 371–79.

Fabian, Johannes. 1983. *Time and the Other: How Anthropology Makes Its Object.* New York: Columbia University Press.

Fabian, Johannes. 1991. *Time and the Work of Anthropology: Critical Essays, 1971–1991.* Abingdon, UK: Harwood Academic.

Farquhar, Judith. 1994. *Knowing Practice: The Clinical Encounter of Chinese Medicine.* Boulder, CO: Westview Press.

Faubion, James D. 2011. *An Anthropology of Ethics.* Cambridge, UK: Cambridge University Press.

Faubion, James D. 2013. "The Subject That Is Not One: On the Ethics of Mysticism." *Anthropological Theory* 13, no. 4: 287–307.

Fishman, Andrew. 2018. "Jair Bolsonaro Is Elected President of Brazil: Read His Extremist, Far-Right Positions in His Own Words." *Intercept*, October 28. https://theintercept.com/2018/10/28/jair-bolsonaro-elected-president-brazil/.

Forbes, Clarence A. 1945. "Expanded Uses of the Greek Gymnasium." *Classical Philology* 40, no. 1: 32–45.

Foucault, Michel. 1980. *Power/Knowledge: Selected Interviews and Other Writings, 1972–1977.* Edited by Colin Gordon. Translated by Colin Gordon, Leo Marshall, John Mepham, and Kate Soper. New York: Pantheon.

Foucault, Michel. 1993. "About the Beginning of the Hermeneutics of the Self: Two Lectures at Dartmouth." *Political Theory* 21, no. 2: 198–227.

Foucault, Michel. 2003. *The Birth of the Clinic: An Archaeology of Medical Perception.* Translated by A. M. Sheridan. New York: Routledge.

Freston, Paul. 1994. "Popular Protestants in Brazilian Politics: A Novel Turn in Sect-State Relations." *Social Compass* 41, no. 4: 537–70.

Ghosh, Bishnupriya. 2011. *Global Icons: Apertures to the Popular*. Durham, NC: Duke University Press.

Gibson, James J. 2015. *The Ecological Approach to Visual Perception*. New York: Taylor and Francis.

Greenblatt, Stephen. 1983. *Renaissance Self-fashioning: From More to Shakespeare*. Chicago: University of Chicago Press.

Harding, Susan. 2000. *The Book of Jerry Falwell: Fundamentalist Language and Politics*. Princeton, NJ: Princeton University Press.

Heller-Roazen, Daniel. 2002. "Speaking in Tongues." *Paragraph* 25, no. 2: 92–115.

Heo, Angie. 2018. *The Political Lives of Saints: Christian-Muslim Mediation in Egypt*. Berkeley: University of California Press.

Hervieu-Léger, Danièle. 1995. "O Bispo, a Igreja e a Modernidade." In *Nem Todos os Caminhos Levam a Roma: As Mutações Atuais do Catolicismo*, edited by René Luneau and Patrick Michel, 291–322. Petrópolis: Vozes Editora.

Hirschkind, Charles. 2006. *The Ethical Soundscape: Cassette Sermons and Islamic Counterpublics*. New York: Columbia University Press.

Hirschkind, Charles. 2011. "Media, Mediation, Religion." *Social Anthropology* 19, no. 1: 90–97.

Hirschkind, Charles, Carlo Caduff, and Maria José de Abreu. 2017. "New Media, New Publics? An Introduction." *Current Anthropology* 58, no. S15: S3–S12.

Holbraad, Martin. 2012. *Truth in Motion: The Recursive Anthropology of Cuban Divination*. Chicago: University of Chicago Press.

Holden, Emily, Andrew Restuccia, Aaron Lorenzo, and Ted Hesson. 2017. "Trump, the Indecisive." *Politico*, September 26. https://www.politico.com/story/2017/09/26/trump-business-climate-indecision-243074.

Hollywood, Amy. 2012. "Performativity, Citationality, Ritualization." *History of Religions* 42, no. 2: 93–115.

Irigaray, Luce. 1999. *The Forgetting of Air in Martin Heidegger*. Translated by Mary Beth Mader. Austin: University of Texas Press.

Ivy, Marilyn. 1995. *Discourses of the Vanishing: Modernity, Phantasm, Japan*. Chicago: University of Chicago Press.

John Paul II. (1979) 2006. "The Redemption of the Body and Sacramentality of Marriage (Theology of the Body)." Catholic Primer. https://stmarys-waco.org/documents/2016/9/theology_of_the_body.pdf.

Johnson, Barbara. 1986. "Apostrophe, Animation, and Abortion." *Diacritics* 16, no. 1: 26–47.

Kafka, Franz. 1954. "Fragments from Notebooks and Loose Pages." In *Dearest Father and Other Writings*, translated by Ernst Kaiser and Eithne Wilkins. New York: Schocken.

Keane, Webb. 2007. *Christian Moderns: Freedom and Fetish in the Mission Encounter*. Berkeley: University of California Press.

Kierkegaard, Søren. (1843) 1964. *Repetition: An Essay in Experimental Psychology*. Translated by Walter Lowrie. New York: Harper.

Kramer, Eric W. 2001. "Law and the Image of a Nation: Religious Conflict and Religious Freedom in a Brazilian Criminal Case." *Law and Social Inquiry* 26, no. 1: 35–62.

Kumler, Aden. 2011. "The Multiplication of the Species: Eucharistic Morphology in the Middle Ages." *Res: Anthropology and Aesthetics*, nos. 59–60: 179–91.

Kungurtsev, Igor, and Olga Louchakova. 1997. "The Unknown Russian Mysticism: Pagan Sorcery, Christian Yoga, and Other Esoteric Practices in the Former Soviet Union." *Gnosis* 31: 20–27.

Lambek, Michael, ed. 2010. *Ordinary Ethics: Anthropology, Language, and Action.* Chicago: University of Chicago Press.

Lambek, Michael. 2016. "Anthropology and the Study of Contradictions." *HAU: Journal of Ethnographic Theory* 6, no. 1: 1–27.

Largier, Niklaus. 2007. *In Praise of the Whip: A Cultural History of Arousal.* Translated by Graham Harman. Brooklyn: Zone.

Largier, Niklaus. 2014. "The Art of Prayer: Conversions of Interiority and Exteriority in Medieval Contemplative Practice." In *Rethinking Emotion: Interiority and Exteriority in Premodern, Modern, and Contemporary Thought*, edited by Rüdiger Campe and Julia Weber, 58–71. Berlin: de Gruyter.

Larkin, Brian. 2008. *Signal and Noise: Media, Infrastructure, and Urban Culture in Nigeria.* Durham, NC: Duke University Press.

Lee, Benjamin. 1997. *Talking Heads: Language, Metalanguage, and the Semiotics of Subjectivities.* Durham, NC: Duke University Press.

Lefebvre, Henri. 2013. *Rhythmanalysis: Space, Time and Everyday Life.* Translated by Gerald Moore and Stuart Elden. London: Bloomsbury.

Lloyd, Geoffrey. 2007. "Pneuma: Between Body and Soul." *Journal of the Royal Anthropological Institute* 13: S135–S146.

Louchakova, Olga. 2005. "Ontopoiesis and Union in the Prayer of the Heart: Contributions to Psychotherapy and Learning." In *Logos of Phenomenology and Phenomenology of the Logos*, edited by Anna-Teresa Tymieniecka, Analecta Husserliana, vol. 91, 289–311. Dordrecht: Springer.

Low, Chris, and Elisabeth Hsu. 2007. "Wind, Life, Health: Anthropological and Historical Perspectives." *Journal of the Royal Anthropological Institute* 13: S1–S18.

Luneau, René, and Patrick Michel, eds. 1995. *New Todos os Caminhos Levam a Roma: As Mutações Atuais do Catolicismo.* Petrópolis: Vozes Editora.

MacIntyre, Alasdair. 2007. *After Virtue: A Study in Moral Theory.* 3rd ed. Notre Dame, IN: University of Notre Dame Press.

Mahmood, Saba. 2005. *Politics of Piety: The Islamic Revival and the Feminist Subject.* Princeton, NJ: Princeton University Press.

Malabou, Catherine, and Judith Butler. 2010. *Sois Mon Corps: Une lecture contemporaine de la domination et de la servitude chez Hegel.* Paris: Bayard.

Marion, Jean-Luc. 2003. *The Crossing of the Visible.* Translated by James K. A. Smith. Stanford, CA: Stanford University Press.

Marno, David. 2016. *Death Be Not Proud: The Art of Holy Attention*. Chicago: University of Chicago Press.

Marx, Karl. [1852] 2012. The *Eighteenth Brumaire of Louis Bonaparte*. Translated by Daniel de Leon. Overland Park, KS: Digireads.

Masco, Joseph. 2012. "The End of Ends." *Anthropological Quarterly* 85, no. 4: 1107–124.

Masco, Joseph. 2014. *The Theater of Operations: National Security Affect from the Cold War to the War on Terror*. Durham, NC: Duke University Press.

Massumi, Brian. 2002. *Parables for the Virtual: Movement, Affect, Sensation*. Durham, NC: Duke University Press.

Maurer, Bill. 2002. "Repressed Futures: Financial Derivatives, Theological Unconscious." *Economy and Society* 31, no. 1: 15–36.

Mauss, Marcel. 1934. "Les Techniques du Corps." *Journal de Psychologie* 32: 3–4.

Mauss, Marcel. 1967. *The Gift: Forms and Functions of Exchange in Archaic Societies*. Translated by Ian Cunnison. New York: Norton.

McAllister, Carlota, and Valentina Napolitano. 2019. "The Powers of Powerlessness." *Political Theology Network*, January 28. https://politicaltheology.com /the-powers-of-powerlessness/.

Merleau-Ponty, Maurice. (1945) 1962. *Phenomenology of Perception*. Translated by Colin Smith. New York: Humanities Press.

Meyer, Birgit, ed. 2009. *Aesthetic Formations: Media, Religion and the Senses*. Basingstoke, UK: Palgrave Macmillan.

Meyer, Birgit. 2011. "Mediation and Immediacy: Sensational Forms, Semiotic Ideologies, and the Question of the Medium." *Social Anthropology* 19, no. 1: 23–39.

Meyer, Birgit. 2012. "Religious Sensation: Why Media, Aesthetics and Power Matter in the Study of Contemporary Religion." Inaugural lecture. Free University, Amsterdam, December 19.

Michel, Patrick. 1995. "O Último Papa: Reflexões Sobre a Utilização do Politico sob o Pontíficado de João Paulo II." In *New Todos os Caminhos Vão Dar a Roma: As Mutações Atuais do Catolicismo*, edited by R. Luneau and P. Michel. Petrópolis: Editora Vozes.

Mitchell, W. J. T. 1996. *Picture Theory*. Chicago: University of Chicago Press.

Mitchell, W. J. T. 2005. *What Do Pictures Want? Essays on the Lives and Loves of Images*. Chicago: University of Chicago Press.

Mondzain, Marie-José. 2005. *Image, Icon, Economy: The Byzantine Origins of the Contemporary Imaginary*. Translated by Rico Franses. Stanford, CA: Stanford University Press.

Mondzain, Marie-José. 2009. "Can Images Kill?" Translated by Sally Shafto. *Critical Inquiry* 36, no. 1: 20–51.

Mondzain, Marie-José. 2010. "What Does Seeing an Image Mean?" *Journal of Visual Culture* 9, no. 3: 307–15.

Morris, Rosalind C. 2000a. *In the Place of Origins: Modernity and Its Medium in Northern Thailand*. Durham, NC: Duke University Press.

Morris, Rosalind C. 2000b. "Modernity's Media and Mediumship? On the Aesthetic Economy of Transparency in Thailand." *Public Culture* 12, no. 2: 457–75.

Morris, Rosalind C. 2013. "Theses on the New Öffentlichkeit." *Grey Room*, no. 51: 94–111.

Morris, Rosalind C. 2017. "Mediation, the Political Task: Between Language and Violence in Contemporary South Africa." *Current Anthropology* 58, no. S15: S123–S34.

Muehlebach, Andrea. 2009. "*Complexio Oppositorum*: Notes on the Left in Neoliberal Italy." *Public Culture* 21, no. 3: 495–515.

Muehlebach, Andrea. 2012. *The Moral Neoliberal: Welfare and Citizenship*. Chicago: University of Chicago Press.

Napolitano, Valentina. 2015. "Anthropology and Traces." *Anthropological Theory* 15, no. 1: 47–67.

Napolitano, Valentina. 2016. *Migrant Hearts and the Atlantic Return: Transnationalism and the Roman Catholic Church*. New York: Fordham University Press.

Ng, Emily. 2020. *A Time of Lost Ghosts: Mediumship, Madness, and the Ghost after Mao*. Berkeley: University of California Press.

Norget, Kristin. 2014. "Neo-Baroque Catholic Evangelism in Post-Secular Mexico." In *The Transatlantic Hispanic Baroque: Complex Identities in the Atlantic World*, edited by Harald Braun and Jesús Pérez-Magallón, 273–90. London: Ashgate.

Oosterbaan, Martijn. 2017. *Transmitting the Spirit: Religious Conversion, Media, and Urban Violence in Brazil*. University Park: Penn State University Press.

Otto, Rudolf. 1923. *The Idea of the Holy*. Translated by John W. Harvey. London: Oxford University Press.

Pandolfo, Stefania. 1997. *Impasse of the Angels: Scenes from a Moroccan Space of Memory*. Chicago: University of Chicago Press.

Pandolfo, Stefania. 2018. *Knot of the Soul: Madness, Psychoanalysis, Islam*. Chicago: University of Chicago Press.

Paraguassu, Lisandra. 2018. "Brazil's Andrade Gutierrez to Pay $381 Million Fine to Settle Graft Charges." *Reuters*, December 18. https://www.reuters.com /article/us-brazil-corruption-andrade/brazils-andrade-gutierrez-to-pay-381 -million-fine-to-settle-graft-charges-idUSKBN1OH22U.

Peters, John Durham. 2015. *The Marvelous Clouds: Toward a Philosophy of Elemental Media*. Chicago: University of Chicago Press.

Perniola, Mario. 2004. *The Sex Appeal of the Inorganic: Philosophies of Desire in the Modern World*. Translated by Massimo Verdicchio. New York: Bloomsbury.

Povinelli, Elizabeth A. 2006. *The Empire of Love: Toward a Theory of Intimacy, Genealogy, and Carnality*. Durham, NC: Duke University Press.

Povinelli, Elizabeth A. 2011. *Economies of Abandonment: Social Belonging and Endurance in Late Liberalism*. Durham, NC: Duke University Press.

Povinelli, Elizabeth A. 2012. "The Will to Be Otherwise/The Effort of Endurance." *South Atlantic Quarterly* 111, no. 3: 453–75.

Rancière, Jacques. 2005. *The Politics of Aesthetics: The Distribution of the Sensible.* Translated by Gabriel Rockhill. New York: Continuum.

Reinhardt, Bruno. 2016. "'Don't Make It a Doctrine': Material Religion, Transcendence, Critique." *Anthropological Theory* 16, no. 1: 75–97.

Roitman, Janet. 2013. *Anti-Crisis.* Durham, NC: Duke University Press.

Robles-Anderson, Erica. 2012. "The Crystal Cathedral: Architecture for Mediated Congregation." *Public Culture* 24, no. 3: 577–99.

Rossi, Padre Marcelo. 2010. *Ágape.* São Paulo: Editora Globo.

Rossi, Padre Marcelo. 2013. *Kairos: Tempo de Deus.* São Paulo: Editora Globo.

Rossi, Padre Marcelo. 2015. *Philia: Derrote a Depressão, o Medo e Outros Problemas Applicado Phili.* São Paulo: Editora Globo.

Rossi, Padre Marcelo. 2016. *Ruha: Quebrando o Paradigma de Que Gordura e Saúde e Magreza e Doença.* São Paulo: Editora Globo.

Rossi, Padre Marcelo. 2018. *Metanoia Wi-Fé: Descubra a Senha Que Vai Mudar a Sua Vida.* São Paulo: Editora Globo.

Sánchez, Rafael. 2001. "Channel-Surfing: Media, Mediumship, and State Authority in the Mariá Lionza Possession Cult (Venezuela)." In *Religion and Media,* edited by Hent de Vries and Samuel Weber, 388–434. Stanford, CA: Stanford University Press.

Sánchez, Rafael. 2016. *Dancing Jacobins: A Venezuelan Genealogy of Latin American Populism.* New York: Fordham University Press.

Sanchis, Pierre. 1994. "O Repto Pentecostal a Cultura Católica Brasileira." In Alberto Antoniazzi, *Nem Anjos, Nem Demônios: Interpretacões Sociologicas do Pentecostalismo,* 34–63. Petrópolis: Vozes.

Schmitt, Carl. 1985. *Political Theology: Four Chapters on the Concept of Sovereignty.* Translated by George Schwab. Cambridge, MA: MIT Press.

Schmitt, Carl. (1923) 1996. *Roman Catholicism and Political Form.* Translated by G. L. Ulmen. Westport, CT: Greenwood.

Schneider, Manfred. 2001. "Luther with McLuhan." In *Religion and Media,* edited by Hent de Vries and Samuel Weber, 198–215. Stanford, CA: Stanford University Press.

Sedgwick, Eve Kosofsky. 1985. *Between Men: English Literature and Male Homosocial Desire.* New York: Columbia University Press.

Sedgwick, Eve Kosofsky. 1993. *Tendencies.* Durham, NC: Duke University Press.

Serres, Michel. 2007. *The Parasite.* Translated by Lawrence Schehr. Minneapolis: University of Minnesota Press.

Serres, Michel. 2012. *Variations on the Body.* Translated by Randolph Burks. Minneapolis: Univocal.

Silverstein, Michael. 1976. "Shifters, Linguistic Categories, and Cultural Description." In *Meaning in Anthropology,* edited by Keith H. Basso and Henry A. Selby, 11–55. Albuquerque: University of New Mexico Press.

Silverstein, Michael. 1992. "The Indeterminacy of Contextualization: When Is Enough Enough?" In *The Contextualization of Language*, edited by Peter Auer and Aldo Di Luzio, 55–76. Amsterdam: John Benjamins.

Slatman, Jenny. 2001. "Television." In *Religion and Media*, edited by Hent de Vries and Samuel Weber, 216–26. Stanford, CA: Stanford University Press.

Sloterdijk, Peter. 1987. *Critique of Cynical Reason*. Minneapolis: University of Minnesota Press.

Sloterdijk, Peter. 2013. *You Must Change Your Life: On Anthropotechnics*. Translated by Wieland Hoban. Cambridge: Polity.

Spadola, Emilio. 2013. *The Calls of Islam: Sufis, Islamists, and Mass Mediation in Urban Morocco*. Bloomington: Indiana University Press.

Star, Susan Leigh. 1999. "The Ethnography of Infrastructure." *American Behavioral Scientist* 43, no. 3: 377–91.

Stewart, Kathleen, and Susan Harding. 1999. "Bad Endings: American Apocalypsis." *Annual Review of Anthropology* 28, no. 1: 285–310.

Stolow, Jeremy. 2005. "Religion and/as Media." *Theory, Culture, and Society* 22, no. 4: 119–45.

Stolow, Jeremy. 2013. *Orthodox by Design: Judaism, Print Politics, and the ArtScroll Revolution*. Berkeley: University of California Press.

Strathern, Marilyn. 1987. "Out of Context: The Persuasive Fictions of Anthropology." *Current Anthropology* 28, no. 3: 251–81.

Swedenborg, Emanuel. 2009. *A Compendium of the Theological Writings of Emanuel Swedenborg*. Edited by Samuel M. Warren. West Chester, PA: Swedenborg Foundation Publishers.

Tambiah, Stanley. 1981. *A Performative Approach to Ritual*. Radcliffe-Brown Lecture in Social Anthropology. London: Oxford University Press.

Taussig, Michael. 2003. "Viscerality, Faith, and Skepticism: Another Theory of Magic." In *Magic and Modernity: Interfaces of Revelation and Concealment*, edited by Birgit Meyer and Peter Pels, 272–303. Stanford, CA: Stanford University Press.

Throop, C. Jason. 2001. "In the Midst of Action." In *Toward an Anthropology of the Will*, edited by Keith M. Murphy and C. Jason Throop, 28–49. Stanford, CA: Stanford University Press.

Travaini, Lucia. 2015. "Coins, Images, Identity, and Interpretations: Two Research Cases—A Seventh-Century Merovingian Tremissis and a Fifteenth-Century Ducat of Milan." In *Medieval Coins and Seals: Constructing Identity, Signifying Power*, edited by S. Solway, 65–80. Turnhout, Belgium: Brepols.

Van den Hoven, P. J. 2013. "A Chair Is Still a Chair, Even When There's No One Sitting There: About the Semiotics of the Trivial." In *Alternate Construals in Language and Linguistics*, edited by Z. Wasik, P. Czajka, and M. Szawerna, 143–60. Wrocław: Philological School of Higher Education.

Verrips, Jojada. 2006. "Aisthesis and An-aesthesia." *Ethnologia Europaea* 35, no. 1: 29–36.

Warner, Michael. 2002. "Publics and Counterpublics." *Public Culture* 14, no. 1: 49–90.

Weber, Samuel. 1996. *Mass Mediauras: Form, Technics, Media*. Stanford, CA: Stanford University Press.

Weber, Samuel. 2001. "Religion, Repetition, Media." In *Religion and Media*, edited by Hent de Vries and Samuel Weber, 43–55. Stanford, CA: Stanford University Press.

Weber, Samuel. 2004. *Theatricality as Medium*. New York: Fordham University Press.

Weber, Samuel. 2005. *Targets of Opportunity: On the Militarization of Thinking*. New York: Fordham University Press.

Weber, Samuel. 2008. *Benjamin's-abilities*. Cambridge, MA: Harvard University Press.

Weber, Samuel. 2017. "Afterword: The New-Old Media." *Current Anthropology* 58, no. S15: S160–61.

Whitman, Walt. 1961. *Leaves of Grass*. New York: Penguin.

Wittgenstein, Ludwig. (1922) 2001. *Tractatus Logico-Philosophicus*. London: Routledge.

Witte, Marleen de. 2009. "Modes of Binding, Moments of Bonding: Mediating Divine Touch in Ghanaian Pentecostalism and Traditionalism." In *Aesthetic Formations: Media, Religion and the Senses*, edited by Birgit Meyer, 183–205. Basingstoke, UK: Palgrave Macmillan.

Witte, Marleen de. 2011. "Touched by the Spirit: Converting the Senses in a Ghanaian Charismatic Church." *Ethnos* 76, no. 4: 489–509.

Witte, Marleen de. 2018. *Religion and Media: The International Encyclopedia of Anthropology*. Hoboken, NJ: John Wiley and Sons.

INDEX

....

body: bodybuilding, 118, 132–33; the breathing body, 4, 6–7, 9, 22, 26, 58–59; the chest, 123–24; clapping, 65, 66–67; confession and, 70; goose bumps, 111–13, 120–22; language as bodily act, 121–22; as medium of energy circulation and transmission, 46–47; Padre Marcelo and, 114–15; of the Pope, 115; proprioception and, 29; sin somatized in act of passing, 65–67; tremors and trembling, 112–13, 115

Boff, Frei Leonardo, 114, 178, 204n5

Bolsonaro, Jair, 84, 179, 181–87, 209n1

Bolsonaro, Michelle, 183, 186–87

breath: Byzantine rosary and, 116–18; inhaling and exhaling "Acts of the Apostles," 29; Padre Marcelo's aerobics of Jesus and, 117, 119–20, 123–24; Swedenborg on, 199n13; virtue, breath-induced, 28. See also *pneuma*

Brecht, Bertolt, 32–33, 58, 183, 197n6

broadcasts: Canção Nova, 37, 44–47, 52, 85, 196n4; Padre Marcelo, 136; televangelism, 4, 42–44, 193n19; TV Globo, 140, 153, 159. See also *Adoration Hour/Adoration Thursday*; aerobics of Jesus

Brown, Peter, 201n11

building up: empty space and, 161; Padre Jonas and, 26–27; Padre Marcelo's aerobics of Jesus and, 118, 126; Santuário Mãe de Deus and, 142, 145–46

Bush, George W., 187

Butler, Judith, 58, 190n4, 196n6, 208n1

Bynum, Caroline Walker, 171, 200n9

Byzantine, the: Brazilian Charismatics and adaptation of, 183; exception, nonadmittance of, 152; Padre Marcelo and bishop as reforming channels of, 143; rosary, Byzantine, 115–18, 121–22; theology of compromise and, 7–8

Byzantine icons. *See* icons

Cachoeira Paulista, 36–39

Caillois, Roger, 197n7

Camargo, Hebe, 174

Canção Nova Community: Acts of the Apostles and, 29–32; Bolsonaro and, 209n1; community, theorizations of, 21–22; digitalization of, 196n4; directness and transparency, Padre Léo's sermon on, 34–35; finances and self-referential publicity, 44, 47–49, 75–76; intermarriage within, 193n15; main base of, 37; Masses of cure and deliverance, 67; as network, 36; oil, chrism, and, 40–41; Padre Jonas and beginnings of, 23–29; proprioception and, 22–23, 26–29; Seminar in the Holy Spirit, 21, 24, 37; setting in Cachoeira Paulista and Paraiba Valley, 36–39; stages of, 27; televangelism and Padre Jonas's vernacular tactics, 41–44; theatrical form of, 32–33; *Wednesday Mass of the Audio Club*, 44–47; youth events, 40. See also *Adoration Hour/Adoration Thursday*; PHN (Por hoje não) festival and confession; Poor Clares

Canetti, Elias, 161–64

Cardoso, Fernando Henriques, 96

Carlos, Roberto, 118, 204n8

Carlson, Thomas A., 200n17

Catholic Charismatic Renewal (CCR): about, 2; as Catholic Pentecostalism, 156; *corpus ecclesia* and, 183; gravitas challenged by, 173; name of, 40; National Congress of, 194n20; rift with progressive Catholicism, 193n19. *See also* Canção Nova Community; Jonas, Padre; Marcelo, Padre; Santuário Mãe de Deus

Catholic Church: elasticity of, 73, 199n16; rationalization and opacity of, 192n10; Santuário Mãe de Deus and, 138–40; tension between paradigm change and, 4–5

Certeau, Michel de, 78, 93, 122, 132, 200n17

chairs, monobloc (Santuário Mãe de Deus): All Saints' Day Mass and,

159–64; arrival of chairs, 165–69; containment and, 157–58; as context-free, 158; contradictions of, 158–59; gravitas and, 169–74; host, community, and, 171; Padre Marcelo's in wheelchair and, 174; Padre Marcelo's resistance and acceptance, 160, 162; Pentecostalism and, 156–57; sitting, act of, 157, 160, 164, 173–74

Charismatic renewal movement. *See* Catholic Charismatic Renewal

charity, 47, 194n24

chrism, 40

Christology, 12

circulation: body as medium of energy circulation and transmission, 46–47; communication and, 62–63; PHN festival and, 74–77; *real* coinage, wafers, and real presence, and, 96–100; Santuário Mãe de Deus and, 131; of sin, 54–55

citational practice, 10, 190n4

Clare of Assisi, Saint, 81–82, 89–94, 101–5

Coffee Shops of Jesus, 51, 195n1

Cohen, Anthony, 21

coincidentia oppositorum, 199n17

communication: circulation and, 62–63; community constituted through, 14, 22, 49–50; compassion and, 186–87; elasticity of opposites and, 6–7; Monsignor Beltrami and, 208n4; Paul and association of body with, 29–30

community, theorizations of, 21–22

complexio oppositorum, 5–8, 49, 199n17

Comunidade Canção Nova. *See* Canção Nova Community

comunidades de vida, 192n14

confession, 53–54, 70, 77–78. *See also* PHN (Por hoje não) festival and confession

Congregation for the Doctrine of the Faith, 204n5

containment, 14, 70, 168, 172

contemplation and adoration. See *Adoration Hour/Adoration Thursday*

Crary, Jonathan, 200n5

Csordas, Thomas, 68, 121–22

Derrida, Jacques, 190n4, 196n6

devils, 75

de Vries, Hent, 102

Diderot, Denis, 198n10

directness, 34–35, 48

Dougherty, Eduardo, 26, 42–43, 47, 50, 179

dramaturgies: Bolsonaro and, 179–80, 187; Canção Nova and, 27, 32, 48; PHN and, 62, 66; power of shock and, 3; Santuário Mãe de Deus and, 130, 154, 162; standing and, 174; structure of empathy and, 12–13. *See also* theatricality

Dunga, 51–53, 56–64, 68–71, 75, 200n20

Eastern Orthodox Christianity: acts vs. figurative content and, 12; aerobics of Jesus and, 2; *complexio oppositorum*, 5–8, 49, 199n17; Mary, the Son, and the Spirit in, 131, 141; Padre Marcelo, Bishop Figueiredo, and, 113–14, 143, 203n3; vigils and, 90. *See also* Byzantine, the; icons; Theotókos

Edmilson, Padre, 45–47, 75

elasticity, 2, 5–8, 73, 199n16, 208n1

electricity and spirituality, 37–38, 74

empathic identification, 12–13

energy crisis, 40–41

enrapturing, 112–13, 125

eschatology, loss of, 9–10, 189n3

Eucharist. *See* Mass and Eucharist

evangelicalism: baroque aesthetics and, 187; Brazilian party politics and, 97; Charismatics and, 30, 100, 179; "kicking of the saint" (*o chute na santa*), 1–5, 97, 138, 144, 182; monobloc chairs and, 156; Padre Marcelo compared to, 141; PHN confessional contrasted with, 75; televangelism, 42–44, 193n19; tension between Catholicism and, 4–5, 75, 140; third person as difference between PHN and, 75

Evaristo, Paulo, 42

Expedito, Saint, 167

Fabian, Johannes, 9
Figueiredo, Bishop Fernando, 120, 132, 135, 139, 143–49, 159, 203n3
flâneurs, 149–50
Flaubert, Gustave, 197n7
Foucault, Michel, 207n14
Francis of Assisi, Saint, 80, 81, 90, 101, 201n14
Freire, Paulo, 30
Freud, Sigmund, 69

Geração PHN program, 52
gesture, 68, 185–86
Gibson, James, 208n1
glossolalia. *See* speaking in tongues
goose bumps, 111–13, 120–22
grace (*kharis*), 24–25, 31, 114
gravity, 169–74
Greenblatt, Stephen, 32
Guerra Santa controversy, 1–5
gymnasium, Charismatic: about, 2–5; the abstract/concrete and, 8; articulation and, 13, 29; body of Jesus as gymnastic model, 124; Bolsonaro and, 185; Canção Nova and, 56, 66–67; clapping at PHN festival and, 66–67; elasticity of opposites and, 6–8; Greek language and, 177; John of the Cross, Ignatius of Loyola, and, 41; Padre Marcelo and, 111, 148; Paul and the Greek gym, 25, 33, 132, 194n26; Pope John Paul II and, 204n5; theology on the run, 177–80. *See also* aerobics of Jesus; Santuário Mãe de Deus

Habermas, Jürgen, 50
Heller-Roazen, Daniel, 59, 78, 200n22
Heo, Angie, 193n16
hiéron vs. *hagion*, 193n16, 195n1, 198n11
Hirschkind, Charles, 11–12
Hollywood, Amy, 197n6
Holy Spirit: *Adoration Hour* and, 88–97, 104; anointment by, 35, 91, 190n3; authorship, displacement of, 61–62;

baptism in, 24–25, 40–41, 123; Canção Nova and, 39–40, 45; as complex network, 157; electricity and, 38; militias of God and, 83–84; Padre Edmilson and, 46; Padre Jonas and, 26; Padre Marcelo and, 120–21, 125, 141, 157; Pentecost and, 22; PHN and, 60–62, 65, 70–71; *pneuma* and, 119, 173; Pope John Paul II on, 204n5; rosary and, 117; Santuário Mãe de Deus taken over by, 146–47; Theotókos and, 133; as third person, 11, 53–54, 75, 124; unction of, 40, 157; wind of, 24, 48, 124, 175

icons: alternative theory of, 145; Bolsonaro and, 187; iconopraxis, 145; Maiani fresco at Santuário Mãe de Deus, 153–55; Mondzain on *perigraphé* vs. *graphé*, 206n11; operatic compromise incarnated by, 97–98; powers of aperture attributed by Nikephoros to, 198n11; sculptures vs., 144; as space-occupying physical beings, 133; stained-glass virgin of contact, 145; Theotókos, 72–73, 130–33, 146
Ignatius of Loyola, 41
impoverishment, stylized, 7
incarnation, 12–13, 48, 194n26
Innocent IV, Pope, 103–4

Jacobs, Ken, 204n4
Jericho, walls of, 24
Joaninha, Nora, 87–89
John of the Cross, Saint, 8, 41
John Paul II, Pope, 34, 111, 114–15, 138, 159, 163, 165, 192n11, 204n5, 208n2
Johnson, Barbara, 184–85
Jonas, Padre (Jonas Abib): *Adoration Hour* and, 94; baptized in Holy Spirit and filled with grace, 24–25; Bolsonaro and, 179; economic praxis and, 48; healing of, 25; at National Congress of the CCR, 194n20; Poor Clares and, 81–82, 103; proprioception and, 26, 29; in

Padre Marcelo. *See* Marcelo, Padre
parade of souls, 162
Paraíba do Sul River Valley, 25–26, 39
parataxis, 57
partaking, 10, 49, 71
Paul, Saint: Areopagus Sermon, 161,
    208n2; aspiration to act in accordance
    with, 29–30; charismata listed by,
    194n24; directness and transparency,
    35; Greek gym and, 25, 33, 132, 194n26;
    as model actor, 33; Padre Jonas on, 25;
    Peter vs., 192n11; spirit as articulator,
    194n26
Peirce, Charles S., 191n8
Penderecki, Krzysztof, 204n4
Pentecost: flame of, 38, 39; oil and, 41;
    Padre Jonas and, 22, 24, 26; *pneuma*
    and, 30, 44
Pentecostalism: the Byzantine and, 7, 115;
    Catholic, 21, 23, 156, 183; mass media
    and, 110; monobloc chairs and, 156–57;
    Padre Marcelo and, 141; Santuário Mãe
    de Deus and, 139–40; Sisters of Adora-
    tion and, 82; tension between Catholi-
    cism and, 12, 77, 139, 145
Perniola, Mario, 167–68
Pessoa, Fernando, 95
Peter, Apostle, 192n11
Petrobras, 137, 206n7
Philia (Padre Marcelo), 178
PHN (Por hoje não) festival and confes-
    sion: about, 51–55; auto-affection, sin,
    and collective autoimmunity (day 2),
    64–72; description of scene, 55–56;
    Mass and circulation (day 3), 72–77;
    repetition, tautology, and rapping (day
    1), 55–64
Pinheiro dos Santos, Lúcio, 197n9
Pius V, Pope, 90
Pius XII, Pope, 82
plasticity, 208n1
pneuma (air, breath, or spirit): adapt-
    ability and, 40; "aerobics of Jesus" and,
    2; articulation and, 13, 25; balanced

economy of, 69; the breathing body, 4,
    6–7, 9, 22, 26, 58–59; centrality of, 9;
    community and, 22; engineering power
    of, 11; as noun and verb, 28; Padre Jonas
    and, 25–26; Padre Marcelo's aerobics
    of Jesus and, 119–20; Pentecost and, 30,
    44; as source of energy, 39–40; tension,
    conflict, opposition, and, 6–8; theol-
    ogy of mechanisms and, 6–7; virtue
    and, 28; walls of Jericho and, 24; youth
    events and managing flow of, 40. *See
    also* breath
pneumatoliberalism, 195n27
Poor Clares (Sisters of Perpetual Adora-
    tion), 80–81, 89–91, 94, 100–105
Prayer of the Heart, 109, 118–20, 123–24,
    161
proprioception, 22–23, 26–29
PSDB (Partido da Social Democracia
    Brasileira), 84, 96–97
PT (Partido dos Trabalhadores), 84, 97
publicity, self-referential, 47–49
publics, 1, 30, 92, 182, 191n1, 197n8

Rahm, Father Haroldo, 24, 43
rapping, 55–64
Ratzinger, Cardinal Joseph. *See* Benedict
    XIV, Pope
real, 96–97
real presence, 82, 97, 202n16
reproducibility: *Adoration Hour* and, 87;
    the host, Eucharist, and, 98–99; law
    of, 55; mechanical, 3, 29; presence and,
    99; singing and, 61; TV filming and,
    78
rhythmanalysis, 65, 197n9
Rita, Sister, 81–83, 89, 101–4, 201n15
Roberto, Father, 51
Robles-Anderson, Erica, 205n5
Roitman, Janet, 16
rosary, Byzantine, 115–18, 121–22
Rossi, Marcelo. *See* Marcelo, Padre
Roussef, Dilma, 137–38, 182
Ruah (Padre Marcelo), 178

empathic identification, 12–13. *See also* dramaturgies

theosis, 119

Theotókos (Mother of God): Chapel of Our Lady of Theotókos, 143–44; Santuário Mãe de Deus and, 133–34, 141–47, 151–52; stained-glass virgin of contact, 145

Theotókos icon: name of, 133; in PHN festival procession, 72–73; sacrificial *hiéron* and, 193n16; Santuário Mãe de Deus and, 130–33, 142, 146

third person. *See* Holy Spirit

Thomas Aquinas, 99

Throop, Jason, 126

Toca de Assis (the Cave of Assisi) movement, 44, 51

transparency: economic, 47–49; Padre Léo's sermon on, 34–35; Santuário Mãe de Deus and, 132; "seeing through" and, 190n4

tremors and trembling, 112–13, 115

Trump, Donald, 184, 187

TV Century XXI, 42

TV Globo, 140, 153, 159

unction, 40, 157, 193n16

ungendering, 55

Universal Church of the Kingdom of God, 1–5, 139, 182, 205n5

vigils, 90–91

virtue, breath-induced, 28

voice: *Adoration Hour* and seeing through the voice, 91–96; middle voice, 76, 200n21

Von Helder, Pastor Sérgio, 1–5, 97, 144, 182

Warner, Michael, 62–63, 197n8

way of Mary (*o caminho de Maria*), 144–45, 206n10

Weber, Samuel, 194n26, 195n2, 200n3

Wednesday Mass of the Audio Club, 44–47

Williams, Linda, 204n4

Wittgenstein, Ludwig, 57, 196n3